Praise for *Award Winning Austi*

'*Award Winning Australian Writing* provides readers with an opportunity for discovery — not just of great writing, but of tomorrow's literary stars. And what a journey of discovery it is!'
— Lisa Dempster
Director, Emerging Writers' Festival

'Read the collection. Here and there you will discover a gem, a passage or observation that will open up a new slant on things, a tiny moment of revelation. This is the reward of reading such a diverse collection.'
— Arnold Zable

'Awards enable writers to be recognised and become a launch pad for many writers. It is anthologies such as *Award Winning Australian Writing* that keep those winners' works alive.'
— Philip Rainford
President (1999–2010), Fellowship of Australian Writers

'There's plenty of energy and inventiveness … but there's also a persistent sense of rawness. This collection offers an intriguing snapshot of the coalface of Australian writing.'
— Patrick Allington
Critic and reviewer, *The Advertiser*

'The initiative behind this anthology of short story competition winners is to be applauded. Every aspiring writer or supporter of new literary talent needs to get behind this.'
— *The Sun Herald*

'A worthy collection.'
— *The Age*

Published by Melbourne Books
Level 9, 100 Collins Street,
Melbourne, VIC 3000
Australia
www.melbournebooks.com.au
info@melbournebooks.com.au

National Library of Australia Cataloguing-in-
Publication entry
Title: Award Winning Australian Writing:
The Best Winning Writing from Short Story
& Poetry Competitions Nationally
Managing Editor: David Tenenbaum
Editor: Adolfo Aranjuez
ISBN: 9781877096631 (pbk.)
Subjects: Short stories, Australian.
Australian poetry.
Australian literature.
Dewey Number: 820.08004

First Edition: September 2008
Second Edition: September 2009
Third Edition: October 2010

Page layout: Ning Xue
Printed in Singapore

AWARD WINNING AUSTRALIAN WRITING

Edited by Adolfo Aranjuez

M

MELBOURNE BOOKS

Contents

Foreword
Delia Falconer

I have a very soft spot for writing competitions. While the publishing industry gears itself more and more around marketable authors, anonymous competitions — into which stories are entered without any identifying markers of looks, backstory, age or sex — are one of the very few places where the work alone counts. For me they still hold something of the romantic promise of the open Broadway audition known unflatteringly as the cattle call; places where sheer talent outs. This is an increasingly old-fashioned notion, as our big televised talent competitions across every skill concentrate more and more on their contestants' personal 'journeys', ability to describe their 'passion', and their marketability should they win.

Perhaps my outlook remains romantic because of the place writing awards have held in my own life. In 1994 *Island* Magazine announced a national competition to revive the 'personal essay' in Australia, a prize I entered and won with an essay about my father's battle with a variant of Alzheimer's disease. The prize was to be awarded at the Adelaide Writers' Festival; my partner and I, then students at Melbourne University, cashed in my airfare and travelled down by train, staying in a Hindley Street hotel that the literary editor of *The Age* would describe in a hushed voice, when she interviewed me there, as a 'doss house'. Beforehand there was a lunch with presenter Frank Moorhouse at Jolleys Boathouse so good that it saw the panel running indecorously, and still wearing the remains of Balmain bugs and red curry sauce, across the lawns toward the presentation tent. It was here that I was approached by my agent; and Moorhouse would take the first few chapters of my novel, *The Service of Clouds*, to Picador, who offered an advance that would let me complete it. That same year I was also lucky enough to win *HQ Magazine*'s inaugural short story competition. This was a very glamorous and literarily-orientated publication — I still remember its profiles of Bruce Chatwin, and a young Jeanette Winterson, nude and painted as a faun — and my story, 'The Water Poets', set in the eighteenth-century Bath, attracted a good deal of attention. I still relish judge Kate Grenville's description of its style as 'faintly obscene'. All of these things were wonderful. But most empowering of all was the realisation that I not only had something to say — someone else valued it.

Of course these were not the first competitions I had entered. I had also been sending work out to various journals for consideration. But what I had learned, quickly, was to be strategic. Amazing as it is to think about now, when magic realist, postmodern, fantasy, slipstream and 'new weird' fiction have become so mainstream in international literary journals, and writers like Nam Le are celebrated for their imaginative engagement in other places, there were at this time almost no venues that published the kind of work I wrote: often skewed from reality, set in other places and other times, formally experimental or containing its own reflective commentary. Experiential and local realism dominated, with the notable exception of *Island* (and it was encouraging to see *HQ* featuring those staunchly anti-realist 'new exotics', Winterson and Chatwin). It seemed like a good idea, then, to not send out work willy-nilly, but to target those few magazines, and their competitions, whose contents spoke to me. This was not so much about maximising my chances of success, but conserving energy and protecting myself from constant rejection. This is certainly advice I now give to my students at UTS: do your research. Competitions are still the best jumpstart you can give your career, with the potential to get you past those hurdles of being noticed by publishers or finding an agent. But it doesn't hurt to play to your strengths. Nor does it hurt to have a goal or strategy. Do you want to enter into competitions where publication is the ideal end-goal? Or which reward a particular genre? Or that connect you to a particularly community, say of other young writers?

This is one reason why *Award Winning Australian Writing* is such an excellent resource, one that will become increasingly valuable as editions accumulate. As well as featuring winning entries, it includes useful information about the history and reach of each prize; its affiliation with a journal, institution or place; and sometimes its judges. For of course the final decision is always a matter of the judges' tastes. The stories collected here are not reflections of abstract quality, or some adamantine winning formula of story-writing, as I am well aware from acting as a judge many times myself and editing *Best Australian Stories*. In both roles, drawing on a strong sense of the history and possibilities of the short story, I certainly chose those entries I felt were the clear stand-outs. Yet I would often see stories that had just fallen outside of my own shortlist win other competitions or turn up in other anthologies of the year's 'best of's. And that is as it should be. It is always important to remember that if your story is not selected this is not necessarily a reflection on its quality, but on the connection the winner made with one, or several, expert readers.

While some competitions, like those run by *The Age* and *Australian Book Review*, do publish the winning entries, the problem with the majority of competitions is that their workings remain opaque. While many writers enter in the hope of honing their craft, they offer little guidance for improvement. The judge might deliver a report at the award presentation, if there is one, though often attendance is limited to winners and runners-up. So it is difficult to have an idea, if your story is not successful, of what was considered the best. There have been times when I have judged several competitions across a year, and recognised some of the same stories, fatally flawed and un-reworked, entered hopefully into each; and found myself wishing that these writers could be inspired and learn from the winning stories. This is the other great value of *Award Winning Australian Writing*. It demystifies the process of competitions, letting other writers judge the winning story for themselves; and, if it works for them, to take it apart and work out why.

For the record, the stories that don't make it onto my shortlist as a judge are those structured around a payoff or punchline: so intent on steamrolling the reader towards a humorous conclusion, or life-changing epiphany, that there is no space left in their telling for surprises — or that quality that critic James Wood, writing of Chekhov, describes as 'lifeness'. Some of their authors, one gets the feeling, have been told at some stage that there is a formula for a good short story: that it needs a strong plot and a symphony-ending, cymbal-striking conclusion. Yet because of its sheer limitations in terms of space, the short story when it works is the least plotty of forms, and much more a glimpse of a moment in time, the invocation of a mood or feeling. It is about, simultaneously, lightness of touch and strength of voice. A good story, the kind that excites me, at least — whether told in the first or third person — gives the impression of being the tip of an iceberg. It seems to know far more than it reveals, to open a door just a crack onto a fully formed world. A great story possesses me. I am so immersed in the logic of its world, and its unfurling — even if that world is entirely fantastical — that I come to believe that it could not have been told in any other way. It does not try to convince me, or bully me. It takes me for a ride.

That is easy enough for me to say. The delight of *Award Winning Australian Writing*, in collecting together these winning entries, is that it shows what has made each judge's heart jump. And that is the other romance of the competition. The writer or reader who volunteers as judge is in it for this addictive thrill — not to be pernickety, or rule out work that doesn't follow some formula for the well-made story, but to find the true original. Every judge hopes to uncover those one or two pieces that make the world look new, which extend the boundaries of his or her own craft.

Here is a rare chance to see a whole year's cohort of winning stories in one collection. Use it as inspiration, or a tool for seeing trends and possibilities in writing. By all means learn from the skills on display here. If you plan to enter competitions, have a strategy. But don't assume there is a particular 'type' of prize-winning story or try to second-guess what readers want. The truest gold standard is your passion as a reader. The stories that will help you most here are the ones that connect with your own tastes, but perhaps push them higher or further. Most of all, they will be the ones that make you want to write.

Delia Falconer is the author of two novels, The Service of Clouds *and* The Lost Thoughts of Soldiers *(republished in paperback as* The Lost Thoughts of Soldiers and Selected Stories*). She is also the author of the nonfiction* Sydney. *Between them they have been shortlisted for numerous awards including the Miles Franklin, Prime Minister's Literary Awards, and Commonwealth Prize. Her stories have been widely anthologised, including in* The Penguin Century of Australian Stories *and* The Macquarie Pen Anthology of Australian Literature. *She is the editor of* The Penguin Book of the Road, *and* The Best Australian Stories 2008 *and* 2009.

Introduction

This is the first edition of *Award Winning Australian Writing* to include poetry, and the decision has been a long time coming. While in its first, second and third editions the anthology had no qualms about presenting *bush* poetry alongside short stories, under the rationale that both were forms of storytelling, it took longer to break the boundary between stories and poems. Perhaps this can be attributed to the way most of us see storytelling — that is, everyday tales about experiences — as being far removed from poetic approaches to language. Generally, it would be acceptable to say that one was harassed by 'a million mosquitoes' when there was probably no more than thirty. Or to characterise a satay as 'sweet' when there is quite evidently a hint of citrus in there, a trace of fish sauce, a few bitter, burnt nuts. When using language on this pragmatic level, the underpinning criterion is that of intelligibility: *Are my words sufficient to put my point across?* And from there stories qualify as 'good' when they successfully sustain the interest of others, and can produce the intended effect (say, laughter).

In this light, poetry can seem drastically different, almost alien. For when using language poetically, there is a greater sense of responsibility: it's as though one could be assassinated for saying the wrong thing. I'll clarify here that I'm not using the word poetry in the way it's commonly understood (i.e. writing composed of lines and stanzas and rhymes), but rather in terms of a particular predisposition to using words. For to the poetic writer of both short stories and poetry, it is imperative that words — brittle and mutable and fleeting as they may be — are deployed with the utmost concern for both clarity and connotation, understanding and undertone.

In *The Republic*, Plato warns against poetry's power to 'seduce' the intellect and lead it away from the Truth arrived at through logical argument. My use of the capital is deliberate, for by 'Truth' Plato is using the term in its putative, almost oppressive sense — as though it were 'out there', untouchable by human cognition. As poets focus on the sensual and write with cadence and feeling, they are celebrating the world as it is to the 'everyman', not the philosopher. And as such, they are no different to the Sophists, Ancient Greece's masters of rhetoric, who swayed audiences through emotive language instead of logic.

In asserting such a view, however, Plato betrays what ties philosophy with both poetry and rhetoric: the idea that words are immensely powerful. In their various forms and combinations, words have the capacity to inspire and transform, to enrich and enliven. Yet they can also injure, bemuse, denigrate and eradicate. It's this spectrum of effect that poetry manages to access, and in so doing it articulates aspects of the world that elude overly logical and pragmatic thinking. I don't deny that philosophy is crucial to our understanding of the world, and that sometimes it would be excessive to use words with poetic exactitude. But, as Plato himself admits, poetry (as with art in general) does help to foster a proclivity for appreciating beauty: it trains us in the appreciation of Truth.

Writing about poetry's place in contemporary society, Seamus Heaney discusses how it can 'redress' aspects of this world, revealing possibilities and affording us opportunities to see the world in a different — more consoling, more exciting — light. These alternative views, of course, are those of the poets, who draw from their imaginations what they wish to convey. But for these to be tangible to us, poets must tap into a 'new world', so to speak, in which the ideas and ideologies that predominate are theirs. And what results is a Nietzschean 'creation through destruction', whereby the socio-political structures of the 'real world' are usurped by the poets' imagined ones. (Poetry, in fact, comes from the Greek *poeisis*, meaning 'to create'.) It is this that leads to poetry's distinctive use of words. Metaphors and metonyms are not merely gratuitous diversions from convention; rather, they are the indispensable tools with which poets actualise their worlds. How else are poets to describe the particular yellow of a sunrise, or the heaviness of the chest that results from watching a loved one being shot?

To Heaney, then, what poetry does is offer us non-poets 'another truth to which we can have recourse, before which we can know ourselves in a more fully empowered way'. The truth (lowercase, this time) that he identifies may not be universal in the way Plato would've had it, but it is universal in the sense that it highlights the shared-ness of the world being written about. Despite the need to create a world for themselves, poets predominantly still take inspiration from the 'real world' — the world they share with us, their readers. And this 'empowers' us in two ways: first, because we are seeing the same world through the eyes of other people who seem more attuned to it than we; and second, because we can then take on these alternative views as our own. Much like the prophets of yore (and the philosopher Martin Heidegger isn't hesitant to equate poets with prophets), it seems it is contemporary poets who are gifted with seeing a little more than is needed, of hearing whispers in places that seem abandoned, of rousing the populace from their complacency — of offering more truth than Truth can ever provide.

Thus, we can see how Plato's characterisation of poetry can be a little unwarranted. Poets may not bring us Truth, but they do invoke truths of their own creation: truths of a subjective kind. So it's no wonder that, unlike pragmatic communicators, poets are so scrupulous with their words — after all, these words bear the weight of 'prophecy'. A colleague (a fellow editor with a PhD in poetry) once told me that, as an exercise, she tasks the writers she's editing with justifying each word they've used in a stanza or paragraph. The reasoning behind her (arguably severe) method is that poets should know their words intimately, that they shouldn't be just thrown around. Auden encapsulates this idea well when he wrote:

> Language is prosaic [or, in terms of my dichotomy, pragmatic] to the degree that it does not matter what particular word is associated with an idea ... Language is poetic to the degree that it does.

Indeed, truly poetic works are those that have not only mastered this process of refinement, but also revel in it. Their narratives aren't mere *this happened, then this happened* sequences with unpolished phrases and pedestrian themes. Instead, they deliver the world they've conjured to their readers — always *showing* and not *telling*, to appropriate the oft-used adage. And so it is that the short stories and poems in this edition of *Award Winning Australian Writing* have been brought together: each exhibits the attention to detail, the care for selection, and the revelatory insight that is characteristic of poetic writing. For instance, Amy Espeseth's 'Downwind' is an overwhelmingly lucid tale of a pivotal moment in a character's life: every gesture, every movement is amazingly narrated, as if I were in the casino myself. And Tasha Sudan paints a young Buddha wandering vivid landscapes and farewelling his family, but always through the pining eyes of his son, Rahula.

There's also the depictions of family conflict and commitment by Jacqueline Winn, Janeen Samuel and Joan Fenney; the portrayals of childhood and adolescence by Adam Tucker, Sarah Holland-Batt and A. R. Holloway; and the poignant hauntings and final moments told by Kate Gilbert, Christopher Green and Cecilia Morris. We are cheered by Kirk Marshall, Gillian Essex and John Biggs; and shown anger by Louise D'Arcy, Jenny Toune and Eleanor Marney. We are offered renditions of love and loss by Josephine Rowe and Jacqui Merckenschlager. And, of course, there's the closer: Leah Swann's 'Street Sweeper', with its intricately interwoven images and scenes, fluctuating sense of time, and lingering (though inexplicably so) ending.

I'd like to thank all the authors and writing competitions involved in this and previous editions of *Award Winning Australian Writing* for your continuing support and enthusiasm; David Tenenbaum of Melbourne Books for persisting, despite logistical difficulties, with this worthwhile project; and Delia Falconer, for honouring us with her wise and wonderful words. I also thank all my loved ones, especially Aaron, my partner, for his unwavering encouragement; and Maddie, Jodie and Ainslee, who each did a last-minute read-through of this introduction. Finally, I express gratitude to all the bush poetry competition winners and organisers who've supported us: without you *Award Winning Australian Writing* would not be where it is today, and I'm sure my counterpart for the upcoming anthology of bush stories and poetry, Max Merckenschlager, will do an equal (if not, better) job of showcasing your superb and distinctly Australian talents.

Adolfo Aranjuez
Editor

GEMMA WHITE

Picaro Poetry Prize

Wanted: Poet

Who addresses countries as if they're people
in the habit of conversing.
Who's not afraid to offer compliments
to a fair modern maiden.
Who generally avoids metaphysical stuff
such as roses and death and time passing. But,
who may use such imagery in love letters
to tempt me to undress for him.

Who would write a mountain of verse
upon which we could sit and drink tea.
Who only has good things to say even
while his pretty words call me ugly.
Who has the power to stop the clocks
so we might spend longer making love.
Who would descend to hell and back
just to fetch anything I happen to want.

Note: no concrete poets please &
all applicants must like wheelbarrows.

Gemma White is a Melbourne-based poet who creates and edits *Velour* magazine. She has been published in *Voiceworks*, *Page Seventeen* and *Visible Ink*. She had poetry included in *The Green Fuse*, the Picaro Poetry Prize's 2010 anthology. Gemma loves the concept of ragdoll cats and the eye candy of vintage cars from the 1960s. She is also a connoisseur of music festivals. For more info, visit *onlywordsapart.wordpress.com*.

The **Picaro Poetry Prize** is run by Picaro Press and the Byron Bay Writers' Festival. The winning poems are featured in *The Green Fuse*, an anthology published in cooperation with the Varuna Writers' Centre.
www.picaropress.com

WILL SMALL

ANU/Uni Pub Short Story Prize

The Promise

The moon was so low it appeared to be sleeping on the horizon, and so big I could see its smug grin as it did so. It was shining through the crevices in the clouds and parting them like curtains, while the waves below wrestled and tumbled over each other, gracefully rising and falling like children learning to walk. The sand was covered in the pockmarks of crab, bird and human footprints. The persistent bass tone of the ocean hummed.

I was standing in the middle of the beach.

Naked.

The wind was pressing into me, rolling over me, every hair on my body standing stiff like the tips of a dandelion, waiting to break free and find a new home with the breeze. The only thing I was wearing was my watch — and the numbers 2.36 blinked on the screen.

I felt the sand shifting through my toes as they curled around and buried their way under it. Then, I was gone.

Like a crack of lightning, shooting down the sand and into the water; a succession of small splashes as my feet stampeded through the shallows, then one bigger splash as I threw my hands out and dived under.

Cold.

Like falling through that dreaded crack in the ice and feeling your muscles tense up, shocked into compression. Thrashing upwards and breaking the surface again, but finding no consolation in the breeze that whips the water off the tips of the waves and into your eyes.

I stayed in there for three and a half minutes. Submerging myself in the black body of water then bobbing back up to see the four or five odd stars that refused to go unseen even on the cloudiest of nights.

Then I raced back to the sand feeling the full power of the wind on my completely exposed body, taking the whole beach on in three steps so I could scoop up my towel, use it as a weak shelter from the wind, and shiver my way back to the beach house.

When I got there at 3.11 I cranked up the thermostat on the old column heater, wrapped three blankets around my naked body and poured a glass of scotch. With shaking hands I put it down the hatch then pulled the blankets closer. At that point, given the option, I would have gladly had the wool sewn into my body and stitched into place forever.

I'm not a nudist. And I'm not the kind of person who goes swimming in icy oceans just to appreciate the stars and the moon and the mystery of nature. It wasn't a dare. And I really was alone.

I was fulfilling a promise.

✳

The world is full of black holes and dark spaces. You don't have to go out in a spaceship and wander through the legions of stars and moons to find them.

I heard someone say once that if you saw someone walking into a black hole from earth it would take millions of years to watch; but for that person, they'd disappear in a second. I don't understand much — or anything, really — about astronomy, but that time-difference thing wouldn't surprise me. Because the days that crawled by, lying on the couch and only moving to pour another drink, might have seemed like a single 24-hour block to someone else. Yet they were forever and eternity for me. Millions and trillions of years stuck in my black hole.

Let's get the formalities aside. Beyond the late-night skinny dipping and depressing sentiments about black holes and emptiness, I have a name and a face — just like you. The name is Tom. Standard sort of a name. Hopefully standard enough to help you conjure up an image of a Tom-like face — if you need some help, you can use these words: green eyes, short brown hair, white skin, a freckle or two. You can use these ones, too, but I can't make any promises about the truth in them: chiselled jaw, soft nose, straight teeth, Hugh Jackman's stubble. The truth is, I'm probably the guy you just walked past, glanced at and forgot about seconds later. Good-looking enough to turn the odd head; not enough to stop it from turning back. You can imagine I'm stretching out my hand to shake yours now if it helps the introduction. I like to think I've got a good handshake. Warm and solid, but never the kind to break your bones. I can see you've got a good handshake, too. Nice face. Don't bother with the name — I'm no good with them. But for what it's worth, it's nice to meet you.

Last year I turned twenty-four. I was one year out of university with a degree in IT/Communications, and I'd succeeded in using that expensive piece of paper to become an IT consultant. 'Consultant' was a word far too fancy for what I was doing, but I had no problem introducing myself as one. I worked for around five or six firms, rotating between them each week and updating their systems, installing virus protection, doing the easy shit any fifteen-year-old with a half-decent knowledge of computers can do, eyes closed. Still, it paid.

I lived in an apartment looking over the city — the kind of view you see on postcards with glamorous shots taken from a helicopter. I paid most of the rent with ease. My housemate, Callum, chipped in what he could afford, though I had no problem putting in the extra to have him there. Callum had been my pal since way back.

We met in college, travelled together after year twelve then ended up in the same uni. He was still studying, scribbling away at a philosophy thesis, hoping one day he could be the lecturer who got the easy job of asking piece-of-piss questions like 'How do I know I exist?' and, of equal urgency, 'How do I know you exist?' (Callum claimed to be genuinely interested in philosophy, but I wasted no chance to give him shit about it.)

As soon as I'd received my degree my parents had found no hesitation in showing me the door. I'd lived at home all my life, and once the status of poor student was lifted from my head I didn't need any extra encouragement. Neither did Callum.

Neither of us had serious girlfriends. Callum was too wrapped up in his studies to give any relationship the time it needed to grow. And me? I wouldn't have objected to a relationship. But my dating record had been six months long, three years ago. Girls seemed to lose interest in me quickly. But really, who could blame them? An IT consultant — what's exciting about that? And I wasn't ready to use the money I was earning as the bait for a relationship. I was like every other Tom (Dick and Harry) who wanted love for love's sake. If Shrek found love beyond fairytales, then my time would come too (the fact that Shrek himself was part of a fairytale was irrelevant to me).

I guess I was waiting for life to fall onto my plate. I'd set myself up for comfort. There wasn't a lot left to do. So I just waited.

And while I waited, life was what every eighteen-year-old male dreams of — *Guitar Hero*, beer, a lifetime's supply of meat pies, and no women to nag about any of it. I wasn't eighteen, but I told myself I was making up for lost years.

I performed 'consultancies' during the week, pissed away my expendable income, and bothered Callum whenever his fat pile of textbooks came out. I'd taken every one of the steps you're told to take when you're growing up. Do well at school, stay out of trouble, get your year twelve certificate, go to uni, get a degree, get a job, work. The problem is, they don't tell you that if you do all that, you've got a high chance of walking into one of those black holes I mentioned. And that's exactly where I found mine.

See, if you spend your whole life aiming for the next stepping stone, when you get to the last one you're so confused there's nothing after it that you simply walk off and hope something will appear. All the while you're sinking down into the water, watching the last bubbles of your oxygen float to the surface.

✳

It was a Monday morning in May when I realised where I was.

Believe me; I've got no scientific basis for all this talk on black holes. But I'm speaking from experience. You can float around in there for weeks, months even, before you realise where you are. And even then, your mind is hazy from all the floating so it comes in slow.

I was watching the screen and waiting for a program to load. It was going to be another twenty minutes or so before it was necessary for me to click the mouse again. I stood up and walked over to the coffee station — the industrial urn that lives in every kitchenette in every office in the business world. The sachets of sugar, the half-empty jar of nasty coffee, and the plastic spoons that sometimes melt and change shapes when you're stirring in your five sugars. This was where I killed a lot of my time. I made the drink — three heaped teaspoons of coffee and a tiny splash of milk. My favourite moment when making the coffee (yes, I'd gotten to the point of having a favourite moment) was pouring in the milk and watching it invade and transform the landscape of the black liquid.

I walked over to the window while I was still stirring. Across the street, window-washers abseiled down the skyscrapers — a combination of an extreme adventure sport with an extremely mundane profession. It was at that point, looking at those three or four men like frogs on the glass, when I had this profound thought: why do they clean the windows? Cleaning the windows enables all the masses of employees who flick between *Solitaire* and *Minesweeper* once a month to see the light outside. Seeing the light is a reminder that there is an outside world — and once upon a time, you had a dream out there, good sir/madam, and it's somewhere floating in circles on the wind, whistling, watching, waiting for you to throw away your briefcase and dive out the window to catch it. Why on earth would they bother cleaning the windows if there's any chance it could lead you through that thought process?

And that was when I realised I had fallen for it. I'd walked into the black hole. I was lost. Forgotten. The millionth sucker to buy the lie and let my dreams rest in the bin with my crumpled-up paper cup and bent plastic spoon.

I hated my job. And as the thought latched onto my brain like an unshakable claw, I hated the fact I was realising that I was another one of those people. The 'I hate my job' mentality is a disease, an epidemic, the most contagious virus out there — and I didn't have the software to fix it. I tried to convince myself otherwise, but failed miserably. Money just doesn't hold weight after a while. All the people in the world who work shitty, uninspiring jobs do it by thinking about the pay cheque they'll walk home with at the end of the fortnight. But I'd bet you every cent of my one, it doesn't make any of them happy the way they think it will.

✴

I stormed into the apartment that night. There was Callum, lying on the couch reading something with a question for a title.

'Hey Tom.'

'Callum. I'm going off the deep end.'

'Going or gone?'

'It's always a question for an answer with you, isn't it.'

'It was always a question for an answer with Jesus. And Plato.'

'Answer this one. Why do they clean the windows?'

'Even Jesus wouldn't have answered that with a question. Dirty windows look like shit. Speaking of which, when do they clean ours? The birds have been bombing again.'

'No, Callum. I demand a better answer. Why do they clean the windows where people work?'

I broke it down for him completely. Shared my revelation, my epiphany, my moment of divine truth. He didn't have an answer. From outside the black hole it obviously didn't seem so significant. There I was, being sucked into my eternal prison, but for him it would take millions of years watching me before he completely saw me make the transition.

I had another sugary coffee, played some Xbox, then went to bed.

✳

Two months went by before I started to hatch my escape plan. June and July — the coldest months of the year. Sixty-one days. I accepted the blackness and tried to find comfort in it. Black is the colour of elegant suits and top hats. It's the colour that never goes out of fashion. The colour of night and mystery and the vast majority of cool people in the world. But holes are never fun. Green or blue or red holes might be slightly more fun than black ones, but undeniably, at some point, the novelty would wear off and the hole part would sink in. Holes are deep and dark and hard to get out of. Holes are empty and hungry and cold (even when they're colourful). I was suffocating. I started to think dangerous thoughts.

The first of August. I stormed into the apartment again. Callum, reading a different book with a question for a title, was lying on the same couch.

'I've got a brilliant plan, Callum.'

'We invite Mitch and Matty over for *Band Hero*?'

'No.'

'I'll text them. But I'm intrigued. What's the plan, Stan?'

'A trip. Next month. Snowboarding in Canada.'

'I don't have a cent to my name, Tom.'

'And?'

'I'm the one who answers with questions.'

'Seriously. I'll pay for your ticket.'

'You already pay half my rent. I can't take that.'

'Callum, I need to go on this trip.'

'Then go, Tom. Don't let me hold you back.'

I heated up a pie. I was sick of meat pies. Mitch and Matty arrived an hour later.

We played *Band Hero*. I strummed that plastic guitar like I was Hendrix and, for an hour or two, forgot about my black hole.

✳

Black holes become comfortable. You go through days, months, even years, I reckon, for some, where you just let it be what it is. You know exactly where you are, but you float around with your sugary coffee and give up on the idea of getting out. You realise you can't — so you stop being so fascinated with the idea of trying.

That was August for me. I'd spent all that time dreaming up a trip to Canada — what appeared to me to be the perfect escape plan. I'd go away for a month or two, enjoy the beautiful things in life, and come back with a fresh attitude, as pure and white as the snow I would have found it on. But Callum was a key component in that plan. I was not a lone traveller. And the sad truth of it was, I had no-one else to ask.

So I sunk into my black hole and began giving up on the idea of changing it.

✳

Come September, I had a brilliant yet dangerous idea. Callum was working on a philosophy thesis. I didn't want counselling or anything like that — but there was an opportunity there and I wanted to give him a chance to prove there was any worth to that sort of degree.

'Callum. Use me to answer one of your questions.'

'What on earth are you talking about, Tom?'

'Philosophy ... all you ever do is ask questions ... then go in circles without really getting anywhere. A million hypotheticals and no real-life experimentation. Let me be that experiment.'

'First of all, philosophers do experiment. It's not all talking, Tom.'

He paused for a moment.

'And second ... I think I've got an idea.'

Ten minutes later I thought Callum deserved a bullet through the head. His solution was far from what I had expected.

'You think the money is the problem?'

'Shit yeah! You hate your job — you only do it for money. What good does money do you?'

'For starters, it pays the rent. Then it feeds me. Then it holds me at night when I'm alone in my bed.'

'Exactly. Maybe if you weren't so concerned with having the money put you to sleep, that could be a person. Take an indefinite amount of time off work ... Figure out what you actually like doing. I think you'll start to answer your own questions.'

'That's it? You spend all this time reading those books, having those endless discussions ... and your solution to a real problem is that I just quit my job?'

'It's just my advice, Tommy. I don't mind if you take it or leave it.'

✳

I started to notice a girl. She worked at one of the places I consulted for, and I often bumped into her when I was making my coffee. She was a tea girl herself — one sugar, no milk. She had hazel eyes and her long hair was lost some beautiful place in between blonde and brown. I'd stand at the window pretending to watch the window-washer frogs like usual, but every couple of minutes I was stealing glances at her sitting in her cubicle, typing away softly in between sips of her tea.

One day she approached me at the window. At first, I couldn't believe she was actually coming to talk to me. Then I remembered why I was there.

'Excuse me. Can you come take a look at my computer?'

I stood for a minute, trying to hide my disappointment that she had not come merely to discuss tea with one sugar and no milk, or men who looked like frogs washing windows.

'Sure. Which one is it?'

She took me over and explained some problem to do with her internet connection. I nodded politely, knew how to fix the problem immediately, but let her stretch it out into long, melodic sentences while I took in her workspace. Controlled mess. Lots of papers, lots of books, lots of everything — but it was all neat and harmonious and balanced somehow. Beneath her computer screen there was a picture of a child in a blue frame. When she had finished talking, I clicked a few things on her computer.

'Should be good as new.'

'That quick? Thank you very much.'

'You're welcome.'

In my mind I took her hand gently, kissed it and told her I wanted to take her for a drink and get lost somewhere in between blonde and brown. In reality, I gave her an awkward nod and walked away.

I went home feeling better than usual that night.

*

Two weeks later we were having lunch together. Natasha was her name. She'd asked me to fix her computer again, and somehow I'd fumbled the words out my mouth. Or was it just the word? There's a chance all I said was, 'hungry?'

No. It had to be more. Otherwise she wouldn't have been there in front of me, sipping lemonade and eating wedges. Either way, my black hole had temporarily turned itself inside out and I was watching the moon as I flew over it.

Halfway through the conversation I couldn't help but ask.

'I saw the photo of the child on your desk. Is he yours?'

I instantly regretted saying it. Who was I to ask that kind of a question on our first 'date' (lunch during work hours — what would you call it)?

She laughed.

'No, no. That's Paul. He's a child I sponsor. Were you thrown off by the fact he is white? There are a few whites in the world who starve too, believe it or not. He lives in Cambodia. His parents moved over to do aid work and ended up falling pregnant while there. The mother died giving birth. The father was hit by a car three years later. Paul's parents' colleagues tried to get him back into Australia, but there were immigration issues — as always.'

'That's horrible.'

'I'm going to visit him this year. Next month actually.'

'I'm sure he'll appreciate it.'

It didn't sound appropriate. But I didn't know what else to say. I wanted to tell Natasha she was wonderful. Instead I insisted on paying for her lunch.

＊

I waltzed up to the door of the apartment that evening, whistling. I rarely whistled. But for the first time in months, I felt like there was something in my life to look forward to. Natasha. That was all I was thinking about. Get through another week and I'd be there, by the urn. I'd tell her how cute the window-washing frogs were, and how glad I was they kept the windows clean. They gave all the people who worked hard at computers all day some sense of satisfaction and hope. She'd wholeheartedly agree and we'd take that coffee/tea break elsewhere.

That's what I was thinking as I whistled and found my key.

People sometimes say it's funny the way life works. I beg to differ. Life is cruel. Life is one black hole after another.

Because I put my key in the apartment door that night, went inside, heated up something frozen to eat, then went to bed. Five hours later, I woke up to the phone ringing.

Callum had been in a car accident.

✳

Back then I'd had no doubts I'd be mates with Callum forever. We'd been through enough years and spent enough time together to guarantee that sort of thing. We never said it. But we both knew it. It was more than beers and pies and an apartment. We were always going to be mates. Forever.

The thing, though, about being friends with someone 'forever' is that no one lives forever. You might be friends for eighty years if you're lucky. Even fifty's a damn good run. I don't know what happens after you die; maybe you become friends again. But as far as friendship in this life goes, it's got an expiry date.

Callum had been driving home from helping some third-years with an assignment. At the library. Sensible Callum, up late helping other people study. Hops in the car to drive home, makes it through two out of three traffic lights. Gets the green on the third, keeps his foot on the pedal, until out of nowhere, shooting through the red, a drunk shithead who thinks he's invincible hits him driver side. Both cars totalled. Both drivers dead. That is a black hole.

Life isn't funny. It's cruel. It's one black hole after another.

✳

Lying in the dark with all the curtains closed in your musty little apartment, waiting for life to come and find its way back into your body, you remember strange things. The fact I'd been lying there on the couch for two weeks straight, occasionally moving to the fridge and back to eat whatever cold, mouldy shit I could scrape together was insignificant. I just continued to lie there, my eyes working slow shifts of open and closed, open and closed. And in between those long stretches of open or closed, that's where the memories would come and make their visit.

I remembered all sorts of shit in those two weeks.

I remembered that Callum used to be obsessed with oranges. Rain, hail or shine he'd eat an orange every day, all year round. Always went on about the vitamin C and how important it was for keeping you healthy. I didn't eat oranges every day and I never noticed any real health difference between us, but all I could think now was how I hoped Callum had died and woke again in a giant orange.

I remembered driving to the coast together once and talking about *The Matrix*. It was Callum's favourite movie. I used to hate it. Now I wanted to love it. When I got up from that couch, whether it was in two more weeks or two more years, I told myself the first thing I'd do was watch *The Matrix*, in honour of Callum.

Callum told me to quit my job. So I did. They called me when I didn't show up for a week. I told them to fuck off, Callum was dead. Didn't they understand?

✳

Natasha called after four weeks. I still hadn't left the apartment. I'd survived off one big Coles online grocery shop. All the frozen crap you can imagine.

She knew I'd left my job for personal reasons. But that was all she'd been told. No-one knew. Who was there to check up on me once Callum was gone? Mitch and Matty had been around once. But it was awkward. They were his friends. They patted me on the back and drank a few beers with me. I hadn't seen or heard from them since.

I told Natasha what had happened. I unleashed. Told her about Callum's thesis. Told her about the time we'd spent together overseas. Just talked. She was the closest person in my life at that point. And it was only our second real conversation. That made me fall even deeper into the black hole. What kind of lonely life had I set myself up for?

She asked, 'Can I come visit you?'

'Yes.'

I did my best to clean up for her. I took out the mountains of garbage and recycling. I sprayed deodorant and opened the windows. I actually had a shower.

She knocked at the door three hours later. I smiled for the first time in weeks. A little smile — nothing serious. She came in and looked around.

'It doesn't smell too bad.'

'It doesn't smell too good.'

She smiled.

'Want a tea?'

'Sure.'

We sat on the couch, looking out at the postcard view. We didn't talk much, but it was the nicest hour I'd had since the last time I'd seen her. Then she brought me back to earth.

'I wanted to come and see you because I'm going to visit Paul. I leave tomorrow. You're a nice man, Tom. I wanted to say goodbye.'

My gut plunged back down into darkness.

'How long for?'

'Indefinite.'

Deeper darkness.

'Call me.'

'I will. Goodbye, Tom.'
A soft kiss on the cheek.
'Goodbye, Natasha.'

✳

The day after she left, I watched *The Matrix*.

The day after that, I took a long walk outside.

The next three days, I relapsed. Couch again.

The sixth day, I went into Callum's room. There on his bed was a giant stack of papers. The words 'final draft' were scrawled across the top. The title was *Money and Happiness: Pressure to Succeed in a Materialistic Society*. His thesis. I spent the morning reading it. Then I cried, realising just how much I looked up to my best friend.

✳

She called me a month later. Her warm voice reminded me it was summer.

'What's it like?'

She took a long time to answer.

'Like skinny dipping at 2am, in cold water.'

'What do you mean?'

'At first you're excited. You don't know what to expect. You know it will shock you; knowing doesn't lessen the shock at all. You go in running, but before long you're up to your knees in it. You trip, stumble and fall in and under. It's suffocating. You forget why you're there. You're naked — nothing to give. Empty-handed. You try and stay in, find the worth in it. Then you get scared and run. Back to whatever warmth and familiarity you can find. Scared. Silent. Trying to get the water out of your ears for days.'

'Sounds scary.'

'It's terrifying.'

'Then what's the point?'

She paused.

'It wakes you up. I've been sleeping for years.'

'I wouldn't mind waking up.'

'Then come. See what it's like.'

'Maybe I will.'

'Promise me you will.'

My tongue moved without consulting my mind.

'Alright. I promise.'

✳

The next day I went to the bank and took out a quarter of my savings. I walked over to the travel agent to buy a ticket to Cambodia. I tried to tell myself I wasn't going crazy.

Money and Happiness: Pressure to Succeed in a Materialistic Society. Callum would have done it.

I bought the closest ticket I could. Three days away.

I packed a bag then drove to the beach. South — where the water is cold all year round. I paid for one night in the first available beach house I could find.

My alarm went off at 2.00 am.

I walked outside and saw the moon sleeping on the horizon.

I was naked.

✳

It's 3.40 am. The column heater is waking up. I no longer feel the need to stitch the blankets into my skin.

Tomorrow I'm driving home. The day after, I'm going to Cambodia. I'm going to meet Paul. I'm going to tell him all about Callum. I don't know what comes after that.

But I'm out.

I'm out of my black hole. I've done the impossible. I've broken away from the darkness and swirl, and flung my way back into the galaxy — a piece of space junk heading back to earth, past the moon, up and over, spinning round the Milky Way and falling towards the green and blue. Broken. Tired. Unemployed. Undone. I could fall apart at any minute.

But for this one, I'm free.

Will Small grew up in Canberra, and still manages to love it. Passion for language was bestowed upon him by his mother — a librarian and writer herself. Will considers himself primarily a poet, and was a finalist at the Australian National Poetry Slam in 2009. 'The Promise' was the first short story Will had ever actually finished. Will is studying English, philosophy and film studies at the ANU, and works as a chaplain at Hawker College. He recently asked a girl to marry him (she said yes). Will's not entirely sure what the future holds, but hopes it will involve mucking around with language for a long time to come.

The **ANU/Uni Pub Short Story Prize** has been offered since 2007, now in its fifth year. It is very generously funded by the proprietors of the Uni Pub in Canberra. Open to all students enrolled at the Australian National University, with free choice of topic, 5000-word limit and a first prize of $5000, the 2010 competition attracted more than 125 entries. The award panel included Professor Allan Hawke (the immediate past ANU Chancellor), Professor Penny Oakes (Dean of Students), Vic Elliot (immediate past ANU Librarian) and representatives of Uni Pub.
www.anu.edu.au/dos/competitions_events.htm

THERESA LAYTON
Perilous Adventures Short Story Competition

The Afghan Hook

A ida wakes early to *ticks ticks* on the window. A giant wood moth flutters against the glass.

George's indifference to their anniversary has bothered her all night. She adds it to a long list. Her case against him has built, slowly, in sedimentary layers. This morning, as she wakes to their fiftieth wedding anniversary, the evidence has finally formed into something solid.

She has decided to leave.

Aida neatens her quilt, pads into the kitchen, and notices three lorikeets on the clothesline chattering expectantly in green, orange and purple. She wonders why George hasn't fed them.

As she leans forward and opens the window, she spots him collapsed and wriggling under a camellia bush. His hand is stretched out to a lorikeet that walks pigeon-toed up and down, up and down on the grass. It pecks at George's blend of whiskey-soaked sunflower seeds spilt in the fall. George makes *tsk tsk* noises, holds his hand out to the bird, but it's more interested in the seeds.

George hoists himself onto one elbow, sways for a moment and falls back to the grass. Turning away Aida fills the kettle. She pours the water, jiggles, squeezes, stirs. Finally sips. She makes toast — butters, spreads and cuts neat soldiers. One by one she eats them.

Only then does she walk down the steps of the old Queenslander to the garden.

Since the stroke he's prone to falling, where he stands, crumpled. She looks down at him, square-on. The grass smells warm, mossy. The lorikeet looks up at her, squawks and flaps up, slightly drunk, to the clothesline. Only when he brings himself to look her in the eye, accept the humiliation, does she slowly offer her hand. As he reaches for her wrist she thinks of pulling away, letting him fall back again.

The warmth of his hand is surprising.

George's mouth remains tight as he rights himself. Always tight.

'That's alright, George,' she says, 'anytime. Really, it was no trouble.'

'It's a low form of wit,' he replies. 'Suits you.'

She stares at him. 'I'm going to leave you.' Her voice is slow and quiet.

'Better do it soon.' George looks at her straight-on, deadpan.

There must be something more to say but Aida's words seem all used up. She tilts her head to one side and fiddles with a pair of dressmaking scissors in her pocket.

✳

By late afternoon, parsley and leftover sandwiches dry out under the dining room fan and a red '50' candle lies discarded on a paper plate. In the kitchen, the siblings wash and dry dishes while their husbands and some of the grandchildren play totem tennis on the front lawn. The youngest two lie on the sofa, playing with a collection of small toys.

While Aida crochets, George listens to a small transistor radio. He sits frowning and slightly bent, with his bad arm resting on a pillow.

'Caitlin, come and sit with Nanna,' says Aida, as the newsreader begins the headlines.

George turns up the volume.

'Grumpy old man, isn't he?' she whispers to the grandchildren with a wink.

George lifts the radio to his ear.

A strand of wool wriggles from Aida's afghan hook into a wicker box. Caitlin, the youngest, puts down her Nintendo and worms in next to Aida.

'I'm not really crocheting … I'm actually fishing,' Aida whispers. 'Inside this magic box is a whole ocean filled with fish, sea anemones and giant squid.'

Caitlin looks at her, eyes wider than wide. 'Can I look in there?'

'It's dangerous in there. Maybe when you're older.'

Caitlin tilts her head to one side. 'Not as old as you, though.'

'Gosh no, not that old,' says Aida, laughing. 'Maybe when you are three.'

'That's only two weeks.' Caitlin shows two plump fingers and runs back to the sofa to tell her cousin.

The family leaves in a flurry of Tupperware, quick kisses and the singsong *see you*s of the children.

At 5pm exactly, George fumbles open the lid of an old film canister labelled *Sunday pm* and pours out an assemblage of coloured pills. They fall into the creases of his palm. They look pretty: a kaleidoscope of old age. With one swallow of his whiskey they are gone.

'You're still here,' he says.

＊

They were married during the war. Lucky to have a man at all, her sister had said. Her mother hadn't been so sure. 'That man was born under a miserable sky,' she'd warned, but Aida knew best.

There was no honeymoon; George thought it a waste. Aida had agreed — it was 1943. They moved into a new fibro-and-tile home on a rare, scorching day in September. It felt like the first day of something exciting. They drank lemon cordial on upturned boxes and Aida chattered about what she might do to the house.

George handed Aida an envelope. On it was written *Housekeeping* in neat, tight loops.

'There'll be the same every week,' he said.

She fingered the envelope. Opened it. Pulled out notes. It had seemed a lot of money at the time, though she would have preferred flowers.

He was absent a lot in those first years. Somehow, she knew not to ask. George never spoke of it. 'Nothing I can talk of,' he said, 'war business.' It was a matter of family shame that he never left Australia, never saw active duty, never put his body on the line. And George never explained himself.

When the war ended, the unexplained trips grew less frequent until he took a job with a firm that made laundry detergent, something in accounts. 'Those clothes are bright,' he'd say over dinner.

'Yes,' she'd reply and offer more gravy.

The laundry powder, of which Aida had an endless supply, was cheap, waxy and smelled slightly of fish.

It seemed there was money in detergent. George bought them bigger and bigger houses and they moved closer to the river, closer to the city. It was hard to complain.

With each child, the housekeeping envelope got slightly thicker, and as Lucy, Joan and then Francis left home, one by one, the envelope shrunk again. Every Friday it was there, on her dresser, always just enough. Just.

✳

The next morning George is in from the garden by the time Aida gets up. His shoulders lean over the *Courier Mail*. He moves a giant magnifying glass over the text; he's reduced to the headlines these days. The blindness creeps like a solar eclipse. It is surprising how quickly the shade comes.

Aida takes her tea and a scotch finger into the sunroom where she hooks on in 8ply.

She calls Betty. The words tumble out fast. 'I've had enough,' Aida finally says. 'I think I want to leave.' The stiches fall off the afghan hook.

Betty says she understands, she knows. 'You will come and stay with me,' she says.

'That man,' adds Betty, 'always had a great talent for misery and small talent for marriage.'

Aida fingers the tube that is becoming a giant woollen squid for Caitlin and wonders how many tentacles it will need.

✳

After a restless night, Aida does 40 miles per hour on Fig Tree Pocket Road and hooks left into Clayton Avenue. Her spotted hands grasp at the top of the wheel and her sun-browned face cranes to see over the bonnet despite a foam cushion. The speedometer on her 1957 Fiat hits *40 mph* for the first time in years.

She picks up Betty on the way. Betty lost her licence five years ago. So did Aida.

'Fifty years to that man!' Aida says, leaning forward and failing to slow down at a *Give Way* sign. 'Fifty years.'

'Fifty is a long time,' says Betty.

'I hope he collapses in the cactus,' says Aida. 'I just might not be there to pick him up,' she adds. The speed feels good.

'Not *might not*,' says Betty, '*will not*!' And she nods and thumps her handbag to make the point.

After the supermarket, Aida and Betty emerge slightly bruised and blink, bewildered, into the car park.

A man is hovering around the Fiat, walking around it. He is middle-aged and a bit tatty.

'Nice wheels,' he says as they approach. 'It's the condition I'm impressed by … I'm guessing one owner.'

'Yes,' replies Aida, 'not a scratch. And the inside … well …'

Aida, Betty and the man peer into the car where purple, cream and pink crochet squares cover the steering wheel, gear stick, rearmirror stem, floor mats, dashboard, indicator stick, headrests, front seats, back seats, parcel shelf.

'All your work?' he asks.

'She did every stitch,' says Betty proudly.

'I'd give you good money,' he says. 'Call me if you're interested.' He presses a business card into Aida's hand. Aida's ears flush.

'How thrilling,' says Betty as they pull out of the car park.

Aida might do with a new zippy red car like her granddaughter. As she drives Betty home she calculates how many housekeeping envelopes she's received in fifty years of marriage. The number is sobering.

✳

Two days pass and the weekly envelope appears. It sits neatly on the dresser. His handwriting is shaky and old but still mean.

Loop, hook, drop.

A red tropical fish takes shape at the end of her hook.

She imagines herself walking out with nothing but the crochet box. Maybe the box and the photo albums. Maybe the box and the photo albums and a small suitcase. Her life in the boot of the Fiat. Or the new red car.

The idea of leaving George is moving into her muscles, into her bones.

She looks around the room. She will sell things. All his things. All the things that have meant nothing to her and something to him. His stamps first.

She grabs his stamp albums, puts them in the bottom of her bag, and as she walks past the dresser she pushes at the envelope with her hand. Makes sure it doesn't sit quite so parallel to the table.

✳

At Doug Sholl's Stamps and Coins, a man, who looks a bit like her son, peers over the stamps. 'Where did you get these?' he asks, opening the first album.

Betty places her hand over the plastic pages. 'Firstly,' she says, 'are you *Douglas Sholl*?' Betty pushes her glasses up with her ring finger.

'Present and accounted for.' He smiles.

'Right,' says Betty. 'They belonged to her late husband and we need a valuation.'

'I'm sorry,' he says, looking at Aida.

'Thank you,' Aida replies. The gap between his front teeth seems honest.

'You'll need to leave them with me. A week. I'll give you a receipt.'

Aida nods. A week. George's glaucoma is on her side. He mostly prefers television these days.

As they leave, Betty squeezes Aida's arm.

'How thrilling,' says Betty.

'You're a good liar,' says Aida.

'Of course I am; I was married forty-six years.'

Aida laughs. Things always seem possible around Betty.

✳

The valuation comes in. The numbers are big. Betty and Aida pore over Doug's neat columns at Liz's Diner. The albums sit between Aida and Betty, leaving nowhere to put the tea and carrot cake when it comes.

Aida scrapes back her chair. The feeling of anger is not entirely unexpected but the sense of shame is so unsettling that she finds it hard to say anything. She hears herself snapping. 'Well. That is just impossible!' Wanting to get away from the humiliation of his wealth in the light of her weekly scrapings, of being his housekeeper, of being part of something so lowly. She walks quickly towards the Fiat, leaving Betty starting after her.

✳

George is out at the Club. Aida lays out the albums and hunts for the stamps. Doug has marked pages with Post-it notes: little yellow flags flap beside the most valuable stamps. She pulls them out, one by one, with her bathroom tweezers, and places them on a piece of blue airmail paper.

She scrutinises them, pauses to take in their colours and shapes. Such strange little paintings. Presently, she takes out her small scissors.

She opens and closes them in the air, finds their snip satisfying. Then she cuts a vague replica, matching rough colours from the pile of junk mail next to her. She cuts each forgery to size and places it in the little empty space in the album.

In the heat, her upper lip beads and she turns on the overhead fan.

The stamps flutter off the table and float to the carpet. Butterflies out of the net. It takes her half an hour to find the final stamp pressed up against the foot of a lamp. She examines it; a small, faded kangaroo marked *Two Pounds*. It's worth more than a year's housekeeping. She replaces it with a replica cut from a local tradesman advertising gutter cleaning at *best mates rates*. The match is good. Good enough.

She cuts and replaces. After two hours she stares at her handiwork.

She places the real stamps into an envelope in the crochet box, under the squid and half-finished tropical fish. The albums sit back on the shelf and look down at her as though nothing has happened.

By the time George comes home from the clubhouse, his mood dark and drunk, Aida is in bed. She stares at the ceiling and feels as though she has stepped into another world.

✳

Every few days Betty and Aida visit Doug Sholl after the shopping. Finally, the first stamp sells.

'We got a great price,' Doug says. 'There was an American bidding on the phone. Pushed the price right up. Did us a great favour! Ta da.' He puts a cheque on the counter with a flourish.

'But I wanted cash,' Aida says. She has no bank account for the cheque. She knows she sounds ungrateful.

'I can cash it,' soothes Betty.

Aida smiles apologetically at Doug.

'Next instalments in cash,' says Doug. He gives her a wink.

All the way home she can't shake the feeling that she is making a mess of it all.

✳

As she comes up the stairs, George is at the dining room table leaning over his stamp albums. She freezes. What were the chances? The cash-filled handbag swings on the crook of her arm. Her breathing is fast, shallow; she watches and races with *what ifs*.

He leafs through the albums but isn't really looking; his fingertips tease memories from the familiarity of the pages. The magnifying glass lies on the table next to him. He stares into the distance, sighs, and tenderly places his good hand on top of the albums. Just like Doug Sholl did.

Her breathing slows. Aida takes the final two stairs, walks past him into the kitchen. 'Cuppa, George?'

'Too bloody hot,' he grumbles.

He's right, but Aida boils the kettle anyway.

✳

Blue sea anemones tangle across her lap in the afternoon sun as she sips her tea. She is out of wool.

Late in the afternoon she joins George in the sitting room and settles into the well-worn green corduroy of her chair. George watches the TV while Aida flicks through *Crochet!* magazine.

She expects to feel plump with revenge, warm at the thrill of the cash and the idea of escaping. But in the late afternoon her decision to leave, which felt so solid during the day, becomes fragile.

George gets up, pours two whiskeys and feeds the parrots. As the early news begins he places Aida's whiskey on a blue crocheted coaster and, with a shaky hand, places her pillbox next to it.

'Down the hatch,' he says.

Outside, parrots flutter slightly drunk into the windows. Aida begins to feel a little warm. Perhaps it's just the whiskey.

She begins to knit a starting chain. Inside the wicker box at her feet, sea creatures float beside balls of wool and remnants in snap-lock bags. Underneath that are old copies of *Crochet!*, and below them fat envelopes, each filled with cash from the sale of the first stamp. Each envelope is marked in Aida's hand and reads *Housekeeping.*

While George drops into sleep open-mouthed and wet-lipped, Aida closes her eyes and begins to crochet. She imagines a tropical sea where seaweed drifts weightless and fish dart between corals. Stiches fall off the afghan hook in blue-green seaweed strands.

After a while she pauses, opens her eyes, looks down. The stiches are flawed, dropped, uneven, and the seaweed pulses wide then thin then wide again. She should pull out the hook and let the stiches unravel, start again. But it's late and she is tired. Instead she ties off, pulls the knot tight and cuts the wool. George stirs and settles again.

As she fingers the seaweed a single thread comes loose, goes its own way. She takes out a yarn needle and weaves it back into the seaweed, invisibly binding it to the hundreds of stitches that went before. Then she places it in the wicker box.

Theresa Layton is an emerging writer who lives in Canberra. Her short story 'The Other Side' was published in *Award Winning Australian Writing 2010*. She has won the Perilous Adventures Short Story Competition two years running, and won the Common Thread Long Short Story Competition in 2011. She is currently working on a collection of short stories. Theresa wishes she could hold a tune, grow tomatoes and tell a good joke.

The **Perilous Adventures Short Story Competition** is an annual competition for short stories up to 5000 words in any genre. The competition's focus is on recognising and rewarding writers of outstanding short fiction, and supporting them in further developing their profile and career. The prize is announced each year during the Brisbane Writers Festival. Prizes include publication and mentorships. More information is available at *www.perilousadventures.net*.

AMY ESPESETH

QUT Creative Writing Prize

Downwind

It was a problem of inheritance: Downwind. The name implied stench, *stay downwind*, and sneakiness at the same time. White folks seemed to imagine a sly creeper, a shifty stinky *Injun* skulking forward on moccasin tiptoe, and for most of Adam's life that's what his last name — his father's name — meant to him, too. He didn't remember all that much; he'd been too little, just turned six, when the tall man drove away in a souped-up Chevy. Adam thought he might recall a rotting jack-o-lantern with a crooked smile and maybe a soft, grey bunny pelt, but those memories might've just been his mother's. She talked a lot about him — the first Adam Downwind — when Adam was little, but she'd stopped carrying on the last few years. There were still those pictures — a skinny man carving pumpkins, then him again skinning rabbits — on the fireplace mantle, framed for the funeral but faded from twenty years of Sunday dusting and daily sunlight. But lately, it seemed his mother had finally moved on.

He hadn't thought much about him — or maybe hadn't thought that much of him, his father, to be honest. It wasn't his bloodline: there wasn't no shame in being Chippewa, not in these parts. He caught more stick at school from his mom being white, always accused — whether it was his curly hair or slouchy way of walking — of trying to pretend like he was white too. Adam's half-breedness was trouble on the reservation and off: too white inside the section lines and a bit too red outside. After a few teenage years of First Nation pow-wows and mainly futile attempts at language and dancing, since high school he generally tried to blend wherever — and with whomever — he was.

Dealing cards at the casino, Adam heard much more about Downwind: *good sausage makers,* an old woman refilling the toilet paper told him when she read his name tag; *hell of a sense of humour,* from a man who'd known his dad from 4-H. These were folks off of the same reservation where his dad had been raised, and they'd known the Downwinds for generations. Now, with Adam being the only son of an only son, it was both a pleasure and a duty for them to recall those times with a young man barely recognisable as theirs. It seemed like every old person with a story felt like they owed him that much. For Adam didn't look like a Downwind; his almost black hair helped but his blue eyes threw plenty off the scent. And, of course, you didn't have to be Chippewa to work at the casino, so lots of white workers didn't even notice him or his name. But the folks like him — the half-of-something, half-of-another — and the real Indians seemed to see him, look down deep inside. They saw Downwind, and those that knew and remembered told him about his name.

Tuesday nights were rarely busy. Mostly a few depressed regulars: feed cap shit-kickers losing their farms at blackjack and blue-haired ladies pouring their retirement quarter by quarter into the blinking and squawking machines. The battered walleye and shrimp brought some locals in, but it was usually a quiet evening for the staff. Restock and clean, that's what management expected; rest and recover, that's what the kindly pit boss allowed. And they needed it, the dealers, with the weekends being crazy as deer season approached. Folks were up from Chicago, overexcited about hunting, and locals were just starting to settle into both the respite and desperation of the coming winter. A man could rest seeing the corn was harvested and the hay was cut, but there was always the fear of not making it through to spring. Worries kept folks awake: not knowing if the barn was full enough or if the money for fuel oil would last until spring — it going up all the time, and costing an arm and a leg already. Wisconsin winter's a long time to wait on the thaw. But if a guy can't sleep, he can always go to the casino.

Already worn out from six hours of standing, Adam was just leaning at the rail and looking at his empty chairs when his mother sat down at his poker table. She'd dolled herself up — shiny dress, lipstick and black lashes — and didn't look half bad. 'We've feasted on fish!' she said, over-pronouncing 'feasted' in a way Adam knew she thought sounded regal, but just made her seem dumb. 'Lavonne's in the restroom, so I thought I'd take full advantage of our outing and check on my favourite son.' Always, the old girl had to put a shine on everything: restroom instead of bathroom, the favourite son was her only child. He knew he was too hard on her, but he couldn't help it. She'd filled his childhood with camping trips that never came and broken promises of birthday bikes and big parties. Even her great outing was just a cheap fish meal designed to lure in locals and turn them into gamblers.

'I really can't visit while I'm working, Mom.' Her lowered head and crushed mouth made him regret the roughness in his voice, so he added, 'Glad to see you out having fun, though.' His mother looked up from her pink nails and smiled again; she made an I-won't-bother-you-none face and put her hands in her lap. He took out a rack of chips and made a show of reordering them, pulling out and putting back into place pieces that were already perfectly arranged. Then he smoothed the green felt with his hands and drummed his fingers on the table. His mother relaxed in the middle of the empty chairs, contentedly humming an old torch song and watching him with pride. Her eyes followed and appreciated his every move, and she nodded approvingly like she had taught him everything he knew. She beamed like he was a heart surgeon. Adam sighed aloud while silently wondering how long it usually took for Lavonne to use a toilet.

He could smell her almost before he could see her: Lavonne's cheap Jovan musk and sweet liquor scent were one of the few mainstays of his childhood. She'd been his mother's childhood friend and — other than a misunderstanding right around the time of his father's death — constant companion. They were inseparable. Now that they were nearing forty, they were almost difficult to tell apart: same frosted blond hair, round Scandie faces, and figures that were almost enough to convince a guy to ignore the age difference. Lavonne reached across the table, touched his face and winked, 'Good to see you, Adam.' Then she turned to his mother and changed her tune, anxiously whispering, 'Sheila, I think I've seen a ghost.' She plopped down into the chair nearest his mother and began to fan her face with her hands.

Oh, the drama. If Adam had had a nickel for every overplayed emotion that he'd witnessed out of Lavonne, he would sure as hell be on a yacht right now, not dealing cards. If his mother had had a nickel for the same, she'd probably be feeding those coins into a slot machine; she always believed the lie. While Adam shrugged and turned away, glancing at the understanding pit boss but still rolling his eyes in exasperation, Sheila took the bait. His mother was shivering with excitement. 'What do you mean?' The whispering was ridiculous. 'In the restrooms?' And here Adam leaned back in toward the table and listened; this ought to be good. Lavonne's response was sure to be either a self-aggrandising description of a shared mirror with a gorgeous lipstick re-applier who could have been her as a young girl, or a passing dashing man with whom she'd christened a long-ago backseat.

'It was the young cop,' Lavonne kept a hushed tone, but twisted her head on her neck and scanned the room as if checking for spies. 'But he's old now, older than us.' She leisurely crossed and uncrossed her long legs on the stool, a habitual attention-getter even when sharing a secret. Adam watched his mother's expression swing from anticipation to shock. Sheila bit her lip and went white.

This was not the spicy way-back story she'd been expecting, and she looked as if she might cry.

'Oh, Lord Jesus,' Sheila said, 'maybe he'll finally make it right.' And then whatever had held back the tears broke, and his mother slumped down into her chair as her mascara began to run. Lavonne retrieved the Kleenex she always kept up her cardigan sleeve and handed it to Sheila. Dabbing at her eyes, Sheila struggled to regain control; after several minutes of quiet crying, she looked up at Adam. 'You have to go make him admit it. He's the only one who can.' After a deep breath she fished a mirror out of her purse, cleaned beneath her eyes with the tissue, slicked on her lipstick, and steeled her face against the world.

Adam had seen this simultaneous rearranging of features and circumstance before: late rent transformed into another month's grace by a seductive smile, or cut-rate tyres further discounted by heavy lashes. His mother had often relied on the loneliness of strangers, especially the lustful kindness of men. But she was telling him to do it this time, to go and offer himself up. Adam wanted to pretend that he didn't know who they were talking about, but the 'young cop' had been a key player in many of the women's fantasies, both get-rich-quick and revenge. And he'd never convince them he didn't know; their trailer had been too small for secrets, and Adam's black-and-white television was never enough once they got going. The history of the young cop and Lavonne and his mother's hopes for man's part in their future were always discussed too loudly to ignore.

He wasn't going to do it, walk over to the stranger and demand an explanation, try and force the man to admit he was — at the very least — a witness. He wasn't going to do anything. But when Adam looked again at his mother, her eyes were following Lavonne's outstretched arm as the woman pointed to a rangy man with a grey crew cut. The man was in his fifties with generic glasses over a squat nose. He was settled at a blackjack table, holding his cards tight in one hand with his other wiry arm wrapped around his waist. And they'd always known who he was, anyway; his name had been listed in the police report. Theirs was too small a town to not know who people were. Adam remembered some screaming phone calls his mother had made, and he was ashamed he'd looked up Kowalski in the phone book himself. So when he saw his mother start crying again, unable to stop even after Lavonne pulled her into a smothering hug, Adam stood up away from the table rail and moved toward the blackjack table.

As he wove between the tables that separated his station and where the formerly young cop sat, Adam reheard all of the women's late-night scheming: a lawsuit against the county would pay out big; wrongful death or hate-crime or something of the like. The way Lavonne told it — and hers was the only word they had to rely on — his father had survived the crash. There had been the snow and, yes, lots of beer, and bad tyres on the truck and low lights. The other car had come speeding around the corner and both vehicles had crossed the centre line. Lavonne always teared up when she talked about the tiny car: three packed across the front seat — eyes glowing like deer in the headlights — the shiny faces of two young girls and the boy driving. The ice, and then the horrific noise of the truck hitting the car, and the screaming and the sleet still pounding down. Lavonne climbing out of the truck, crawling on her hands and knees on the icy gravel, bleeding from her head and trying to find the first Adam Downwind. He'd been thrown clear. She remembered picking glass out of her face, seeing flashlights and hearing Adam moan and moving towards him, but then laying down in the snow alongside the road. When she awoke, Adam was less than a couple yards away, and a man's boot was crushing his throat. An old policeman was saying, 'That's the last you'll drive.' And behind the old man who was murdering her friend stood the young cop, shaking, but trying to hold steady a flashlight on the scene. Lavonne saw the young cop's eyes and knew that he knew he couldn't stop it.

Adam was shaking himself, and he didn't know what he was

doing. He wasn't walking over to Kowalski for no money, but he didn't know why he was walking over at all. He'd heard the story so many times that he could feel the snow melt on his arms and pick the glass out of his own face; he never felt the boot crushing his windpipe, though. When Adam remembered the death of his father, it was always as Lavonne, his mother's best friend forever; and when the women relived the night, it was never quite explained why the wrong woman was in the truck. It was always something about needing more beer and his mother didn't drink, or there was mention of the baby — him — being sick. And it was always partially why Adam had stayed away from liquor. As he walked toward the gambling man, the young cop who had heard his father gurgle and struggle for air, Adam wasn't thinking of money or revenge. He only thought that he might finally be ready for a drink.

When Adam got to the blackjack table, he stood about a foot away and stared at Kowalski. Adam watched the man finger the edges of his cards, squint at his chips, and lay down his bets. The dealer shot Adam a look that let him know that the gambler had started sliding downhill, and Kowalski's slumped shoulders told him the same. The game ended as Kowalski slapped the table and swore; the other player quietly stacked his winnings and walked away. Adam stood and pressed his hands into his elbows and thought he could smell tyres burning. He knew it was now or never, that if there was anything to be done it would be have to be done now. He took a step toward the old man, reached out his hand and touched his shoulder.

Kowalski turned to Adam, but his eyes barely glanced up as he rubbed his grey head. 'I'll have a Coke,' he said and then turned back to the dealer. 'Let's do this again.' Then the old man raised his eyebrows and laughed in way that was more of a cough; it seemed to be part of the struggle against showing how much he had bet or how much he had lost. The tall dealer brushed his long braid back over his shoulder and began to reshuffle the cards. He nodded at

Adam and gave him a smirk that said he knew his co-worker had been slighted with the drink order, but that the gambler would pay for it eventually. Adam stood with his hand still stretched out and waited for a moment; he was waiting to feel something and then decide what to do. When he felt nothing and waited and felt nothing again, finally he turned and walked away.

Adam walked toward the bar. He looked across the room and saw his mother and Lavonne smiling and chatting animatedly to two men in crumpled suits and loose neckties — businessmen up from Chicago. The bells of a slot machine were ringing and an old lady was collecting the coins in a plastic casino bucket. Waitresses in short skirts were walking by, carrying pop and juice to the tables. A dishevelled young man was passed out in one of the deep leather seats near the bar. Adam got the bartender's attention, pointed toward the blackjack table where Kowalski sat, and ordered the old man his Coke. Then he sat down, took off his nametag, and ordered himself a whiskey. The bartender, having worked with Adam for a couple years, looked surprised. Then he poured the man his drink and said, 'Here you go, Downwind.'

There are some things a man puts off but can never be shook or fully ignored. Adam had been too young and there weren't any pictures to help him, but he had the creased obituary in his wallet. He took it out and unfolded the yellowed paper on the bar. He could remember waiting all that winter, hoping for the thaw. His father's burial had been put off — 'spring burial', the newspaper said — until better weather and softer ground. Once the graves dug in fall were filled, everyone had to just sit tight. It was putting off for tomorrow what should be done today. Adam drank his whiskey and ordered another. The employees — native or white the same — weren't allowed to gamble at their workplace, but they sure as hell could drink. And there was no reason to worry about the thaw. Better weather never comes. The old newspaper clipping was disintegrating, sopping up the rings of condensation on the bar. It will stay cold here forever, he thought, always cold.

Amy Espeseth was born in rural Wisconsin in 1974 and immigrated to Australia in 1998. She holds a Master of Arts in creative writing from the University of Melbourne, where she is a sessional tutor and PhD student. Her fiction has appeared in various journals, and she received the Felix Meyer Award for Literature in 2007. Amy's first novel, *Sufficient Grace*, was awarded the Victorian Premier's Literary Award for an unpublished manuscript in 2009 and will be published by Scribe in 2012. An extract from her second novel, *Trouble Telling the Weather*, won the QUT Postgraduate Creative Writing Prize in 2010. Amy is the new publisher at Vignette Press. Continuing Vignette's sub-cultural journal series including *Sex Mook* and *Death Mook*, *Geek Mook* is scheduled for launch in late 2011. She lives in Footscray.

The **QUT Creative Writing Prizes** offer $2000 each for the first-place winners of the Postgraduate and Undergraduate categories. In addition to the cash prize, Highly Commended certificates are awarded to all shortlisted candidates, and the final entries are published in the annual QUT Creative Writing and Literary Studies journal, *Rex*. Entries may be in the form of a short story, creative nonfiction, a literary or professional writing essay, or poetry. Submissions are limited to 3000 words of prose or 50 lines of poetry.

KIRK MARSHALL

fourW twenty-one *Booranga Prize — Best Short Story*

Bear vs. Plane!

We were sitting with calculable comfort at about 3000 feet, our feeble human engineering warping from the relaxed atmosphere of our immediate surrounds, the cabin lights dimmed in a subdued, sleep-aglow sort of way, and the earth rotating beneath us was now not *even* a memory, but a rumour or a myth.

I think it's only precise to suggest that we were all succumbing to the mid-flight possibility of unerring bliss when the plane banked left with a sudden sharp logic, and the craft began to shudder, a nauseating momentum. A bear was on the wing, and it was sinking its legend of bladed teeth into the skybus carapace, plunging holes into the cabin through which its thermal-deranged eye roved, bloodshot and foaming, fascinated by the horrified human cargo trembling and yowling within.

I'd seen a bear once, or maybe read about one, but the experience had constituted an apparently unprofound and spurious event because I knew nothing of merit about such animals, except that they excrete a noxious mixture from a foot-shaped gland; though for what it's worth that could have been mountain goats. Not possessing an interest in the particulars of zoology, or things of this breed, I did not feel certain about the most effective way to intervene in the turbulent fear of the moment, so I slunk out of my seat into the aisle and grimaced, like a marathon athlete distressed by the lacklustre gloss of his or her performance.

'We should trade with it!' I suggested, as oxygen masks vaulted from the ceiling in a weird clusterfuck of pneumatic pipe and plastic.

Stewardesses were somersaulting like bulbs of forest pollen, their white uniforms brazen and distinct among the red abundance of screaming mouths. I felt, for a glee-drunk second, that all these bright, swift, softly-phosphorous women were dashing themselves at my feet because of the image of a gallant hero-bandit that I presently commandeered, but I am not so dispossessed of intelligence to forget that I am fat, short, nervous and equipped with a nose capable of inviting comparisons with a small bowel. For these reasons I merely entertained an obscene fantasy to put me at ease, in which I swam naked with these fleet-pleated females in a lake that bristled with the greenest orbs of floating apples, and within a passage of panicked seconds I felt sufficiently restored in my miraculous purpose to propose another solution.

'I think I watched a documentary once that advises victims of a bear attack to transform into hedgehogs and roll away. Actually, I think it was a school play I was once involved in. Never mind!'

This, too, did not generate the stutter of generous applause nor the graphic spontaneous nudity that I was striving to catalyse, so I scowled and plundered my pockets for warmth. The bear had sheared a considerable hole in the side of the aircraft at this point, so that we could all collectively observe the rapid articulations of the beast's paws as they monstered the exterior alloy and thrust talons the size of sunsets through the gap in the metal.

It was a mild, unclouded day outside, and the high-octane whistling of debris and upholstery being set astir by the stratospheric winds reminded me of swallows whistling, though it might have been kikes warbling.

'I've got it!' I yelled, my head frothy and raging with the adrenaline of my conviction. 'Why don't we paint stripes on ourselves to make us resemble zebras? Bears don't eat zebras, and that's a simple fact of chemistry!' I was incommunicable with pride at this theoretical injunction, and I probably would've been swarmed by in-flight hostesses startled into arousal by the catastrophic theatre of our present dilemma, but the bear chose that moment to lunge at a passenger hoarse with terror, cowering in her seat, and the berserk creature managed to pull her, despite her convulsive kicks, through the gash in the plane's exposed side.

The woman was accelerating to her murder, and this realisation went down sharp in me, like a slice of lightning pie. I could only glimpse a tangle of visual cues outside the periphery of the nearest convex window, but the thrashing passenger seemed to be grappling with the bear out on the wing, blood fanning rivers of carotid-crimson through the incendiary fire of the daytime sky.

The bear was feasting. I could not abide this, particularly not directly following my brilliant scheme to disguise the entire airborne convoy as economy-class zebras, so I careened down the aisle, artfully darting past the sinewy blooms of the oxygen masks, capering above the glade of golden hair thicketing from the screaming scalps of one hundred sex-fierce flight attendants as they marvelled at my Sisyphean ascent. Soon the planets glided through my legs like a basketball being dribbled to the cosmic net by a Harlem Globetrotter displaying the wings of a condor.

I thundered down the aisle, between fright-blighted faces, a thousand docile drugged-up irises swifting in their sockets to watch me dare the ghosts of adventure, yet I continued harrying up that band of carpet without pause, until I reached the emergency supplies strapped fast to the wall at the nose-end of the plane. I prized the flare-gun from its bracket and, without a further regard for self-preservation or even the expression on my ex-wife's face when I disturbed her in the throes of orgasm with a census collector, I dove through the hole in the aircraft and hooked onto the ligature of the left wing.

The bear looked up, haunted, a mutilated sneaker dangling like the first fruit of misery from its blood-clovered jaw. It roared at me then, at my compulsion to disrespect its efforts to kill the whimpering, shallow-breathing woman travestied in a splay of wounded limbs on the shark-shaped extremity of the aeroplane.

I grinned, clambering to my knees and triumphantly locating my feet. I waved the gun, an arc of propulsive colour, and narrowed my gaze at the great swollen animal hulking toward me. 'You're smoked, cubby,' I crowed, pulling the trigger, thinking that I should aim for its heart, but wondering whether that applied to bears or tigers. The sky pulsed a stroboscopic red.

Kirk Marshall is an emerging Brisbane-born, Melbourne-based writer. He has written for more than sixty publications, both in Australia and overseas, including *Wet Ink*, *Going Down Swinging*, *Voiceworks*, *Verandah*, *fourW*, *Mascara Literary Review*, *Word Riot* (USA), *3:AM Magazine* (Paris), *(Short) Fiction Collective* (USA), *The Seahorse Rodeo Folk Review* (USA) and *Kizuna: Fiction for Japan* (Japan). Kirk was the first-prize recipient of the 2010 Booranga Prize from Charles Sturt University for Best Short Story. He edits *Red Leaves*, the English-language / Japanese bilingual literary journal. Kirk's debut short-story collection, *Carnivalesque: And, Other Stories*, will be published by Black Rider Press in October 2011.

The **Booranga Prizes**, one for fiction and one for poetry, are awarded each year for the best short story and poem in the current issue of *fourW*, the annual anthology of new writing and graphics published by fourW press, out of Charles Sturt University's Booranga Writers' Centre. The competition judges are comprised of the *fourW* editor and the selection panel. The School of Humanities and Social Sciences at CSU funds the prizes, worth $250 each.

TASHA SUDAN

Blake Poetry Prize

Rahula[*]

That night, I imagine
underneath my eyelids —
I saw him.
The lamplight on his hair
shining like black lacquer
the sump smell of his scalp.

He bends over me
(in this vision)
his breath
falls
into that warm hollow
cast from his own.
I make of my throat a well
to house the falling pebble.

In the morning while
the sun scatters through
the lattice of the window,
like beads of yellow oil
spilt on the earthen floor —
my mother wails.

There is a bowl,
goat's milk fresh drunk
on the table.

Its blue skin still glistens.

Later, we would hear
sometimes of him with
boney ribs and sunken cheeks
ranging the lunar landscapes
of a desert
his eyes salt flat
or, on a hillside
the color of ghee
breathing soft as moth.

Her black flow of hair
has white water in it when
finally, we go in search of him.

There are waxy mountains
faceless lakes
places where rocks crack open
in the cold
I could tell you of them
I could;
for days and days
I was fed just by the shade
of her sandalwood silks.

One day, we find him.

He says: *Rahula, close your eyes.*
This pitcher, this hand, the flaxen field —
breathe them in
as if you were the air itself
and empty, completely
your will;
but I have his breath in a chamber of my chest
that riverstone
that bird with still wings
beating.

I will not let it go.

In the long shallow
noon when there are no shadows
they gather like vultures
on the flanks of the peak.
He holds up the single flower
and his eyes, roaming over
those bent, bare heads
(fingers twirling the chalky stem)
speak only to one man:
he has chosen.

When did he become
a space that simply houses me
in him, beside the squat lamp
black ponds, rising birds — a horizon
beyond its own line?

Rahula

I sit in the still field;
I feel nothing at all.
His breath is a broken rock
in my chest.
Nor can I empty, completely, when
from the swollen hillsides
the color runs
down into the rivers where
the women wash cloth
spreading his word
in the rushing currents.

They know nothing of us:
my mother and I
in the bruise of the dusk
our white robes making
morning stars of us
shedding a light that falls
unseen on the field
on the thronging grass
and the loyal soil;
on the black well
with the pebble
that was once
(in this vision)
a jewel.

So close, we are invisible.

---

* Given by the Buddha to his son before renouncing his family, the name can be translated as 'bond' or as 'fetter'.

Tasha Sudan comes and goes from Ulladulla on the south coast of New South Wales. She spent four years in residential training at the Zen Mountain Monastery in the Catskill mountains of upstate New York, which began as a Zen arts training centre. She has worked as a radio journalist and recently in screenwriting. She is currently in residence at Toshoji, a Soto Zen temple in the mountainous Okayama prefecture of central Japan, where she was ordained a monk in September 2010.

The **Blake Poetry Prize** is a national award, now in its fourth year, offering a cash prize of $5000 for a new poem that best explores the religious or spiritual. The prize, named after the visionary poet and artist William Blake, is non-sectarian and encourages Australian poets to write a new work of up to 100 lines displaying a critical awareness of, or sympathy for, the concepts of religion or spirituality.

The Blake Poetry Prize is presented by the New South Wales Writers' Centre and Blake Society, with the generous support of Leichhardt Municipal Council.

www.blakeprize.com.au/galleries/the-blake-poetry-prize

KEREN HEENAN
Hal Porter Short Story Competition

Beyond the Bay

When I see the stranger in the distance, coming down the sandy track, I know that everything from now on will be different. All day I have looked to the headland and the pale trail leading down to the beach; afraid that someone may come, terrified that they won't. If I am alone for much longer in this wild place I am not sure what I will do. Yet if I am not alone my purpose in being here is bent, confused. My jaw is sore from clenching and unclenching.

Last night the thunder crashed and rolled around the sky all night long, and lightning flared the tent into daylight. It seemed that even through my eyelids I could see the gnarled fingers of trees above the tent, stark against a violet sky. Before sunrise the rain started, solid drops like boulders falling on the thin sheet. I stared into darkness, imagining the water rising around the tent, loosening the pegs and floating me away into silvery-blue. I felt as if some other substance was running through my veins, mercury or treacle, but not blood. I tried to find patterns in the dark, some spaces of lesser dark to link together. But it was all darkest dark.

Some time after dawn the rain stopped, and when I peered outside I could see small puddles reflecting a lemony glow. My head felt heavy and I think I'd been dreaming: lots of hills and running and stubble that felt like glass underfoot.

I have been on edge all day, waiting and watching, as if I have known all along that someone will come. I have gathered sticks and pebbles, seed pods and shells, and sat in the clearing, sorting through them. I chose a smooth, white pebble with a vein of palest caramel and placed it in the centre, surrounded it with seed pods, eight in all, ran a twig from each pod outward, another pebble at the head of each twig, working around the circle. But today even this pattern hasn't pleased me the way it should. It was jarring and bare. I left it there and returned to the beach. And now the stranger is here.

I watch the small, dark figure becoming taller, larger. There's something odd about him and I can't work out his arms. As he comes closer I see his arms are raised, crucifixion style. I stay tucked in among the trees, watching him coming closer, wondering if it's some *Passion Play* being enacted, or perhaps some lunatic carrying his own cross. I slide in behind the tree trunk. I have no time to pack up my camp site. I dare a look out and see now that it is a man with a backpack, and a stick behind his neck and his arms looped over it at the wrists. He has long, curly hair and a hat that covers his eyes. I don't know where to run.

When he reaches the small rise near where I'm standing he pulls the stick from his shoulders and stares at me in surprise. 'Oh,' he says. 'I thought I'd be the only one here.' I nod. 'Ah,' he says and walks past me, sliding his pack off his back. I turn and watch him go to the far side of the cleared space, pausing only briefly to glance down at my circular design. He pulls things from his pack and shakes tent pegs from a pouch, looking up at me as I stand in the same spot. I look away quickly and move to the beach. I'm worried now about how I must look. It is almost two weeks since I have used a mirror and I haven't washed for days. I go to my tent, my head down to avoid his eyes, and take soap and a towel.

Down by the water I'm all a-fluster: should I pack up and move, or stay? should I ignore him or speak to him? Indecision crashes around me and tears prick my eyelids. For one brief moment I would like Marcus to be here. Just so he could hold me, and then be on his way. But he will never be here. There is nothing to bind us any longer.

It doesn't feel as if I've made a decision but I walk around the pebbly point to the sheltered side where the creek runs into the bay. The water is shallow and warm from the sun. I wash my hair. I even wash the clothes I'm wearing, wrap myself in the towel and return. The stranger is not there. Perhaps he is in his tent, or walking up the mountain to the rear of the clearing. The tent is too hot so I dress and go to the beach to sit and watch the curved patterns of light flicker endlessly.

He is there. Halfway around to the headland I can see him twisting his body into strange postures. Yoga, he is doing yoga. I watch for a little while then lie down to doze.

I hear the soft brush of sand and a shadow passes over me, returns, and hovers. 'Seems silly to have two separate fires,' he says. 'Do you mind if we share one?'

When I look up at him I can't see his features, just a fuzzy halo of hair in the blinding light. I squint and shade my eyes. 'Ye-es,' I say, 'I mean, no, okay.'

He nods. 'I'm making a cup of tea.'

I'm not sure if that's an invitation or not, so I nod. He moves away, picking up sticks. I close my eyes again and lie for some time in the sun until I feel my face burning. If the mention of tea was an invitation I have probably missed the opportunity. I stand and stretch, moving off towards the headland to prise mussels off the rocks. I still have rice; I can offer him dinner just in case he has expected me to come and drink his tea.

When I return to the camp I see a second cup by the fire. He has expected me to have tea with him after all. He looks up from his book and says, 'Tea's cold, sorry.'

I shake my head, splaying the fingers of one hand, and drop the mussels on the ground in my towel.

'Have you taken a vow of silence or something?' he says. 'Sorry,' he adds. 'It's just that you're not very talkative.'

How do I tell a stranger that in silence there is a blueness that comforts. Even as it blurs into a kind of whispered black. And this is strength until I can haul myself up again. Long ago when my mother died she was wearing a blue dress. The ambulance roared off into the night while my grandmother held me quietly. And together we fell into some kind of blue silence where I thought of nothing but my head resting in those soft folds.

He's still looking at me as if I am a child who has just done something quaint or endearing. I shake my head. 'No. It's just … I've been here a while by myself.' I rush on, 'I'm cooking. Do you like mussels?' I flip the corner of the towel to show the purple-black shells.

His eyes light up. 'Yes, I do, thanks … I hope that's not presumptuous. You were inviting me to eat with you?'

I nod, 'Yes.' He turns back to his book, his head propped up on a stump padded by his sleeping bag. I want to know what he is reading, but if I don't ask I can pretend he's not here.

While we're sitting, eating, he says, 'How long have you been here?'

I didn't want him to ask questions, but I knew he would. I look into the flames and watch the patterns of orange flare and die. He's stepped over my circular design of sticks and pebbles without disturbing it so I can finish it tomorrow. Yes, I must finish; it will look so much fuller with something chunkier between the twigs, perhaps …

He's looking across at me still, and one question alone is harmless. 'Nearly two weeks.'

'Oh, is that all. I thought it might've been months,' he says. 'I stayed here for a month once. I only had one visitor. The hike over the mountain stops people. You have to be committed to isolation to come here.' He looks at me quizzically, one brow raised. 'Been here before?'

'Once,' I say. 'For a short time.' I remember turning and

looking back along the curved bay as I left, committing the place to memory: the still blue of the bay, the wide silence of the sky. And later, when my mind screamed for refuge, it was this memory that flooded in.

When we finish eating we sit by the fire and stare into the flames. 'You weren't afraid?' he says. 'Camping here alone.'

I shrug. 'No. There's more to be afraid of than camping alone.'

He laughs. 'True. What do you fear most?'

I could tell him that I fear everything. But I think I fear loss the most. I even fear for the loss of those things I don't yet have. 'Those sorts of questions,' I say.

He laughs again. 'Yes, I can tell. You make conversation hard work, don't you?'

How could I tell him what I couldn't even tell Marcus. That when he talked and talked and asked questions about things I could never know the answers to — the burial, what to dress his tiny body in, what to do with the cot, his toys, this grief — it left no silence in which I could fall into blue. I'd said, *Be still, and just hold me,* but he did not understand.

'I'm sorry,' I say. 'I know you didn't come all this way for a conversation with a stranger either. And you've been very ... considerate.'

I want to ask him what he does, who he loves, or has lost, but instead I ask if he'd like a cup of tea. He says no, he only drinks tea during the day, and I'm glad because there's no water and I'd have to find my way to the creek. I have a torch but there are always sounds behind me in the dark.

'Do you know how long you're staying?' he says, then adds, 'or is that an unwanted question, too?' He looks at me then says, 'Ah, a smile.'

'I haven't thought about how long I'll stay, but I don't have much food left.'

'And you're sharing it with me? That's no good. Tomorrow I provide the food, okay?'

I nod. 'Thanks.'

He puts his hands on his knees and stands. 'Well, time for bed. G'night.'

'Good night.'

Before he goes into his tent he looks across at me and says, 'You know, the world is bigger than the things you can't talk about.'

By the light of his torch I see his silhouette moving about in the tent, twisting his body this way and that to remove trousers, shirt, sliding into his sleeping bag. Then the light goes off, and he sighs contentedly. I sit gazing into the dying embers of the fire, then I pour the dishwater and watch the fire splutter and hiss.

✳

Some time through the night the wind shifts. I wake to the change in cadence and lie listening to its rising murmur. If I were home I would hear light furniture moving on the deck outside, voices perhaps, shifting grasses and leaves — a sea of sibilant sound. But I am here, all adrift on a thin mattress, just a flimsy plastic sheet between me and the dark world outside. I wonder what Marcus is doing: is he sleeping? has he, too, woken to the rising burr of the wind? But he is a long way away. I couldn't tell him when he asked where I'd be. *Then I can't tell you where I will be either,* he said. *But I won't be here.*

I take one hand in the other, spoon-like, hefting it lightly. How much is the weight of one hand? one heart? I've seen a sheep's heart. But I mean a *heart* — the one that breaks. And then you have to live. An eternity of *living* stretches before me. It will be done because it must be. I turn on my side and hold emptiness in my arms. And I wonder suddenly, what is the stranger's name.

✳

He has gone from the camp site when I wake. He doesn't return till midday. All morning I have waited for him to appear, on the beach, on the path from the creek. But he has disappeared, and if it wasn't for his tent I'd think I had dreamt him up. Suddenly I hear his cheerful humming and whistling. 'I've just been up the mountain,' he points back over his shoulder. 'Amazing view.'

'Yes, I know,' I say, as if I haven't been anxious for his safety — a fall, snake bite — and wondered where to start searching first.

'Right, my turn for lunch,' he says and rummages in his pack, coming out with packages and tubes of things that he sets up near the fire. 'I'll be out of your way soon,' he says. And I think he means here, now, from the fireside. But he adds, 'I'm heading back to town today.'

'O-oh. I didn't mean … I didn't want to drive you away.'

'No, no, I was only ever staying till this afternoon. Have to work tomorrow.'

✳

I'm standing on the sandy rise, leaning against the tree, watching him walk away. He is almost halfway around the curve of the bay when I remember. 'Wait!' I call, and he pauses, turns. I run along the sand to catch up to him. Panting, I say, 'I don't know your name.'

He says, 'I have told you, you know, but I don't think you took it in.'

'I'm sorry, I don't remember. I'm Elsa.'

'James.' He laughs and shakes my hand. 'We seem to have done this in reverse order.'

I watch him walk away, his figure becoming smaller again. He reaches the track over the headland, turns and waves. I keep watch till long after he has disappeared from sight. I imagine him turning, seeing me as just a speck on the sand, and I wave again though I know he's gone now. Silence thrums painfully for a moment then I turn and face the water. Beyond the bay, the distant horizon is a pale shimmer.

Keren Heenan is a part-time teacher of the Arts living in Melbourne. She has been awarded the Hal Porter Short Story Competition 2010, the Southern Cross Literary Competition 2009, and the Ellen Gudrun Kasten (short story) Award 2007. She has been published in *Overland*, *Island*, *Wet Ink*, and in other Australian magazines and anthologies. She is a member of Io Writers' Group and is currently working on a novel.

September 29, 2011 marked the twenty-seventh anniversary of Hal Porter's death. To celebrate his literary life, the East Gippsland Art Gallery and the Hill of Content Bookshop launched the eighteenth **Hal Porter Short Story Competition**, with a national prize of $1000 for the winner and book prizes and certificates for shortlisted stories. The competition has been sponsored by the Hill of Content Bookshop, Community College East Gippsland, Collins Booksellers (Bairnsdale), East Gippsland Newspapers, East Gippsland Institute of TAFE, and Porters Electrical. It is also auspiced by the East Gippsland Art Gallery (EGAG) and supported by the University of Queensland Press. For more details, contact founder and organiser Peter Millard via *pedrom53@bigpond.net.au* or visit the EGAG website at *www.eastgippslandartgallery.org.au*.

Jacqueline Winn

Banjo Paterson Writing Awards

The Dangers of Swimming

Rosie never learned to swim. Though, God knows, she tried. Her father insisted that fear was the key. So, when he threw her over the side of the little rowboat, she fought like crazy against the slimy waters of the inlet, that great mangrove-stained bowl of tea, that muddy brew of fish and weed. She thrashed her arms and kicked her feet, desperate for hold against the sinking. But the water sucked her down until her stomach was bloated from so much swallowing and her chest was begging for just one long, dry rush of air. Her father's angry grip pulled her up from drowning and back into the boat to face his scowl of disappointment.

When her coughing and wailing subsided, Rosie looked up to see her twin brother Robert grinning back at her from the stern. He had managed to get back to the boat under his own strength, and their father had helped him back onboard with a kinder hand before slapping his back and shouting his praises. As she pushed her shaking fists into her eyes, squeezing out the tears with the brackish water, Rosie heard her father's disparaging whisper: 'Girls.'

There was only ever one swimming lesson. That was the limit of her father's patience. But Rosie's failure didn't even nibble at the joy of fishing with Robert the next morning, off the end of the little jetty that struck out into the curve of still water below the holiday shack. Every day of that summer break was another long, blue sky burning the skin off their noses and drying their hair to straw as they perched, legs dangling, toes tipping the cool water, fingers flicking at cork-wound lines.

The inlet fish had long been wise to jetty children. Only the puffer-fish fell for the wormy bait and the twins exacted a misplaced revenge by flipping each catch onto the splintery boards and whacking them with a fierce-wielded thong. But not until the fish had filled itself with as much air as it could hold, not until its prickled throat had swelled to twice the size of its body, not until they could almost see its innards through the balloon-thin skin. Robert held his thong high until Rosie judged the moment when the puffer could puff no more. Then she yelled 'Now!' and they greeted the almighty pop with a great circus of leaping and shrieking.

'The best yet!' Robert declared every single time, and Rosie grinned her agreement.

In the afternoons, their mother laid towels on the thin strip of beach and their father speared the sand with a rainbow-coloured umbrella for shade. At first the twins played together, but, after the swimming lesson, Rosie found herself paddling alone at the foamy fringes while her brother stretched his newfound skills further out. Their father pushed him on by swimming a distance, then standing and waiting for Robert to meet the challenge. Deeper and deeper each time. Until one day they strode out of the water together and the boy announced, 'Dad's taking me fishing. Out in the boat. Out in the channel. Tomorrow.'

The disappointed quiver of Rosie's lip went unnoticed among the torrent of objections from their mother. 'No, Bill, the boy's only eight. I don't mind you taking them out on the calm waters. But not the channel. He's too young.'

'C'mon, Emmy, you've seen him. He's a champion. And I'll be there to watch over him. It's time he learned to catch some real fish.'

Any further motherly concerns were smothered by a whirlwind of whooping as Robert tore back into the water and plunged, fingers outstretched, toes disappearing, as neat as a dolphin.

'See,' their father assured. 'Swims like a fish.'

Rosie ducked her head and wandered along the edge of the water. One chance, that was it, and she'd wasted it. She should have tried harder to stay above that sucking water. Tomorrow morning there'd be no fishing from the jetty and she'd be the only one missing it. She kicked at the wet sand, refusing to look up at Robert with his splashing and yelling.

'Rosie, look at me! I'm a fish!'

'You're an idiot,' she whispered, not meaning a word of it.

Rosie heard them leave before dawn the next morning, hushing and shuffling around in the kitchen, clicking the door softly closed, crunching along the gravel path down to the jetty. Then the slow-fading slap of oars.

She mooched her way around the longest morning. A few pieces placed in the holiday jigsaw, a half-hearted game of snap with her mother, a postcard written to Gran. She sniffed at her mother's suggestion to go down to the beach before lunch but followed all the same.

While her mother spread towels on the sand, Rosie peered across the inlet. A long smudge of mangroves marked the far side and she could make out a dip in the horizon, a gap in the rim. The channel. She wondered how many fish they'd caught already. Real fish, no puffers. Her father would go again tomorrow. And he'd take Robert again, most likely.

It suddenly occurred to Rosie that she had time right now to practice her swimming, away from the critical eyes of her father and the jeering teases of her brother. She waded out just over knee-deep and crouched in the warm, clear water. Then she reached down and pressed her palms onto the spongy sand, before locking her elbows and slowly stretching out her legs. Her chin just dipped the surface as she kicked up her feet, and immediately she felt her body rising to the surface. Floating at last. She started to hand-walk back and forth, and, when she was sure she had this much mastered, she stood and looked back at the beach. Her mother was nodding and miming a round of encouraging applause. Getting there, she was certain of it.

'Watch, Mum!' she yelled out, before throwing herself into a lunge, fingers outstretched, no hands touching the bottom this time. For a brief moment she was gliding over the surface. But the next instant, she was sinking, water surging in her open mouth and rushing up her nose. She flailed with arms and legs until her knees found the sand and her head pushed through the surface. Then, spluttering, shaking, warm tears welling, she stumbled back to the safety of the beach.

'Never mind, honey,' her mother cooed, wrapping her in a sun-warmed towel. 'Give it time. You'll get there.'

But not today. She'd had enough of the water and she nodded gratefully at her mother's suggestion that they go back and make some sandwiches ready for when the hungry fishermen returned. The piled-high plate had just made it to the table when gravel-footsteps drew Rosie to the window. There was Robert holding high a silver-glistening fish, big enough for dinner, and she couldn't help conceding a grudging smile of approval.

Over lunch, Rosie suggested the jetty but Robert shook his head. 'Nah. Just a bunch of puffer-fish. Who wants to catch rubbish?'

Rosie put down her half-eaten sandwich and sat in silence for the remainder of the meal. She sneaked sideways glances at her brother, envying his salt-crusted hair, his wind-red eyes and his easy chatter with their father. Robert had been out in the channel and she didn't count anymore. He was Dad's mate now.

Next morning, her brother and father were already gone when she woke, and by the time she'd finished breakfast she'd decided to go to the jetty. Why should she miss out just because Robert wasn't here? And anyway, she could whack puffers with her own thong. Nothing hard about that.

'Not in the water, Rosie,' her mother insisted. 'Not by yourself. Stick to fishing off the jetty.'

But once she was sitting on the edge of the rough boards, she didn't feel like putting in a line. She peered over the edge and stared at the jetty ladder for a while, and wondered how deep the water might be down there. She might be able to touch the bottom.

A second later, she was stripping down to her swimmers and climbing foot-over-foot down into the water until she was perched on the lowest rung. Cool ripples lapped at her waist as she peered at the shafts of sunlight flickering over the sandy bottom. But it wasn't so easy to tell how deep that might be. Moving her hands down to the last dry rung, she stretched one leg down into the depths. Even with her toes pointed to their limit, she couldn't touch. She shivered at the thought of all that water beneath her and quickly drew herself back up, pressing her cheek against the safety of the ladder.

Her mother's warning suddenly dropped into her head, and she screwed up her nose. It was because she was a girl. She'd heard her father say it. She was the same age as her brother, but Robert could swim, Robert was allowed to go fishing in the channel. She was left behind, alone on the jetty, because she was a girl.

Without another thought, she took one long breath and lowered into a crouch, fingers tightening on the ladder, toes curled around the bottom rung. Then she let both feet slip their hold and kick out. The harder she kicked, the more her body rose to the surface until she was floating there, arms outstretched, fingers clinging to the rung. When her legs began to tire, she stopped kicking and was surprised to find she didn't sink. Then she let go one hand. Gripping tighter with the other, she swept her free arm back and forth until she was facing the beach, parallel with the jetty. She could see the shack from there, and hoped her mother wouldn't look out and see what she was up to.

But it wasn't her mother at the window that suddenly made Rosie kick her legs and thrash her arm, desperately straining for the safety of the ladder. It wasn't the two men shouting and running up the gravel path that made her gulp great mouthfuls of salty water. It wasn't her mother flying through the door, barging past the men and tearing down to the beach that made her feet windmill against the deep, searching for the lifeline of the bottom rung.

It was her mother's screaming, over and over, that made Rosie haul herself up hand-over-hand, until she stood on the jetty, legs trembling in a puddle of her own dripping. She threw up her arms, waving and yelling between splutters, 'Mum, I'm here!'

But it didn't stop the screaming, and it was only when Rosie started to run along the jetty towards the beach that she realised her mother wasn't even looking in her direction. She was wailing across the inlet, crying out to the channel gap. And it wasn't Rosie's name she was calling, but the names of her brother and her father.

Rosie never learned to swim. Not like her twin brother, clawing at the chilly deep of the channel, kicking against the drag of swirling eddies, filling his lungs with water until he was weighted with the swell and drifted like a weed along the sandy bottom. Not like her father, diving again and again for his boy, until his arms gave out and he floated facedown on the outrunning tow.

High tide tumbled their bodies onto a surf-scoured beach, days later. Rosie was not allowed to see, but she heard whispered snippets. And she could imagine. They swell up, bodies that have been sucked down, held without breath for too long by the sea's selfish grip.

Learning to swim can be dangerous, and after so many long, blue summers it's something Rosie still believes. It's something she repeats over and over as she stares across the inlet and thinks of her brother, burn-peeled nose, sun-strawed hair, stranded on the sand like a puffer-fish.

Jacqueline Winn lives on a farm at Possum Brush on the Mid-North Coast of New South Wales, Australia. When she's not busy with cattle and goats, vegetables and fruit trees, she writes short stories, novels, poetry and scripts. She has won awards for short stories and poetry in Australia, New Zealand and UK. Many of her stories have been published in anthologies and literary magazines in Australia, UK and Ireland. She has two collections of short stories: *Once More with Feeling* and *Salt & Pepper*, published by Ginninderra Press. More about Jacqueline and her work at *www.jacquelinewinn.com*.

Each year, beginning in 1991, the **Banjo Paterson Writing Awards** have been held to honour the great Australian writer Andrew Barton 'Banjo' Paterson. The awards are launched on the anniversary of Banjo's birth (17 February) and close in April, with winners announced in June. The awards are run by the Orange City Council, Central West Libraries, and Central West Writers' Centre, supported by the *Central Western Daily* and ABC Central West Radio. There are cash prizes to be won, and the winning short story entry is published in the *Central Western Daily*. There is an entry fee of $10 for adults and $5 for children per submission, and entry forms are available from Orange City Library.

JANEEN SAMUEL

Katharine Susannah Prichard Short Fiction Awards

Lifesavers

In the end, of course, the girl comes with them to the Cove. 'She doesn't have to,' Elizabeth has said to Susan last night, 'if she doesn't want to. She could stay here. We're only going for the day.'

'Mother! You can't leave a child out here on her own all day.'

I'm here on my own all day, Elizabeth thought of saying. Day after day. Year after year. But what would be the point? It was by her own choice.

Instead she answered, 'She's hardly a child: she's nearly fourteen. In some cultures she'd be a married woman by now.'

'All the more reason,' said Susan darkly, as if the empty countryside were bristling with Lotharios just waiting for a duenna's back to be turned. 'She's *my* responsibility, remember.'

And Elizabeth sighed and said no more.

Now: 'Do I have to come?' asks Jess, as Elizabeth has known she would.

'Of course you're coming. I'd have thought a girl your age would love a day at the beach.' Susan's voice has the tone one might use with a child ten years younger than Jess, and the girl's sullen look darkens to a scowl: *Just like a three-year-old,* thinks Elizabeth, and suddenly she is remembering Alex, Jess's father, in this very kitchen, refusing to go to kindergarten.

'You'll like it when you get there,' she tells Jess. Probably the same words she used to Alex. 'It's a lovely spot. You can bring along your lifesavers if you want.'

'My what?' The scowl lifts a fraction as the girl stares at her grandmother in perplexity.

'Lifelines, I mean. Your electric gizmos. Your telephone and your ePod.' With Alex it was a little wooden horse.

'*i*-Pod, mother,' says Susan. 'She won't want them at the beach. What's the point of going to a place like that and burying yourself in electronics?'

And with Susan it was books, Elizabeth remembers. When she was older than Alex in his kindy-refusal days, of course. Coming up to Jess's age, in fact.

Later, in the car, she thinks: *Yes, it was on this very road, on the way to the Cove.* Susan in the back then, not the driver's seat: a lumpy, sulky teenager, nose in a book the whole way, emphatically distancing herself from parents, little brother, the whole family outing. Giving herself a sick headache so that by the time they reached the Cove all she would do was lie under the umbrella and complain about the sun in her eyes.

Best not to bring that up now, perhaps. Susan is finding the charge of her niece hard enough as it is.

Behind them in the back seat, Jess has her eyes fixed on her phone. The stone walls and black-and-white cows they are passing interest her no more than the sheep and wide paddocks they have left.

'How many bars have you got now?' Elizabeth asks her. It's one thing she's learned this last week, as she's watched Jess prowl around the garden and out to the barn, climb on the tank stand with the phone held above her head, even walk up the hill in the top paddock. It's the only outdoor exercise she gets, as Susan has several times remarked.

'Only two. No, three ... No, it's dropped back to one.' She sounds like a shipwrecked mariner watching sails disappear over a horizon.

I should get her to explain the bars to me, Elizabeth thinks. But then she's shot through by a pang of sadness. *That's not how it should be, not yet: not her explaining to me. What about all those earlier times? The little girl on her grandmother's knee: 'Here's a little bar, then another bar, and here's another; how many bars does that make? Count them with Gran: one, two, three bars. What a clever girl!' Those times never happened. There I was one moment,* she thinks, *holding my new granddaughter, giving her my finger to clutch in her tiny fist; next thing, here I am trying to make polite conversation with this prickly teenager who so plainly doesn't want to be with us — with me — and watching her thumbs flicking away at a piece of technology I don't begin to understand.*

Presumably Jess got all that — the cuddling and the 'one-two-three' and the rest of it — from her other grandmother. It's to be hoped so, at least. Elizabeth only met the woman once, at Alex's wedding, and she looked like a walking vinegar bottle. But perhaps she only looked sour because she thought Penny and Alex were making a mistake. In which case she was quite right.

The car breasts the last rise and there it is before them: the Cove, sudden and surprising as ever. For a moment Jess is forgotten, and Susan; it is Len in the seat beside her, and the lift in her heart is the same as the very first time they came over this hill and saw it, the two of them, that unexpected bite of blue sea between orange cliffs.

'There,' says Susan. 'Isn't that worth coming for, Jessica?'

Jess doesn't answer. But the moment is over. It is Susan beside her, though the ghost of Len is there still, in Susan's profile, in the timbre of her voice, in the very set of her shoulders as she swings the wheel. She deserves to be here in her own right because she was present, after all, on that first visit. She was here in utero, a six-month foetus, holding all the promise of a first longed-for child.

She didn't turn out as they hoped and dreamed, this solid, righteous middle-aged woman who is now levering herself out of the driver's seat while turning to frown at her niece. Nevertheless,

Elizabeth knows, with absolute certainty, that if Susan had been the very epitome of their dream-child she could not have loved her more.

At the top of the steps Elizabeth stops, as she always does, to read the plaque about the shipwreck.

Susan has already started down, burdened with umbrella, esky, picnic basket, and the beach bag Elizabeth made her for her fourteenth birthday. At the first landing she looks back. 'You've read that a hundred times,' she calls. 'You must know it by heart.'

'No, I don't; I'm getting old and forgetful.' Which is a lie, but some truths are not for speaking. It's a small ritual she never omits, this telling over the bones of the old tragedy. A propitiation of the spirits of all the women and children for whom this cove was a place of horror and death.

Jess has come up beside her and is reading too. 'That's so sad.'

Elizabeth stiffens. Is *sad* one of those code words of the young — like *wicked* or *cool* — that means something different? Something derisory?

But the girl's face is solemn. She's not mocking. She is making her own small attempt at bridging the gulf between them. A nineteenth-century wreck should be far enough away from both of them, goodness knows, for a common view. Only it's not, because Elizabeth has taken possession of this tragedy and she doesn't want to share it with a stranger, even of her own blood. Anyway, it's too late; the moment for a spontaneous reply has already passed, and she can think of nothing to say that would not sound fatuous or forced. And below them on the sand Susan is calling, 'Come on, you two.'

By the time they reach her she has the umbrella erected and has shed her clothes to reveal her well-muscled body in a bathing suit.

'I won't wait for you,' she says. 'I like a nice long swim before I have my lunch.'

They watch her stride through the shallows then plunge into a wave. Jess is still standing beside the umbrella, dangling her small day-pack from one hand. Elizabeth sets up the low chair she has brought and sits down. She runs her fingers through the dry sand, familiar as a lover's hand.

'I don't think I'll go in just yet,' she tells Jess. 'Your grandfather always said there are icebergs in that ocean. I'll wait till the day warms up a bit more. But I expect you want a swim.'

The girl turns her head, taking in the little stretch of empty beach between the two cliffs. Is she liking it? Hating it? She has her sunglasses on and Elizabeth can't read her expression. 'I guess I'll just look around,' she says, and wanders off.

Elizabeth watches her. So many times she has sat on this beach keeping an eye on children, her own and others, as they clambered among the rocks at either end of the bay or tried to scramble up the cliffs. She seldom called them back even though sometimes she had to bite her lips to stop herself; children must be allowed their freedom even at the expense of a little peril.

Back then she always assumed, without really thinking about it, that someday she would be here watching a tribe of grandchildren. But there is no other grandchild but Jess. And Jess has never been here until today.

She doesn't need watching; she isn't going to do anything venturesome. She drifts along the shoreline, aimless as a jellyfish. Elizabeth has often done the same herself, picking up shells or losing herself in the pattern of the waves. Content to be alone with the sea. But Jess is not content. You can see it in every line of her body. She is mooching and drooping along the beach as she has mooched and drooped about the house and garden all this past week. 'Sulking,' Susan has said, more than once.

Not sulking, Elizabeth says now to herself. *She's sad.*

'Sad!' She can imagine Susan's reply. 'What's she got to be sad about?'

Why shouldn't she be sad? Thirteen years old and expecting to spend three weeks with her father — whom she's seen little enough of, heaven knows, in her lifetime. Instead, at the last minute 'something came up' and now he's off overseas. 'To Mongolia,' he told Elizabeth when he phoned. 'Not the sort of place you can take a child.'

I don't see why not. She thought of saying that, quoting his own words back to him from thirteen years ago. But he wouldn't have remembered his response to her horrified 'Dubai! That's no place to take a newborn baby.'

In fact, she has no evidence that Jess did anything but thrive in Dubai. It was the marriage that suffered. Or would it have happened anywhere? All she knows is that after two years, when Alex renewed his contract, Penny left him and brought her daughter home.

Elizabeth has never blamed her. She remembers too well what it was like for her out here in the beginning, fresh from the city and with a new baby. She went to see Penny once but the visit was not a success; Jess had a cold and was fractious, Penny was stiff and defensive, Elizabeth could find nothing to say. *I should have kept trying,* she thinks now, but at the time it was too difficult. Susan had just launched on that dreadful affair with the married man, and Len was beginning to be ill. She had no energy left for building a relationship with an ex-daughter-in-law. She saw Jess briefly a couple of times when Alex made one of his rare visits to Australia, but the long gaps between meant that each time she was meeting a new little stranger. Then, when Jess was nine, Alex moved to Hong Kong and Jess began flying there to see him. Susan went with her the first time — it must have been just after her affair finally petered out — but Elizabeth couldn't leave Len.

She's been hoping things will be different now that Alex has moved back to Australia. But Alex himself is not going to change. His career comes first and no argument. 'Susan says she'll take charge of her,' he told her in that phone conversation a week ago. 'She can bring her down to stay with you, same as I was going to. There'll be other holidays. Maybe I'll take her up to Cairns in July.'

And maybe by July she'll have given up on her father. But she didn't say it. When it comes to her children these days, she seems to spend a lot of time not saying things.

Jess has drifted back to the umbrella. She's still wearing her jeans and several overlapping upper garments which look, to her grandmother, like underwear. *If I had tried to make Susan wear any one of those in public,* thinks Elizabeth, *I would have been the world's worst mother.* Jess pulls off the outermost one, produces sunscreen from her pack and applies it to her bared forearms.

Susan comes jogging up from the sea, her brown skin glistening. She towels herself briskly, frowns at Jess's fingers languidly rubbing in cream. 'What happened to you two? I thought you'd be in right after me.'

'It's still a bit cool for my bones,' says Elizabeth. 'I'll go in after lunch.'

'What about you, Jess? Why don't you have a quick swim and give yourself a nice appetite for lunch?'

The girl shrugs. 'Not now.'

'Don't you like swimming?' Susan asks it as one might demand, *Don't you like Christmas?*

Elizabeth is about to intervene; why should Jess swim if she doesn't want to? But the girl's head comes up suddenly. 'I won the under-thirteen breaststroke in our school carnival last year.'

'Did you really!' says Susan warmly. 'That's great. You'll have to go in now and give us a demonstration.'

'But that was in a pool. This is ...' Jess's sunglasses do another quick scan back and forth along the empty beach. 'It's, like ... there's no-one here.'

Susan looks as if someone has slapped her in the face with a wet fish. Elizabeth is almost as taken aback.

'But that's the nicest part about coming here,' she says. 'We're lucky to have it to ourselves today. You wouldn't like it crowded with people?'

'It's not safe to swim on your own,' mutters Jess.

Susan explodes. 'I don't know! You young people seem to want mollycoddling the whole time. I suppose you want lifesavers and flags?'

Jess is silent but her expression says: *Yes,* that's just what she does want.

Susan draws breath for what is sure to be a scornful tirade. Elizabeth says quickly, 'I once had a boyfriend who was a lifesaver. When I was not much older than you, Jess.'

The sudden switch throws them both. From Jess's face it's plain she can't imagine her grandmother as a teenager, let alone with a boyfriend. Nevertheless, after a moment she says, as if conscious some effort is called for, 'What was he like?'

'He was a bit of rat, actually. He threw me over for somebody else. I was furious. So I went down to the beach when he was on duty — you know, standing to attention in his ridiculous cap and those flimsy trunks they wore. But he wouldn't even look at me. He just kept on staring out to sea and ignoring me. So then I got really mad. I was wearing my new two-piece bathing costume and I stood right in front of him and I said, "What about this then? You were all over me like a rash until that Dawn came along." He just gritted his teeth and looked straight through me. So ...' — she is staring out to sea herself now, not daring to look at Susan — '... so I started rubbing myself up against him. I even took off my top. He couldn't do anything because he was on duty. He just had to keep standing to attention with his hands at his sides and muttering through his teeth, "Stop it, Beth. Go away, Beth," and trying to pretend nothing was happening. Only it *was* happening and it was perfectly obvious in those skimpy trunks.'

There is a choking sound from Jess. Her face is red and her hand is over her mouth. She meets her grandmother's eyes and it's too much — the laughter bursts out of her. Elizabeth collapses too. They laugh together, the girl rolling in the sand, while Susan watches in blank amazement.

'Did he get back with you?' Jess asks when she can speak.

'No fear, I wouldn't have wanted him. I'd made my point. So to speak. Oh dear!' And they're both helpless again.

Suddenly they're aware of voices above them. A group of people is coming down the steps. It looks like an extended family party: grandparents, several sets of parents, a gaggle of children. And three teenagers: two boys and a girl.

Jess sits up and reaches into her pack. 'I'm so hot. I'm going in the sea to cool off.' In no time she has stripped off her jeans, pulled up a swimsuit, and shed the rest of her clothes. She doesn't wait to put on sunscreen; she runs lightly down the sand at an angle that will take her below the newcomers.

'What on earth did you tell her that for?' says Susan.

'Oh, well, it just seemed to come up. So to speak.' She represses a snigger.

'It wasn't true!'

Just for a second Elizabeth hesitates. Should she give in to temptation? Susan has such a strong streak of prudery, in spite of that affair of hers.

'Not exactly,' she replies. 'It did happen, but it was someone I worked with.'

Jess is running into the water, splashing it up around her slender figure. One of the boys is moving down the beach towards her.

'We'll need to keep an eye on her.'

'Yes,' says Elizabeth happily. And she settles back to watch.

The majority of **Janeen Samuel**'s published works have had titles such as 'The normal oral flora of the mouth of macropods'. When she is not getting enough work as a veterinary pathologist, she tries her hand at fiction instead of fact, and some of the results have been published in various magazines and anthologies. In 2010 she had stories published in the anthology *Shades of Sentience* and *Andromeda Spaceways Inflight Magazine* No. 44. She lives in South West Victoria.

The Katharine Susannah Prichard Writers' Centre is run under the auspices of the Katharine Susannah Prichard Foundation Inc. It is located in the Perth Hills, in the former home of Katharine Susannah Prichard, the internationally celebrated author of *Coonardoo*, *Working Bullocks* and many other novels, stories and plays. The centre encourages and facilitates services for writers at all levels of the craft. The **Katharine Susannah Prichard Short Fiction Awards** have two sections: the Open Awards, and the Mundaring National Young Writers Awards (for entrants twenty years old and under).
kspf.iinet.net.au

Ray Tyndale
Salisbury Writers' Festival Writing Competition

fossil-hunting

Aberlady, east of Edinburgh

the fossil-hunters
scramble over loose rocks
on the firth beach
calm water lapping gently
sharp mewling of oyster catchers
cormorants standing wings wide

there's a seal sunning itself
on its back on a sandbank
beside eider ducks and banded stilts
hoverflies suck dog daisy nectar

all this lazy beauty
might not be there
the fossil-hunters have eyes
for nothing but ancient corals
trilobite tracks and ferns
things with long latin names
that lived and moved in this place
millions of years ago
for this novice an idea
hard to grasp

the fossil-hunters head home reluctantly
bags bulging with rocks
I carry only my memories

Ray Tyndale started writing poetry and literary fiction in the 1990s when studying for her MA in creative writing at the University of Adelaide, and has continued to publish all manner of words while gaining her doctorate. There are always women in her writing, although they are rarely young. Ray is multi-skilled and has led many lives, all of which enrich her several books. *Farmwoman* and *Sappho at Sixty* are her latest works, both published in 2008.

The **Salisbury Writers' Festival Writing Competition** is run as part of the Salisbury Writers' Festival, a joint project between the City of Salisbury, SA Writers' Centre and the Salisbury Library Service. The competition is open to South Australian residents in two categories: Aged 17 and over; and Aged 16 and under. Prizes amount to $1200 across both categories, and winners are announced during the festival, held in August each year.

www.salisbury.sa.gov.au/Our_City/Events/Salisbury_Writers_Festval

JOAN FENNEY
Poetry Unleashed Festival — Adrian Kavanagh Award

Learning to Breathe

I was born into a family where words
could attack without warning, aided by pauses
as chilling as words. I was five before I took sides,
chose pauses, not words. Pauses seemed safer.

My newlywed parents were awaiting my birth
in their renovated two-bedroom home at Stokes Bay
when my recently widowed grandmother appeared
with a truckload of furniture and cases of hidden hostilities.

At eight I learnt to navigate my way around conflict.
It was a journey I would take until I was eighteen.
I became an observer of the daily taunts that were fired
between my parents and grandmother.

Our house could no longer hold the tension within.
My grandmother built a bungalow in our backyard
and borders were erected around us. We had no anchor
but drifted in turbulent seas.

We still ate together and I held my breath.
Tried to shield myself from the faces my grandmother
pulled at my father during mealtimes and the mutterings
that were served up as regularly as our food.

My mother was caught between her mother and husband
her days spent untangling the bitter lines they cast
at each other. She tried to steer a path through
but remained trapped by the nets enclosing her.

I escaped into books, to words of my own choosing,
into a world of fairytales woven into my dreams.
I believed I could cocoon myself forever
but was unravelled by the barbs circling me.

My father rarely drank but my grandmother said
she smelled liquor on his breath and ordered
my mother to empty his beer down the sink
like she used to do with my grandfather's whisky.

At school I stayed on the outside,
remained quiet when I should have spoken up,
fearing my words would be used against me.
I had no defence for that.

In her eighties my grandmother rarely left
her bungalow but the borders built around us
could not easily be dismantled. Hostilities
still cast shadows over us.

As a teenager I could no longer stay silent.
I weighed in with my own words, pleaded
for an end to the battles that were never
resolved.

The last time my grandmother left our house
for a rushed trip to the hospital
my father opened the car door for her.
She said 'thank you' and briefly held his hand.

.

Joan Fenney's award-winning poetry has been published in newspapers, magazines and journals throughout Australia. Her first poetry collection, *Marilyn Monroe by the Brooklyn Bridge and Other Portraits*, was published by Ginninderra Press in 2009. Joan's poetry is also included in a number of anthologies including *That Which My Eyes See* (2011) and *Season of a New Heart* (2010). Joan has been a journalist for more than twenty-five years in both electronic and print media. Joan's love of the written word has even resulted in her and her husband opening a second-hand bookshop in Adelaide.

The 2010 **Poetry Unleashed Festival** was the fifth biennial poetry festival conducted by the City of Onkaparinga and the SA Writers' Centre, with the support of a number of partner organisations. The festival's aim is to raise the profile of South Australian poets, their work and poetry within the community. The festival provides entry points for people of all ages, reading and writing abilities through a range of mostly free events in traditional and non-traditional arts venues throughout the city. The Open Poetry Competition in 2010 was renamed the Adrian Kavanagh Prize in honour of the festival's first organiser.

ADAM TUCKER

Australian Literature Review *Best Rural/Small Town Short Story*

How Would They Get Rid of Him?

Winter had passed into spring. Frost still crackled across the ground occasionally, snapping at the lawn's mid-year excess, but the jasmine had started to blossom. It walled the cutting yard, clouding it in toilet freshener. A halo of new life circling stacked deadwood, the space where the dog had met its end.

The Boy doesn't know where the dog is buried. Just knows where it died. Isn't sure how to pay his respects so each Saturday he sits in the chopping enclosure. He isn't religious, hasn't been to church a day in his life. Most times at school he finds an excuse not to attend RE. He isn't sure how to pray; he just sits on the block where it'd happened. Spent an hour mumbling apologies for his father's actions. For his own inaction. Thinks it might help, knows it can't hurt. Feels the jagged surface of the wood block, all the toothy axe scars, bite into his bum. Somehow knows this isn't something that can be done comfortably. He picks apart the red wood chips littering the ground like tears. Splits them along their grain until he holds one sliver. Then pricks it into his palm.

In time he walks inside. Seems he's walked in on something. The Mother and Father stand at opposite ends of the kitchen. The Father's face is red. The Mother's, wet. They both turn to face The Boy. He feels their gazes. Feels an intruder. His mind turns to the dog. The Boy wonders about his own fate. How they would get rid of him? On the chopping block? Probably not.

The Father harrumphs. Walks past The Boy. Out the door. Blundstones thudding. First heavy on the lino, then hollow on the wooden porch.

The Boy closes his eyes. Listens to The Father fade away. Raises his eyes to his mother. Sees the imploring face. Clumps his own way across the kitchen floor. Opposite direction to The Father. Leaves The Mother with her hand stoppering her mouth.

In his room, The Boy sits hidden within the built-in robe. Cradles his clarinet. Thinks of the lunchtime lessons he'd missed. Thinks of the school music room with its *Row Your Boat* sing-along posters and its wet carpet smell. Thinks of the stupid bitch teacher who doesn't know how hard it is. The Boy pulls out the reed. Runs his thumbnail the length, creasing a seam into the fibres. Puts it in his mouth. Bites hard. Feels the wood tear. Starts to chew. Begins to unscrew the instrument. Places the pieces in a pile, next to the long forgotten box of Lego. Studies them. No longer a functional tool, just bits of wood with holes. Smiles. Scrambles onto his knees. Unzips his fly. Pisses on the dismembered instrument.

✳

The family sits at the kitchen table. Each silent. Cutlery clinking crockery. Occasionally a pop emits from the wood stove.

The Boy pushes his Brussels sprout around the plate. The weak leaves falling from the mini cabbage, leaving a trail in the cooling mustard sauce.

The Father stands, coughs past a mouthful of silverside. Dumps a pan of briquettes in the stove. Sinks back on his bench with a sigh.

The Mother attempts conversation. Refers to an item in the local newspaper. An item of discussion at the supermarket. Surprised The Father hasn't heard. A local boy. Missing. Peter Henderson. Does The Father know them?

He nods. Tough family. Talk old man Henderson is a bit rough round the edges. Boy's just done a runner.

'How long's he been gone?' The Father asks.

The Mother thinks two days.

'Be back by tomorrow' is The Father's verdict.

They turn their attention to The Boy. Does he know the Henderson lad? The Boy keeps his head bowed. Gives the slightest shrug of his shoulders, which communicates nothing, and squishes his Brussels sprout into his mashed potato.

✳

The Boy stamps through the ankle-high grass. It is his job to mow the yard but he'd been lax in his chores. Knows he can be. The Father, usually a disciplinarian about these things, has been easy of late. Seems reluctant to enforce anything since he had cut the neck of the dog he no longer wanted. The Boy knows of the reluctance and he is going to exploit it. Feels it is his duty to exploit it, feels The Father deserves it to be exploited.

And he is angry, The Boy. He is angry about everything, but most of all he is angry with Miss Albrecht at the moment. Detention again. Teachers were meant to know everything. Be guiding lights. The older he got, the more he knows they are as thick as The Mother and Father. What good is a fucking music lesson?

He kicks out. Disperses a cluster of dandelion. Watches the spores float up in the air and feels a sudden sadness at having caused their destruction. He catches a spore in his palm and silently apologises. Apologises for the unintended damage. He puts the spore in his pocket for future reference.

The Boy finds the entry point to the hedge and climbs in. The hedge runs along the back length of the property. Three metres high. Two across. He hauls himself up the spine. Emerges at the top, flopping out on the interwoven branches. He spreads himself out. He's seen people make snow angels on the television. This is his hedge angel. His fingers search through the branches. Finds a solid limb. Takes hold and rolls to the side. For a moment he is freefalling over the side. Then the branch retracts and he flings softly into the cushioning pine wall. Lets himself drop. Lands softly on the balls of his feet. Re-enters and climbs back up. All around him, in his clothes, his hair, his nostrils, the scent of pine. The sound of a car pulling in. The old valiant coughing to a stop. The Boy peers through the fern. Begs to be left alone. Can see The Mother. Ducks his head.

'She won't see you.'

The Boy almost tumbles over the side. Regains balance. Edges his way around. The Henderson boy is sat snuggled in the hedge.

'You've run away,' The Boy says. It is a statement not a question.

Henderson shrugs. He looks pale, cold. His hair is damp.

The Boy wriggles out of his school sweater. Hands it over. 'Why?'

Henderson accepts the sweater. Places it beside him. 'Can't tell, just had to.'

The Mother is calling. Has seen The Boy's school bag. Knows he is home.

'Have to go.'

Henderson shrugs again. 'Everyone goes.'

'I'll be back.' The Boy feels obliged. 'I'll bring some food.' He shimmies down the trunk.

'Don't tell anyone.' Henderson peers down at him.

The Boy nods.

✳

The Boy puts the last dish away. Hangs the tea towel on the stove. Can hear the telly in the next room. Father watching the news. In the cupboard, he takes down a packet of arrowroot biscuits. Takes a juice box from the fridge. Puts them up his jumper. Folds his arms. Heads toward the hallway. The Father diverts his attention from the television. Wants to know what The Boy is up to.

'Music practice,' he replies, eyes averted, head down.

And his school jumper, The Mother wants to know. Where is it? Was going to put it in the wash.

'Locker at school,' he says and continues up the hallway. Stops by the linen closet. Checks they aren't following him. Takes down an old blanket. Drapes it over his shoulder. Quicksteps to his room and closes the door behind. He bundles the loot into an old sports bag. Leaves it by the window. Sits on the bed and waits. Watches the staccato movement of the alarm clock digits. How they stare blankly at him, as though stuck in time, and then jerk forward. Each ticks shudders through his body. Doesn't know what he is waiting for. What would be a good time? Mesmerised by the glowing red numbers. Vision blurred. Doesn't hear The Father's footsteps on the floorboards. The door opening.

'Thought you were practising?'

The Boy jumps a little. No time for composure.

'Mother thought I should hear you play.' Still standing by the door, holding the knob.

The Boy stares blankly.

The Father raises his eyebrow. Grows tired of looking at the mute boy. Sees the old sports bag by the window. The one he'd given The Boy to carry his football gear. The Boy had quit. Wouldn't need it anymore. He could do with it back. Strides over.

'I'll have this back,' he says and picks it up. Feels the weight. 'Whatcha got in here?' Unzips.

The Boy follows the movement, says nothing.

The Father takes out the blanket, lets it fall to the floor. Holds the arrowroots in one hand. Drops the bag. 'What's with this?'

The Boy stays silent.

'Running away? With a pack o' bloody biscuits and a blanket.' He shakes his head. 'What's going on, mate? Eh?'

The Boy can't take his eyes of The Father's. Grips the Transformers quilt.

The Father breaks the contact. Brushes aside the curtain. Turns the key in the window lock. Drops the key in his pocket. 'Going to say something? Cat got your tongue?' The Father shakes his head. 'Running away never helped anyone.' He scoops up the bag and the blanket. Walks to the door. Over his shoulder, 'Mother doesn't need to know.' Tosses the arrowroots onto the bed. 'You can keep those. Bloody awful.' Flicks off the light, closes the door.

✳

Days are brightening but the mornings are still cold enough to clean-snap the ends off any brave new buds. The Father, up early, has lit the wood stove before leaving for work. The sun only beginning to peek over the horizon. He is long gone by the time The Boy sits at the table, lethargically dabbing his spoon into porridge. The Mother always in a rush. Never enough time to make The Boy's lunch, have a proper breakfast and get off to work. Had to be there by eight. Shop assistant at Australian Geographic in the big multiplex toward the city. Not much of a career. A limp clasp at a schoolgirl passion. She bangs out the porch door. Yells back a reminder. 'Don't forget that sweater.'

The Boy waits until he can no longer hear tyres on gravel. Dumps his full bowl in the sink. Strides out to the hedge, an apple in hand, school bag over his shoulder. Drops the bag. Calls out as he ascends. Had the apple in his mouth. Needs both hands to get up. Doesn't think Henderson will mind. Up top, can't see Henderson. The sweater lies in a crumpled heap. He feels it, holds it in his lap. It is soaked through with last night's dew. The Boy sinks back in the ferns. It is a clear crisp day. In the embrace of the entwined branches, he closes his eyes. Thinks of nothing but the pale red hum of his eyelids. Dozes.

Wakes with a start. Henderson sits across from him. Has the apple. Thanks The Boy but doesn't bite into the fruit. The Boy gathers himself, wipes the sleep from his eyes.

'Not going to school?' Henderson asks.

'Waste of time.'

Henderson nods sadly.

'What about you?' There is accusation in The Boy's voice. Feels judged.

'Didn't help me.'

The Boy relaxes. Likes Henderson. Is a few years older than The Boy. Maybe thirteen. Fourteen. At school they wouldn't speak. 'You've been in the news.'

'Really?'

The Boy shrugs, 'The local paper.'

Henderson nods. 'Makes sense.' Wipes his damp fringe from his face. Seems paler than yesterday. Colder.

The Boy watches a mosquito settle on Henderson's forehead. Henderson ignores it.

'You should put the sweater on.'

Henderson shrugs. 'It's wet.'

'So why'd you runaway.'

'Can't say.'

The Boy wants a better answer. Knows he won't get one. Has to push on. 'Dad says you'll turn up today. Will you?'

'Be a few days yet. Do you ever feel like running away?'

The Boy hadn't expected to be quizzed. Isn't sure how he feels. Says, 'Sometimes.'

'To get back at your parents. Get back at your dad for killing your dog?'

The Boy's eyes widen. Cheeks redden. A fresh wound. 'How'd you know?'

Henderson smiles his doleful smile. 'Whole town knows. Knows he put its head on the chopping block.'

Tears sting The Boy's eyes.

'You want to get back at him?'

The Boy nods. Doesn't look up.

'I used to want to get back at my parents. Want to know what I did?'

The Boy is eager for instruction. Some wisdom from this pale prophet in the hedge.

'Hurt myself. Tells them they can't hurt you, 'cause you control it.'

'How?'

'Burn yourself. I did it with cigarettes. Just butt it out on your arm.'

'Doesn't it hurt?'

'That's the point.' Henderson sighs. Looks over his shoulder. 'Anyway, gotta go.'

'What?' The Boy reaches out his hand. Withdraws it just as fast. He wants more. 'Where will you go? Home?'

Henderson laughs, the sorrow lifting from his face. 'Not home, not yet. I told you, in a couple of days they'll find me. Just have to hang out for a while by myself.' Eases himself onto the main trunk. Disappears into the heart of the hedge.

✳

The Boy sits at the window. Watches The Mother pull from the driveway. A shroud of drizzle heavy on the valley. Focus draws back to the windowpane. Droplets run and expire down the glass. His vision blurs before he snaps himself from the stupor. Takes his bowl. Rinses the soggy flakes in the sink. Pauses at the bench. Knows he has to go to school but the previous day had given him a taste. Maybe he can avoid ever going back. But not today. He would have to plan that eventuality. He pushes off from the bench. Leaves his inertia behind. Begins compiling a sandwich. Peanut butter and jam. Makes a second. The first, Glad-wrapped and shoved in his school bag. The second, left on the bench. One more task to complete. He takes the fire stoker. Opens the heavy stove door with a mitt. Damps down the coals. The orange beads would smoulder through the day, ready for re-stoking upon his return. He withdraws the stoker. Just put it in the stand and then out of there. His hand hovers. The tool raised before him. With teeth, he draws back his sleeve. Touches the burning metal to his forearm. Squeals. Drops the stoker to the floor. Panics. Grabs at it. His palm snatches at the hot tip. Forces another yelp from him. Eyes burning. Tears welling. Deep breath. And another. Calming. The acrid smell of burning linoleum. Measured now. Picks up the tool. A black smudge melted into the lino. Steels himself. Sinks the stoker into the glowing coals. One. Two. Three. Four. Five. Six. Seven. Eight. Nine. Ten. Withdraws. Touches the metal to his inner forearm. More prepared this time. Fights the urge to recoil. Body trembles but still holds in there. Emits a low growl, rising in pitch. Howls like a wolf and slams the stoker into its stand. Studies the weeping skin. Light-headed. The Boy feels faint and then a rush. Almost invincible as the endorphins release and the adrenaline slaps him on the back like an overeager coach. Light on his feet. Snatches up his bag, the sandwich from the bench. Crashes through the porch door. Crosses the yard at a trot. Slings the sandwich up into the hedge.

'Later, Hendo.'

✳

The Boy sits at the table; clarinet in hand. The Mother leans against the bench; dishcloth in hand. Wants to hear The Boy practise. Doesn't believe him when he says he does it in his room. Doesn't know what he has previously done to the instrument.

It feels sticky in his hand. A faint sour whiff close up. He'd replaced the reed but the mouthpiece tastes salty. The pieces had struggled to fit back together. The wood had swelled. Air escapes through the joins. The Boy keeps stopping to scratch his arm. A ferocious, insatiable itch. The scratching drives The Mother wild. More so than the bum notes being hit. Repeated enquires. Repeated brush-offs. The Boy blows. Stops. Scratches. Blows again. The notes are like jangling nerves tearing the air. The Mother reacts. A tether frayed. Flops the dishcloth down. Snatches at The Boy's arm. He recoils. The clarinet drops to the floor. Discarded. Rests against the leg of the table.

'Show me what's wrong.'

The Boy hard up against the windowsill. The porch door clangs. The familiar tattoo of door banging, boots clumping, oilskin rustling. The Father enters the kitchen. The Boy presses further into the corner. The Father eyes him. Considers the situation. Feels the tension but can't gauge the intensity. Lets it drop. Kisses The Mother. Burning cheeks on his lips. Snatches open the fridge door. Uses it to support his weight. The interior light illuminates his grey-flecked stubble. Retracts a beer.

'They found the Henderson boy.'

Suction of seal on door. Skitters the bottle cap across the bench.

'Oh.' The Mother feels the tone. Knows it's more than a simple runaway. 'Where?' Disgusted with herself. Wants to let the conversation slide by but can't. Needs the information, the details. How else would she cluck and sigh with the others in the supermarket aisle.

'By the river. The bo—'

The Boy hears no more. Already in the yard. Striding across the lengthening lawn. Wet grass seeds pocking his school trousers. Up the trunk of the hedge. Snagged halfway. Jerks free, fabric tearing, skin grazed. Crests the hedge. Flays his hands through the fronds. The sandwich. Nestled in among the branches. Still in plastic wrap. Unopened, untouched. Takes hold. Flings himself over the edge. Hits the ground running. Out the side gate. Onto the narrow bitumen. No sidewalks. Just street bordered by grass. Drizzle falls. Hair plastered to his forehead. Stumbles on the uneven tarmac. Dim lights well spaced. Instinct the only thing guiding him. Somehow knows which part of the river. Down the hill, past the cricket sheds, across the unused paddock and on to the bank. Across the way, the tennis courts, cracked and dishevelled. Tennis courts you would find after the termination of man.

Puffing. Not knowing what happens next. Crouches on the bank. Eyes closed. A noise. At first, maybe, the sound of fish breaking the surface. Then, closer. A persistent lapping. Too loud to be the gentle melding of drizzle with river. The Boy opens his eyes. Something moves closer. Hendo. Thigh deep in the water.

'Knew you would come,' Hendo says, moving closer.

'Dad said—'

'Adults talk shit.' Hendo is emphatic.

The Boy hugs his knees. Bum hovers just above the sodden bank. 'Why're you in the water.'

'Saw it in a movie. Means they can't track you.'

'Thought you wanted to be found.'

Hendo shrugs. Is close enough The Boy can make out his blue lips. The Boy feels as cold and wet as Hendo always looks. 'What now?' he asks.

'Gonna get away. Don't want to be found no more. You comin'?'

The Boy smiles. Pulls back the sleeve of his jumper. Even in the dark the welt is obvious. Raised, weeping. Hendo winks. Turns his back. Begins to wade. The Boy looks over his shoulder. The last chance for adult intervention. The dark is empty. He slips off his shoes and socks. Even in recklessness he is cautious. Ties the laces together and slings them around his shoulders. Slips his left foot into the river. Warmer than he would have thought. The sediment stirs around his foot, envelops it. Hendo is moving away. The Boy commits the other foot and follows.

Adam Tucker studied film and photography at ECU in Perth, and writing and editing at RMIT in Melbourne. His short fiction has appeared in anthologies and collections such as *Block*, *Verandah*, *Visible Ink* and *Pendulum*. He lives in Brunswick and is currently learning how to be a builder and a father.

The *Australian Literature Review* (*AusLit*) regularly runs short story competitions throughout the year. The *AusLit* **Rural/Small Town Short Story Competition,** for the best story with a rural or small-town setting, was part of a round of three competitions: Best Rural/Small Town Short Story, Best Realistic Horror Short Story, and Best Adventure Short Story. As winner of the Best Rural/Small Town Short Story Competition, Adam Tucker received feedback on his story from rural novelist Fleur McDonald and a $250 book voucher.

www.auslit.net

Sarah Holland-Batt

The Adelaide Review / *University of Adelaide Creative Writing Program Short Fiction Competition*

Istanbul

Toby said Istanbul, though not even he really knew where the Maynards had gone. In the end it didn't matter. The point was, they were gone, Jamie was gone; he had taken his scrawny hand-rolled greyhounds and his careless, wolfish mouth with him; and Toby and I were at a loose end all summer. January in Newstead stretched out, dangerous and glittering as the lapis at the lip of an artesian well, deceptively far off. So far off, you felt you could drown before you reached the end of it.

Toby and I played squash that month. We were hardly even friends; he barely spoke to me back at Knox. But there was nothing to do with the hours except waste them, so we met Monday and Thursday afternoons at Ascot and hammered a rubber ball as hard as we could at a black smudge on the wall. Sometimes Toby would feign an injury when he was out of breath.

'Christ,' he would say, bending over. 'My ankle.' He would rub his shin, wincing, then fiddle with his racquet head.

'For Christ's sake,' I would say, exasperated. 'Get on with it.'

We would turn back to the wall. Squash must be the most draining sport on earth. The rhythm of it made everything recede. Toby cut across me, a clean white blur. After a while, I could feel something in me hurtling off and breaking up. A dangerous feeling, a falling away.

*

It was after one of those sweltering games that Toby suggested we go to the Maynards' place. We were in the change room, a dank space where the closed-in smell of men — sweat, Right Guard, menthol salve, Lux — was both arousing and vaguely sickening.

'February,' he said.

I looked up. Toby was eating an egg sandwich. He must have packed it in his bag.

'They're not back until February. Jamie said.' His face was bland, freckly. I knew that expression from school.

'So?'

'They've got a swimming pool.' He angled the sandwich into his mouth artfully, so as not to lose any of the egg.

I tried to imagine it: Jamie's pool. My stomach turned. 'Porter, *you've* got a bloody swimming pool.'

'Not like that. It's half-Olympic.' He paused. 'You've never even been, have you?'

'Why would I want to?'

'I don't know.' He looked at me shrewdly. 'Why would you?'

Toby must have known it even then. There wasn't an instant that summer I wasn't excruciatingly aware that Jamie wasn't here, was out there somewhere, with his parents, with the witch Cecelia. It was a kind of fever: my mind kept reaching out airy feelers, sweeping its corners for some scrap, and returning with dust.

'Fine.'

'I thought so,' Toby said smugly, pulling his shirt off. 'Jamie told me you like swimming.'

I felt a slow burn creep across my face. I thought, quite disconnectedly, that I could kill him, that it would be easy to do it,

'Shut up.'

'God, calm down.' He sounded pleased with himself. 'Look, you don't have to.'

'Piss off. I'm coming.'

I felt for the key in my pocket. No-one would be home. My mother would still be at work; my sister would be at her pottery class, making another one of the lumpy vases that were converging in an unruly line on the kitchen windowsill.

Coming home for the holidays had become an awkward, uneasy affair. I had grown inexorably apart from the both of them; from my mother's solicitous attempts to read my essay on Whiteley's *Summer at Carcoar*; from Katie's pitiable infatuation with David Bowie, her tatty photos cut from magazines and sticky-taped to her school books. I felt further than ever from our house on Kingsholme Street, its chipping gunmetal-green stairs, the tired orange trumpet creeper shrinking against the fence.

Even Brisbane itself had begun to feel limp, burnt out, sun-blasted. As Toby and I left the building, the air was smothering.

Toby swore. 'That bastard.'

'What?'

'That bastard'll be lazing about, being fanned by palm leaves. Jesus Christ.' He grinned. 'They're probably feeding him horses' bollocks.'

'What the hell are you talking about?' I unlocked my bike chain.

'Jamie, idiot. In Istanbul.'

'They don't eat horse, you dunce.' I felt victorious. 'They eat dates and chickpeas. Apricots. It's not China.'

'Whatever,' Toby said casually. 'Anyway, we're going to Greece again for mid-year. To Milos.'

I didn't have anything to say to that. In July I would be killing time back in Brisbane, holed up in the State Library reading Caulaincourt or Horace, or cycling along the river to prolong going home to *Countdown* with Katie and my mother.

'What about you?' Toby said.

'What about me.'

We pulled up at the bottom of the hill. Hamilton rose up in front of us, block by block, sandy brick and cream. There was a patch of green up the top, and an enormous gothic revival house, its roof gleaming in the sun.

Toby was breathing hard. 'What're you doing for the break?'

'Nothing,' I said. It was true.

'You're on scholarship, aren't you.'

'None of your business.'

We pushed our bicycles up the hill in silence. The houses on the road were large and shaded by trees, their fences tall and uninviting. A dog was barking steadily somewhere. I tried to imagine Jamie walking up this hill when he was young, before Knox, but I could only conjure an image of the Jamie I knew, his shirtsleeves rolled to the elbow, his waist slim and firm, his back coolly turned away.

✳

The Maynards' place was just below the hill's crest, a white and brown mock-Tudor monstrosity behind a patterned brick wall. Through the gate, the garden looked mannered and spare; the footpath was lined with mock-oranges, and there was a row of savagely-pruned rosebushes beneath the front windows. I kicked my bike stand and let Toby go ahead.

Inside the gate, a little path of stepping stones led along the side of the house to a lattice gazebo. There was a set of white wicker chairs in there, and an empty glass ashtray on the table. Perhaps Jamie smoked here at night once his parents had gone to bed. I traced the edge of the ashtray. I was in Jamie's garden. I was going to swim in Jamie's pool.

Toby yelled something from around the back.

'Porter?' He didn't answer. I slung my shirt and shorts over a chair, and followed his voice to the pool.

Jamie hadn't been lying: it was half-Olympic. I could see the sky cut up in its surface, splinters of sun peaking and breaking. In the shallow end, Toby was floating on his back in his boxers, which ballooned like parachute silk around his thighs.

'Not bad,' Toby said. He kicked a few times, then cupped his hands behind his head. 'That prick. Not bad.'

As I dived in, the water shattered over my head, cold and clear. Veins of light rippled over the tiles. I swam along the bottom until I could feel my lungs burn, then I pushed up. Hold your breath: it was an old game Katie and I used to play at the Spring Hill Baths. In those seconds before breaking through to air, I imagined I was a corpse, drifting dumbly towards the surface. I dived down again and again, sinking and rising until my heart was hammering and I couldn't swim anymore.

✳

I had probably only been going down to the Knox pool a few weeks before Jamie caught me, although those hours feel endless now, inviolate; nothing can or will ever touch them. The mornings he trained I left the dorm early, in the half-light, and took my books down to the pool. I would crouch in the stands with my scarf wrapping my mouth and nose, then when I picked out Jamie making his way across the grounds, I would pore over my book with a pencil. I never lifted my head until he was in the pool.

The day it happened was clear and cold. It must have been close to six-thirty; I could hear the thin pipe of a whistle intermittently from the oval. My book was open at a colour plate of Zurbarán's Saint Agatha, who was holding her severed breasts on a tray like, the caption said, 'two heavenly pink scoops of gelato'. Her face was pale and soft, and the rich red cloth was spilling off her shoulder like a ribbon of blood. The image was strange, savage; it seemed to me to signify neither revelation nor transcendence.

It was September, so the water would have still been freezing. Lines of flags snapped overhead in the wind. Jamie dived from the blocks and struck out at a sprint. The water churned white behind him, then stilled. I felt a thrill rush through me. Watching him swim was my first apprehension of something approaching beauty: the dark lines of his back, his hands dragging and reaching in the water.

By the time Jamie was finished training there were a few other swimmers, and he lingered with them at one end, his arms folded on a plastic barrier. As always, he was at the centre of it all, laughing with someone in a blue swimming cap I didn't recognise.

At any rate, it was far too late when I realised I was being watched. Two of the boys had seen, and one of them elbowed Jamie. I ducked my head.

'Wentworth,' Jamie yelled.

I stared at the page. The words winnowed and slid.

'Wentworth.'

I could see his chest beaded with water, the sliver of his smile. I lifted an arm.

'You fucking fag.' He was grinning. Behind him, the boy in the blue cap laughed and said something I couldn't hear.

'What's your problem, Maynard?'

'You're a fucking fag.' He was drying his back with a towel. 'What the fuck are you doing down here, anyway?'

'Reading.'

'What?'

'I was reading, in case you hadn't noticed.' My voice sounded reedy, weak. I felt as if I was seeing myself from a great distance — from the future, even — as a wretched, faltering thing, an insect trying to make itself invisible.

'What, *Arsefuckers? Cocks and Frocks?*' Jamie laughed. 'Fuck off.'

'Yeah, fuck off,' one of the others yelled. Anders, from Sinclair. 'Jamie's already got a girlfriend.'

Everyone was watching, now, from the shallow end. The one in the blue cap smiled mockingly at me.

'Get stuffed.' My heart was beating dizzyingly fast. I scrabbled for my things.

'You wish,' Jamie said. Someone whistled. 'Now fuck off out of here.'

✳

From the Maynards' pool, the city was faint as a backdrop in a play. Blocks and bands of light glinted coolly in the sun: windows. And behind them, people working; behind one of them, my mother. Beyond the city, suburbs stretched out in an endless expanse. Hidden somewhere in the cubist mosaic of roofs was our house, but it was impossible to make anything out from this distance.

'Istanbul.' I said it more to myself than to Toby.

'What?' Toby asked suspiciously, propping himself up on one elbow.

'Why would you go to Istanbul?'

'What do you mean?'

'Nothing.'

Toby sighed, then laid back down. His skin was mottling pink in the sun.

'Would you stop that?' he said abruptly.

'Stop what?'

'You're staring at me. I can feel it. Just stop.'

'I wasn't.'

'Why are you always staring at everyone?'

'I'm not. Don't be ridiculous.' I felt a sudden swerve of hatred for him. 'You're going red, you idiot.'

'Don't call me an idiot,' Toby said sharply.

'I'll call you an idiot if I want to,' I said. 'I'll call you one if you're acting like one.'

I could feel the rage roaring up in me. This perilous sliver of time might be the only afternoon I would ever be here, at the Maynards', and Toby, thick, fatuous Toby, was ruining it.

'Porter.' My pulse was thrumming.

Toby shifted his leg slightly and said nothing.

'Porter, you stupid arse. You're burning.'

Up close, there was nothing to like in his face: the disturbing translucence of his cheeks, his fleshy lips, the bulbous flare of his nose. Before Jamie came to tolerate Toby, he used to call him 'Pufferfish', and even once the nickname died, the image remained, lodged in my mind for good.

'What the hell are you doing?' he said. He was the one who was staring, now, dispassionately at me.

'What do you mean, what am I doing?' I said irritably.

'I mean here. What the hell are you doing here?'

'What's your problem?'

'Jamie doesn't even like you. He said he wouldn't piss on you if you were on fire.'

'You suggested this, you imbecile.' I was shaking all over.

'You wanted to come.'

'Of course I did,' I said. 'I wanted a fucking swim! You wanted one too, remember?'

Toby just looked at me. There was nothing to read in the glaze of his eyes, his slack, slightly-opened mouth.

'Everybody knows, you know,' he said.

'What?'

'About the pool.' Toby said. 'Everybody knows.'

I let it sink in once, quickly, then I turned and dropped down into the water. I sank to the bottom and held my breath, then pushed back up to the surface for air. I sank back down again and again, and when I finally turned around, Toby was gone.

∗

It was late by the time I realised Toby had taken my clothes with him. The houses next door were quiet and dark, and the sky was pale and washed out. I could see the lights across the river beginning to flicker in the water's surface. There was nobody anywhere.

I walked around the house a few times, looking for a sign. Nothing. The Maynards' pool was a faint silver, and I could see the lines of the roof cut up in it. The city looked cold and sepulchral over the water, a dark echo of its daytime self.

I thought about going around and smashing in the Maynards' windows, but I didn't do anything. I just sat there.

My mother and Katie would be standing, now, in front of the sink, listening to the radio and clearing the dinner plates, probing my absence like a bad tooth.

I picked the ashtray up. Behind me, the lights in the house clicked on; the Maynards must have set a timer. I let my hand sag with the weight of the glass. I could throw it, now, through one of the second-floor windows — Jamie's, perhaps — so that when the family came home they would find it. They would stand around the bed for a long minute like a nativity, trying to divine some message in the pattern of splinters and shards fanned over the sheets, then someone would gather the glass away.

Sarah Holland-Batt has lived in Australia, the United States, Italy and Japan. Her first book, *Aria* (University of Queensland Press), was awarded the Arts ACT Judith Wright Poetry Prize, the Thomas Shapcott Poetry Prize, and the FAW Anne Elder Award, and was shortlisted in both the New South Wales and the Queensland Premiers' Literary Awards. She is the recipient of the Marten Bequest Travelling Scholarship, an Australia Council Literature Residency at the B. R. Whiting Studio in Rome and, as of late 2010, is the W. G. Walker Memorial Fulbright Scholar at New York University.

Founded in 2009, *The Adelaide Review* / **University of Adelaide Creative Writing Program Short Fiction Competition** represents a collaboration between *The Adelaide Review* and the University of Adelaide's Creative Writing program. Each year it attracts some 400 entries from every state in Australia and a dozen or more countries internationally. Since its inception, the competition has also enjoyed the support of the National Arts Council of Singapore, assisting in raising the profile of short fiction writers in South East Asia. Senior competition judges Brian Castro and John Coetzee are joined each year by a guest judge — in 2009, Olive Senior, and in 2010, Gail Jones. Winning entries each year are published in *The Adelaide Review* and on its website. For more details, contact: *shortfiction@adelaidereview.com.au.*

A. R. HOLLOWAY

Wyong Writers 'Not To Be Taken Seriously' Short Story Competition

When Billy Went Beetroot

B et you can't guess what happened at school today.
We had a new teacher.

Wow. Damien Schultz reckons she was smokin'.

Our regular teacher, The Gremlin — her name's not really Gremlin. It's Gremlich. But we all hate her 'cos she's mean and smells funny, so we call her The Gremlin — well, she was off at some meeting, so we got this new student-teacher for the maths test. That's the test that's supposed to decide what class we go into in high school.

You should've seen all the boys staring at the new teacher. Billy Mumford, he got an eyeful down the new teacher's blouse and went so red we thought steam was gonna come out of his ears. But that was later — after he totally freaked.

The new teacher was just about to sit down when Billy leapt out of his chair so fast he nearly knocked over his desk. His maths book went flying and smacked Fat Mandy in the back of the head so hard it knocked the gobstopper out of her mouth and it landed smack on the front of the new teacher's shoe.

Damien Schultz thought that was hil-arious.

Anyway, Billy was standing there in the middle of the room with his school shirt all hanging out and his big shorts flapping around his knees and the teacher goes, 'What's wrong with you?'

and he goes all pink and says, 'Er ... Spider.'

Well, the whole class cracked up — except for Shauna, who was hiding behind her emo fringe and texting — 'cos Billy's nearly as big as a doorway *and* he's the school wrestling champ.

Billy goes to us, 'Shut u-u-u-p.' And the teacher says she'll have none of that and for Billy to get his book and sit down. Then she goes to sit in her chair again and Billy yells, 'No-o-o-o,' and the new teacher looks at him, her eyes all big like one of those Bratz dolls, and Billy says, 'The spider, it's on your chair,' and the new teacher dances around and screams like she just saw Freddy Krueger.

Well, the whole class cracked up. Except for Shauna — who was texting — and that kid Mikey Bradshaw, the one who used to be friends with Billy Mumford, but now they're not talking 'cos Billy reckons Mikey's a douchebag now that he wears a hoodie and his pants halfway down his bum.

The new teacher looked like she was gonna cry and she says for Billy to tell her his name and to get his book and sit down. So Billy goes to get his book, but Fat Mandy won't give it to him and Billy's going, 'Give i-i-i-t,' and Mandy just pokes out her tongue, which was bright blue from the iceblock she had at recess, and Billy called her a lizard-face. So she stuck his book under her bum and sat on it. Billy goes, 'Keep it, lizard-face. I'm not touching it now. Gross.' And the new teacher tells Billy to sit down and, by the way, she still hasn't got his name. And Mikey goes, 'It's Billy Munster, but we all call him Mummy's Boy.'

Well, the whole class cracked up — except for Shauna, who was texting — 'cos we all call him Billy Munster behind his back and now that Mikey and him aren't friends anymore we all know the story of 'Mummy's Boy'.

See, when Billy went to kindy — that's where him and Mikey made friends — his mum gave him a big kiss at the gate and started crying, and Billy was running across the yard where all the other kids were playing when his mum goes, 'Be a good boy,

Billy. Remember, you're Mummy's boy.' So then everyone started calling him Mummy's Boy.

Billy hates it.

So when Mikey says it, Billy yells, 'Shut up, douchebag. Shut u-u-u-p.' And the new teacher she gets real angry and says she's gonna send Billy to the headmistress's office with a note about his behaviour. And she yanks open the desk drawer — the one where The Gremlin keeps her pens and pencils and all the things she's taken off us — and stuff goes *everywhere*.

Well, the whole class cracked up — except for Shauna, who was texting — 'cos someone had put the drawer in upside down and now there's toys and rubbers and pencils going everywhere.

The new teacher, she's real mad by now, and she's trying not to cry and her skirt is so tight she can't bend over properly so she's kind of crouching and trying to pick up everything. And Billy jumps up, knocking over his chair, and goes to help her — after he punched Fat Mandy in the arm and called her a lizard-face again.

So Billy's got an armful of stuff and he goes to pick up a whiteboard marker that's rolled under the desk, but when he tries to pick it up it jumps out of his fingers like it's on a piece of string or something. Mikey calls him a doofus and Fat Mandy joins in. So the two of them are going, 'Doofus, doofus,' and Billy's trying to pick up the pen and it keeps leaping out of his fingers like a slimy frog and the whole class is cracking up.

So the new teacher goes over to Billy and tells him thanks and he can sit down.

And that's when it happened.

She had on this white shirt and one of the buttons had come undone. And when she leant over and held out the drawer for Billy to drop the stuff into, Billy copped an eyeful.

Damien Shultz goes, 'On ya, Billy,' and starts clapping, and Mikey joins in and even Shauna looks up from her texting. The new teacher looks all confused and then she notices her button is undone and what the class can see, so she grabs her shirt and orders Billy back to his chair like it was his fault her shirt had come undone.

By now the whole class is watching, and Damien and Mikey are clapping and whistling, and some of the kids are laughing, and Shauna's looking at Billy like he's the grossest thing she's ever seen. And Billy just stays there, on his knees, half-crouched over, his face going pink.

The new teacher is practically crying now and she yells at Billy to go sit down and for the class to be quiet. But Billy doesn't move and his face is getting redder and redder. Which is when Terri and Jenni — those girls who always ring each other before school to make sure they dress the same — they start saying, 'Billy better not have water in the brain 'cos otherwise he'll start whistling like a kettle.'

Some of us heard that and we laughed and the teacher must have thought we were laughing at her 'cos she went up to Billy — who was nearly as tall as she was even though he was all crouched over — and she kind of gave him a shove.

Well, Billy didn't fall, 'cos he's used to stuff like that from wrestling, but he had to straighten up to steady himself and that's when we saw it.

At first everyone was dead quiet. Then we all cracked up.

That's when Billy went beetroot.

See, it looked like someone had pitched a tent in Billy's shorts.

Well, that was the end of the new teacher. We never did get to do our maths test. Not that anyone cared. Didn't see much of Billy after that either — though I did see him and Shauna behind the bike sheds, so I guess they're going out again.

They reckon when they find out who pulled all those pranks on the new teacher they're gonna suspend them and maybe make them repeat grade seven. I told them I'm pretty sure those pranks were meant for The Gremlin, 'cos no-one knew we were getting the new teacher that day. But no-one ever listens to me. If they did I could tell them who did it.

Oh, it wasn't me. I'm not that clever. That's why I get to school early, so I can study. And that's when I saw who snuck into homeroom.

If they think about it they'll work it out. 'Cos who else would have made a dick of himself to stop a teacher sitting on a drawing pin except the person who put it there?

A. R. Holloway is an Adelaide-based writer who has devoted herself to writing fiction since 2006. She writes novels and short stories, dabbling in articles and poetry when the mood takes her. Her first novel, a noir mystery, was a semi-finalist in the 2010 Amazon Breakthrough Novel Award. The short story 'When Billy Went Beetroot' won first prize in the 2011 Wyong Writers 'Not to Be Taken Seriously' Short Story Competition, and has since been published in *Signatures* No. 7, Winter 2011.

An autonomous branch of the Fellowship of Australian Writers, Wyong Writers meet in the Wyong Senior Citizens Centre in the grounds of Wyong Old Primary School. They hold competitions, including the **'Not To Be Taken Seriously' Short Story Competition**, to encourage writing, and publish anthologies of members' work. The 2011 competition received seventy-five entries.

BRENT BEADLE
Mardi Gras Short Story Competition

Noah

The holidays dragged on forever. I mucked around half-heartedly with the others. We dug tunnels in the sand hills. We stripped yellow lupins for ammunition to protect the territory. My hair was always full of sand. At bedtime, lupin petals fell out of my underpants.

It was in the last week that Mum announced Uncle Tony and his friend Dick were coming for a visit. I made plans. My cowboy outfit was best for the impression I wanted to make. The curved brim of the hat highlighted my fringe and made my ears stick out. Inclining my head down, the men wouldn't see my blue eyes until I flicked my head up sideways. It would be like a lovely surprise. My chaps with the bronco-buckle held up at a jaunty angle would certainly charm them. I was going to get proper boots next birthday, Mum had said, so bare feet would have to do.

When I sauntered into the kitchen they were eating Mum's blueberry muffins. Dick noticed me first. He was a tall, elegant man with a deep voice. He was just saying, 'Raelene ...' — that's Mum — '... these muffins are dee-licious!'

Amazed at that, all my ten-year-old coquetry went out the window. 'Did — you — say — dee-licious?!' I blurted.

Mum looked blandly from me to Uncle Tony, to Dick and back at me. Uncle Tony smiled. They talked on as I leant against the doorframe squinting intently at my wiggling toes.

A fat, shiny bee flew into the kitchen, zizzing up and down the window.

'Get it out, Noah!' Mum said, 'Get it out, poor thing!'

I got a glass and one of the Christmas cards, and slid it between the bee and the pane. The bee went madder. When I let it out through the kitchen door I turned around grinning. No-one looked. Mum was prattling on and pouring more tea.

Next, I carried a handful of completed jigsaw to the kitchen to be admired for my skill. I called out above their chatter, 'Look, look what I done!'.

'*Did*, sweetie!' said Mum.

I got hot in the face and breathed out through my nostrils.

I went to the front room. Rainbows from the hippie-crystal hovered across the wallpaper. Uncle Tony came in and looked at the completed jigsaw upside down on the coffee table. He tapped the brim of my hat.

When we waved goodbye to Uncle Tony and Dick, the footpath was still warm. I felt a bit sick. I swung on the clothesline to cheer me up. We all watched the usual on telly. After that, the others went out to play. I went to my room and buried my head in my pillow.

Mum came in and sat on the side of the bed. 'What is it, why are you crying?'

'Lassie was so sad!' I said.

She stroked my back a bit. 'Come on, tea's ready. Call the others in, will you?' she said.

Slipping in between the venetian blinds and the window, I rapped on the glass, made cross-eyes and bared my teeth. In the dusky light, the others looked like they were made of felt.

School started back. Some kids called me 'pansy'. I was an easy target. Everything seemed strange, like I wasn't part of it. I left home to go and live in the tree-fort up behind the horse paddocks. On the way I stopped to help the blacksmith. He held a line of nails between his lips. I took them one by one and passed them to his free hand for tapping into the hooves. I was mesmerised by his muscled arms. His singlet hung loosely and I caught glimpses of his ribcage. I kept close so I could sniff him.

Later, when Mum found me up at the tree, she said, 'I don't understand you, son. Why must you be so airy-fairy?'

I didn't know why. 'It's ... It's ...' I tried to start to explain.

Then I followed her home, and she turned around and said, 'Do you have to walk with one foot in the gutter? Can't you just do one little thing normal?'

When I got home there was a postcard from Uncle Tony and Dick. It said:

Dear Hop-a-long Cassidy,

Next holidays, if you like, come and stay with us!

Unpacking my bag, I felt smothered by the scent of lupins. It was then that I thought about moving on for real.

Brent Beadle grew up in New Zealand and has lived in Australia for the last twenty-odd years. Brent thinks the short story competition is a 'very cool' way to be involved in Mardi Gras, and has entered the Mardi Gras Short Story competition for three years in a row. His entry last year, under the pseudonym Bettina Brentano, was subsequently published in *Flaunt 3*, number three of the *lesbian-ebooks* series. Recent unpublished tales include 'Star Man', 'The Lord's Good Work', 'The Skipping Rope', 'Warts and Piss' and 'Glassed'. His works thus far have been autobiographical and seldom untrue.

The **Mardi Gras Short Story Competition** is a national competition for members and friends of the lesbian, gay, bisexual, transgender, queer and intersex community. For the sixth year in row, organisers New Mardi Gras included this competition in the Sydney Gay & Lesbian Mardi Gras festival with the support of The Bookshop Darlinghurst, The Feminist Bookshop, *gay-ebooks*, *lesbian-ebooks*, Gleebooks, NSW Writers' Centre and Sydney Writers' Centre.

The theme of the 2011 competition was 'Home', which authors were free to interpret in any way they wished. Winning entries were presented as part of Mardi Gras's Queer Thinking program.

JOHN HALE

Terri and Hal Moore Poetry Award

Chiaroscuro

1. Against the light

When as a boy I clackety-clicked
my joyous roller skating way
around the streets of Fulham —
no kneepads, elbow guards, helmet,
just me —
sometimes, tapping towards me
I would see a man — stick,
dark glasses, black dog.
I'd stop and press my body
into the privet hedge,
giving them right of passage.
The dog would glance at me.
The man would not.
And I'd skate on.

Now all the world wears dark glasses
even when the sun does not shine.

2. As the cards fall

In the absence of God,
the gods have been kind to me,
have dealt me cards to sift into suits,
hearts always the least plausible,
the most fecund, most profound.
Whoever called trumps wasn't me.
I played the hand as dealt,
the cards falling and I with them falling —
or rising, the ace of hearts between two fingers
and the sun bursting over the waters
of a newborn day.
Each day, like the sun, I looked out spellbound.
At twilight a different game, a different hand —
but the green baize or the ship's bollard
or the upturned packing case
was where the cards would fall.
No taking tricks.
There was more moment in the fall of the cards,
the fall of a lock of hair
and the light ... the light ...

3. Dust

I don't these days much wield the monstrous cleaner.
Sometimes, carpet rambling, I stoop and grunt,
retrieve a rogue intruder
which turns catherine wheel in my palm
before I flick it onto grass.
Unknowable fluff gets less attention,
its provenance obscure,
lying nonchalantly in a wine stain.
I drop upended flies into a scooped-out
wooden bowl from Lombok —
their own sarcophagus.
No, not your meticulous nit-picking.
No clean sweep here. More a stroll
around the perimeter, checking the fences.
Yes, I was more than a boundary rider once.
Economy's the watchword now, conserving
the juices, the zest.
Few more years yet, I reckon, before
the shadows lengthen,
their edge diffused
but still quick.

John Hale is, among other things, a writer who lives south of Hobart, Tasmania, with his sternest critic, a wisely spotted dog. He has travelled extensively under various guises. He is in his ninth decade.

The **Terri and Hal Moore Poetry Award** is an annual competition run by FAW Tasmania. The name of the award honours past members who made a significant contribution to FAW Tasmania and is supported by the Moore family. Poems or a suite of poems of up to 60 lines are eligible.

DAVID CAMPBELL

Bondi Writers' Group Short Story Competition

The Burden of Guilt

The minister didn't mention the way Peter died. Not specifically, anyway. Funerals are like that. Reality takes a back seat to piety. Peter had, tragically, been 'taken from us', and the world was a lesser place as a result. We would all have to find understanding in our own way.

It wasn't hard to see Julie's understanding. Julie was Peter's wife and she was inconsolable, sobbing quietly in the front pew between their two children. Her mother and my parents filled out the row. I should probably have been sitting there, too, but Julie didn't much like me. Never had. I was the layabout brother, the wastrel. The black sheep of the family.

Maybe that's the way it has to be with brothers. Night and day. Yin and yang. Peter was three years older, and a success from the day he was born. Thoughtful, intelligent, hard-working and cheerful, he was universally loved and admired. He did well at school, then graduated from university and became a teacher. He was a deputy principal at only thirty-two. His future was assured. Until he committed suicide.

I got the call at three in the morning, in the middle of a high-stakes poker game. It was my father, even more abrupt than usual. 'You'd better come. It's Peter. He's killed himself.'

They'd found his car up in the Blue Mountains, on a bush track near Blackheath. A hose led from the exhaust to the front window on the driver's side. His wallet and a note to Julie were on the passenger seat. That was Peter. Neat and organised.

Apparently he'd been caught up in a financial scam. Teachers don't earn much, not even deputy principals, so he'd taken a risk by investing in one of those high-return investment schemes that guarantee to make you fabulously wealthy in a very short time. Early results had been so good that he poured more money in, even to the extent of taking out a loan against the value of their house. Julie had gone along with it. After all, this was Peter, ever-reliable Peter.

But then the global financial crisis hit and the scheme collapsed. The money disappeared, and they were about to lose the house. Peter couldn't face the shame, the thought of what he'd done to his family. The irony is that I could have saved him. I could easily have lent him enough to get through the worst, but he was too proud to seek help from his disreputable little brother.

Money is a funny thing. It can bring success, but not approval. I left school at sixteen and worked at a variety of meaningless jobs until I found my true vocation. I discovered that my brain had a special aptitude for calculating the odds in games of chance and became a professional gambler. A very successful professional gambler. I have a comfortable apartment on the north shore, overlooking the harbour. I own the place but, as far as people are aware, I'm just renting. In my business it's better that way.

But to my parents my lifestyle is seedy, decadent and probably illegal. That's their opinion. And Julie's. She and Peter only visited the apartment once, but she made her feelings very plain. 'Well, James, it seems that crime does pay,' she said caustically, gazing out at the view. But Peter was very quiet, and I could see that the situation bothered him. He was envious. I suspect Julie was, too, but she didn't want to let Peter see it.

As I sat in the church looking at the back of Julie's head I wondered if that envy lay behind the risk they had taken. If it had prompted a fatal mistake. And there's another irony. For I would have given anything to enjoy the family life that Peter and Julie had. As I said, money is a funny thing.

So I felt a certain guilt for what happened, and it weighed on my conscience. In my world it helps to know someone who knows someone, and I began to make discreet enquiries, to put out a few feelers. I learnt that Peter had been caught up in a Ponzi scheme, exactly the same fraud that had hit the headlines courtesy of an American gentleman named Bernie Madoff. Madoff's scheme went bust with billions of dollars missing. Peter was caught up in something much smaller, but the results were still devastating.

Peter had been seduced by a smooth-talker named Frederick Winterton — or 'Fast Freddie', as he was known around the traps. Freddie was a flashily dressed young man with a love of the horses and a passion for fast cars. Unlike Madoff, Freddie had been able to insulate himself from the financial collapse by getting out before it all went pear-shaped. Although his fingerprints were all over the scheme, the authorities hadn't been able to muster enough solid evidence to charge him with anything. So he was now swanning around spending his millions. Freddie was definitely no shrinking violet when it came to splashing the cash, and that, to me, was red rag to a bull.

As a gambler, I've had to become a good judge of horseflesh. The casino world is my preferred habitat, but I keep an eye on the neddies and the odds, and sometimes a good thing comes along that's too tempting to resist. Usually it's an unknown horse that sneaks under the radar and, if you get the word early enough, it's possible to make a killing before the rest of the world wakes up to what's going on. It's rare, but it happens.

I began attending the thoroughbred sales, on the lookout for a good horse with sound bloodlines. Nothing in the really big league, for that would have brought publicity. Eventually I discovered a nice little filly named Spring Mist that I managed to pick up for nineteen thousand dollars.

The best way to start a rumour is to let someone in on a secret. Of course, you have to choose the target carefully, and the really good rumour-spreaders are those on the fringes of inner circles, the bit-players who are desperate to work their way up the slippery ladder of favouritism. Such a man was Robert 'Rubbish' Binns, a rotund gentleman with a fondness for pork pies and the hats that went with them. He acted as a gofer for Fast Freddie, and he was also the uncle of one of the lads who mucked out the stables where I decided to keep Spring Mist. The lad had aspirations to be a jockey and made a habit of turning out when he could to watch the early morning track-work and pick up a few tips from the professionals.

It just so happened that I was standing near him one morning when Spring Mist was going through her paces, and I let fly with a low whistle of surprise, just loud enough for him to hear, as the filly completed a circuit. I stood staring at my stopwatch for a few seconds, then, quite forgetting to reset it, placed it absent-mindedly on the running-rail while turning away to grab my mobile phone and make what was obviously a very urgent call. By the time I finished, my young messenger had departed on winged feet.

The message that I hoped was now flashing its way via Rubbish Binns to Fast Freddie was that an unknown filly by the name of Spring Mist had just turned in a gallop that made greased lightning look like a somnolent snail. The perception could never have survived any independent assessment, so it was immediately necessary to remove Spring Mist from the stables to do some specialised training at a secret location. I, meanwhile, was to be seen at all my favourite haunts displaying an unusual degree of good humour and perhaps drinking a little too much. And that, I was pleased to see, soon attracted Fast Freddie Winterton.

The first rule in conning a con-artist is to ignore him. He had to initiate the approach, so I treated him as a non-person. Until he stood rather too close behind me as I turned rather unsteadily from the bar clutching a drink and spilt a quantity of liquid over his very expensive suit. That, quite naturally, prompted mock outrage from Freddie and contrite apologies from me, accompanied by offers of dry cleaning and 'Can I at least buy you a drink?'

Of course he accepted, albeit with much grumbling about clumsy people who don't watch what they're doing. In no time at all, he and I were bosom buddies, laughing at each other's jokes and exchanging tall tales and true about jockeys, trainers and the noble art of horse-racing in general. But I made no mention of Spring Mist. The second rule in conning a con-artist is not to appear too eager. So my first encounter with Freddie ended merely with a promise that we'd catch up again very soon. We exchanged numbers, but I didn't call. He did.

Four days later he was on the phone, wondering if I'd like to come for a spin in his new car. Of course I would … if a week next Thursday in my very busy schedule was okay. It turned out that 'spin' in Freddie's terminology meant exactly that. He had hired a car company's proving ground for an hour and proceeded to put his new acquisition, a red Ferrari California, through its paces. The California, he proudly informed me, cost half a million dollars, had a top speed of over 300 kilometres an hour, and was capable of hitting the ton from a standing start in less than four seconds.

All that meant nothing to me, as what I know about cars could fit on a postage stamp with space left over. But I dutifully sat in the passenger seat while he hurled the car around the track at what seemed fairly close to the speed of sound, rendering my knuckles quite white and almost causing my lunch to make a most unwelcome reappearance. I have nerves of steel at the poker table, but excessive speed is most definitely not my cup of tea. His driving merely added to my list of grievances against Freddie, but my admiration for his skill and daring knew no bounds once we had finally come to a halt, and I readily accepted an invitation to accompany him home for a few drinks.

Freddie's principal residence was in the Hills District and, predictably, it was one of those palaces perched way up high, with large, remote-controlled gates and a long, curving driveway that led past manicured lawns and several ornate fountains. Inside, huge windows framed a rolling landscape populated by similar dwellings.

Freddie opened his drinks cabinet wide and invited me to help myself, which over the next few hours I readily did, until it was possible to give an excellent impression of being three sheets to the wind, as the old saying goes. And that was when, quite clearly envious of Freddie's opulent living quarters, I confided to him that maybe I had a nice little earner that would pay off in the not-too-distant future.

'Oh? What's that?' was his nonchalant reply.

'Ah,' said I, tapping the side of my nose and slopping some more drink down my shirt.

'A nod's as good as a wink to a blind horse.' And with that I laughed uproariously and proceeded to regale him with a series of wild tales about the various ways in which I'd fleeced mug punters out of thousands of dollars at the poker tables over the years. And Freddie took the bait. Ego plays a big part in the life of every crook, but it's impossible to predict precisely how it might manifest itself. I needn't have worried. Freddie belonged in the category that loved to boast and, fortified by the knowledge that his guest was a drunken fool, he couldn't resist bathing himself in a little glory.

'Thousands?' he sneered. 'You took 'em for thousands, Jimmy boy? Chickenfeed! You wanna know what the big boys do? We get into 'em for millions. Whaddya think built this place? All those poor suckers out there just fallin' over themselves to give me their dough. An' you know the best bit, the real clever part? Gettin' out before the old horse manure hits the fan. An' there's nothin' they can do about it … not one bloody thing!'

He sat back contentedly, hands folded over his stomach. I shook my head and gazed at him in admiration. 'Jeez, Freddie. Millions? You're a positive genius, that's what you are!' And Freddie Winterton absolutely oozed satisfaction, to the point where he was still radiating warmth when he poured me into a taxi somewhere close to midnight. We were, by then, the best of mates.

I knew things were going well when I spotted Rubbish Binns hanging around outside my hotel a couple of days later. After the first meeting with Freddie, I'd moved out of my apartment into a cheap hotel in Kings Cross. Appearances are very important. Binns was taking careful note of the quality of my lodgings and, once he had put that together with the rumour floating around that I owed a number of unpleasant people from Queensland a rather large sum of money, I was sure he'd be reporting some valuable information back to Fast Freddie. And so it proved.

The call came the following day. Freddie had a proposition for me, and so once again I ventured through the big gates, this time in my rather battered old Holden.

'Hear you're in a spot of bother.' Freddie didn't beat around the bush.

'Huh?' I looked at him with a blank expression. My best poker-face.

'Money. Our friends up north are after you an' you need some cash real quick or there might be an accident. I know these things. I got contacts.'

I looked suitably chastened and shrugged. 'Just a temporary setback. You know how it is.'

He smiled, a shark advancing on its prey. 'I can help, you know. Better owin' money to a friend than an enemy, hey? Now I'm always on the lookout for new investments, so what say I cover your debt in exchange for Spring Mist? Oh yes,' he said in response to my look of surprise, 'I know all about that.'

I stared gloomily at the floor. 'No, I couldn't ...'

'What choice is there? How much do you owe?'

'Two hundred thousand.' I said it quietly, clearly embarrassed. 'But the horse ...'

'Is only worth nineteen thousand. I know. I checked.' He smiled again. 'Pay me the difference when things improve.'

It took him a good hour and several drinks to convince me that I didn't have an alternative. It was take the money now or suffer the undoubtedly painful consequences. Reluctantly I had to agree, and by the following evening a vet had checked that Spring Mist was in good condition, the paperwork was complete, and two hundred thousand dollars had been transferred to the account I'd nominated. Freddie was a happy man, and I stayed late once again as we celebrated the mutual benefits of friendship.

So it must have been something of a shock when I roused him out of bed very early the next morning with an abusive tirade that accused him of being a liar, a cheat and a crook who'd swindled a lot of good, honest folk out of their life savings, a snake-oil salesman who would very soon be behind bars once I'd delivered to the police the secret tape recording I'd made of his 'confession'. Unless, of course, he was prepared to contribute a further one million dollars towards helping me settle my debts. He had twenty-four hours to think about it. Oh, and by the way … Spring Mist probably wasn't the fastest thing on four legs.

Freddie didn't need twenty-four hours. He didn't even need twenty-four minutes. Rage is the enemy of logic, and Freddie was in no mood for rational thought. A con-artist who thinks he's been conned is an angry man. Still only half awake, he threw on some clothes and ran to his gleaming red Ferrari California, presumably with thoughts of wrapping his fingers around my neck.

Gunning the engine, he activated the remote control for the gates and hurtled down the long, curving driveway. At precisely the moment he realised that the remote hadn't worked and slammed on the brakes, he hit a patch of oil and the car careered into the heavy gates at a speed later estimated to be close to 70 kilometres an hour. In his haste, Freddie hadn't bothered to put on a seatbelt.

His death made the headlines and brought a sense of justice to quite a few people. Media reports indicated that the authorities couldn't say where Freddie was going, or why he was in such a hurry. Nor could they explain the patch of oil and the failure of the gates. The crash, of course, had done so much damage that it was impossible to determine why the remote-control mechanism hadn't worked. 'Just one of those unfortunate accidents' was the verdict. 'A combination of speed and carelessness.' Needless to say, I didn't attend the funeral.

Instead, I was on the receiving end of a telephone call from Julie, who informed me in a dazed fashion that an amount of two hundred thousand dollars had materialised in her bank account and seemed to have come from a company associated with 'that terrible man' who had just died in a car accident.

'The burden of guilt,' was my assessment. 'Probably couldn't sleep at night and was just trying to make amends. Sometimes, you know, people aren't as bad as they seem.' And I left her to think about that.

David Campbell is a Melbourne writer who has won numerous awards in recent years for short stories and poetry (both traditional and free verse). He has contributed to three poetry books for children, and in 2007 published *Skycatcher*, an anthology of original Australian bush verse, and *Morning Light*, a collection of prize-winning short stories. His writing has been published in a number of books and magazines, including *Best Australian Stories 2005* and *Award Winning Australian Writing 2009* and *2010*.

The **Bondi Writers' Group Short Story Competition** accepts stories of any theme of 1500 to 3000 words. No entry form is required, but there is an entry fee of $5 per entry. First prize is $200 while second prize is $50, and results are to be published in *Writers Voice*. Bondi Writers gratefully acknowledges the grant from Waverley Council that makes this short story competition possible.

www.bondiwritersgroup.org.au

IRENE WILKIE

Grenfell Henry Lawson Festival of the Arts Literary Competition

Living Sculpture

All day the ferries rock   and charge the spray
across the bow;
green and crested waters match the rhythm
of the engine thrum inside.

All day the ferries lasso the wharf   salt rope
gunned like a noose
about each post   the strangled twisting chafe
drowns the swash of barnacles.

All day a sculptured girl tries her charm as
travellers
rush to glass-walled canyon streets —
black-suited lemmings   footing it
ignore her studied stillness   the silent art
the hidden breath
the heart that begs for notice in the skill
of immobility
the pretence of marble skin   though it burns
of marble hair
of marble gown
that should not be stirring in the wind.

Across the pavement she steals time to glance.
Yes, I am alive;
look, see this silent shift of hand
slow-rising wink of eye
and the beads of sweat on my upper lip —
are they not real?

All day she dreams of being somewhere else
but hears the meagre clink of coin —
stares ahead when children test for proof
of life or stone.

At five
she breaks her trance   the marble melts
from arms and legs   the rigid hands
discard the chiselled form.

She skips aboard the crowded ferry
its bouncing floor   she rocks and rolls
in perfect time to the engine-throb inside.

The orange-crested waters fade
the voices of the gull
then the harbour bridge lights up
in scintillating points
outdoes the stars

and night comes.

Irene Wilkie's work has appeared in many anthologies and journals including: *Blue Dog, Poetrix, Idiom 23, fourW eighteen, Five Bells, Going Down Swinging, Broadkill Review USA, Australian Reader, Divan* and the *Henry Lawson Festival of the Arts Anthology*. Her first book was *Love and Galactic Spiders* (Ginninderra Press), and her second book of poetry is now complete. Irene is an inaugural member of The Kitchen Table Poets, Shoalhaven, who as a group produced the anthology *Tangents*, which includes the poetry of the seven members. Irene has read her poetry at Shoalhaven poetry festivals at the Shoalhaven Arts Centre in Bundanon, and at the South Coast Writers Centre as a featured reader. Her thanks go to Chris Mansell for a mentorship some years ago and to Varuna for a poetry masterclass.

The first **Henry Lawson Festival of Arts** was held on the June long weekend in 1958, and it has continued every year since to commemorate the birth of Henry Lawson in Grenfell. The festival aims to promote and attain recognition for aspiring Australians in various fields of arts such as verse, story, art, photography and television. Entries close for the Verse and Short Story competitions in March each year. Verse is limited to 48 lines and short stories to 2000 words. Entries vie for the total prize of $3725, with a statuette awarded for the best entry.

www.grenfell.org.au/henrylawsonfestival

Kirilee Barker

John Marsden Prize for Young Australian Writers

The Unreality House

Most people believe the best way to forget someone is to throw them down a well. Or lock them in a room with eight keys. Or bury them at a crossroad in the thirteenth hour. But they're wrong. The best way to forget someone is for them never to have existed in the first place.

Madame Marisol's Unreality House was where you brought people to make that happen.

*

It was a harsh October evening when the strange young man showed up at Madame Marisol's door. This wouldn't have been strange in itself except that no-one ever made the journey across the Whispering Plains after the clocks chimed for nightfall; and yet here he was, standing on her front landing with the nerve to drip on her welcome mat.

Madame Marisol pulled back from the peephole and calmly reached for the loaded musket she kept propped up in the umbrella stand. Then, with equal poise, she put down the book she'd been reading to the occupants of the House, opened the door a crack, and aimed the musket at the strange young gentleman's face.

'You have five seconds, sir,' she said, cocking the gun, 'before you no longer have a head. Use them wisely.'

He took a step back and stared at her through a thick rain-veil he wore attached to his hat. 'You can't be serious.'

'Four,' she said, and poked him in the nose with the musket.

Immediately, he raised his hands. 'There's no need for this.' He gingerly nudged the muzzle away from his head.

'Three.' In response to his actions, Madame Marisol rapped him over the knuckles and then returned the musket to its precarious position. 'You could be taking this time to compose some suitable last words, dearie. I've heard some corkers.'

He just stood there. Some froze, like him. Others ran. The furthest anyone had gotten was the lightning-struck tree by the gate. The gentleman's false teeth were still embedded in the bark.

'Two.'

The rain fell in diagonal sheets, splattering against the weathered timber of the landing. The rain clouds tinged the sky with shades of black and purple, making an artificial night. Madame Marisol tightened her grip on the trigger. Here, where the sun and moon, locked in their unchanging positions in the sky, gave the country the perpetual look of a balmy afternoon, anything darker than twilight tended to be regarded with suspicion.

She wiped a raindrop from the musket with one hand and made a sign against the darkness with the other. 'One,' she told the intruder. 'And I've really given you more than enough time to tell me what you're doing here.'

'Wait, wait, wait,' the young gentleman finally managed to spit out. 'Myname'sQuintalionI'vecomeforthepackageandI'vegot aninvitation.'

He said all this in one breath.

'Zero.' She lowered the musket with a sigh. A little recreational shooting would have brightened her spirits considerably.

'I suppose you'd better come in.' With another look at the sky, she opened the door and beckoned for the young man to follow her inside.

He wiped his boots on the lintel, leaving trails of mud, and stared up at the interior of the House. Madame Marisol watched him out of the corner of her eye as she de-cocked the musket and slid it back into the umbrella stand. She didn't know what people expected from the Unreality House, but it certainly wasn't a modest homestead complete with open kitchen, cheery wallpaper and fat-cheeked cherubs peeking out from the corners.

'What did you say your name was again?' she asked.

He kicked his boots off by the fireplace, removing his hat with its rain-veil and dumping it unceremoniously on the mantelpiece. 'Quintalion,' he replied.

'Quintalion?' she repeated. 'Why does that name sound familiar?' She scratched her neck thoughtfully. Not many travellers found their way to her House these days, although not long ago it had been one of the most visited spots on the map. She cast her thoughts back to the numerous influential families, magicians and, truthfully, anyone with enough money to pay the keeping-house fees. One image in particular stuck out: a tall, dark man and his smiling wife clutching their son's gloved hands. 'You're Quartalion's boy, aren't you?'

He nodded. Removing the rain-veil laid bare the young man's extraordinary features — the tell-tale line down the middle of his face that indicated someone of his kind, born of both mortal and immortal parentage. Although he kept himself swathed in a woollen coat, there was no mistaking that one half of his body was pale and the other half wreathed in shadows.

'Little Squinty!' she exclaimed fondly. 'I'd know that face of yours anywhere. Turning up on my doorstep after all these years … who'd have believed it?'

He pulled at a sleeve awkwardly. 'No-one's called me that in a long time. I'd appreciate if you didn't bring it back into vogue.'

'Now, now,' she told him. 'You can act as grown-up as you want, but to me you'll always be the little boy running around with the chamber-pot on his head.'

'Yes, well …' he brushed the rain droplets off his greatcoat, '… be that as it may, this time I'm not here to play with the porcelain. I'm here on business. Rather important business, in fact.'

She shut the door and fished around in her sleeve for a toffee that wasn't covered in lint — he'd always loved her toffees as a boy. 'And what's that?'

Finding a sweet that looked sufficiently edible, she walked over to him and, standing on the points of her pink slippers, popped it into his mouth.

For a moment it looked like he would spit it out, but he swished it around and dutifully began to suck. 'I've come for a package. *The* package.' His words came out slightly incoherent from the stickiness of the toffee.

Madame Marisol froze. 'You mean it's time already? Goodness, how the years do go by.' The violence of the quiver in her voice shocked her, but damned if she could control it. She patted at her hair, searching for her hair-comb. Having been dipped in liquid wormwood, it was potent enough to floor twenty men.

'Of course …' his voice cut into her thoughts, 'my father knows where I am and is more than willing to take action should events turn sour.'

She subtly took her hand off the comb, one finger at a time. 'Sour? Why should things go sour? We both know the bargain was sealed long ago. I keep the package safe until it's collected. You think I care what happens to it after that? Come on.'

They journeyed further into the recesses of the House, through an archway and past a long mirror, the fixings in the gilt frame empty and flaking gold, the large gem that would have been the centrepiece long gone, before stopping at a red door, set far back into the gloom where the lamplight didn't reach.

'I was sorry to hear about that business with your mother,' she told Quintalion. 'She was a good woman.'

He inclined his head, his gaze fixed upon the door.

Madame Marisol could feel the room's hum of power calling

out to her, but she hesitated with her hand hovering above the ruby handle. 'Is it really that bad out there?'

Quintalion shrugged. 'I daresay there are those profiting from the Tempus's separation of the nine countries ...'

'Such as you,' she commented, raising an eyebrow.

He chuckled, but the laugh didn't reach his eyes. 'Of course ... if I weren't being run out of every town I entered. It seems the natives have developed a little fear of strangers.' He scanned the open hallway and then, as if displeased by what he saw, ran a hand through his hair and grimaced. 'The old ways are dying, Madame. It's only in the forgotten pockets of time that they still exist at all.'

'Like my House.' Madame Marisol's finger unconsciously drummed out a rhythm on the handle as she bit at the inside of her lip.

'Like your House,' he concurred. 'Which is, I must say, looking remarkably similar to the last time I was here, and that had to be a hundred years ago now. How do you manage it?'

'A gentleman shouldn't ask and a lady wouldn't tell.' She exhaled deeply, blowing the air through her lips with an audible smack, and then pushed the door open. It swung silently on well-oiled hinges. 'It's time.'

But then she whirled around to face him. 'Let me tell you this — if you hurt the package, I'll take you over my knee and wallop you as though you were still seven years old. *You see if I don't.*'

✳

Darkness.

The air, which should have been stale and dank, still had that same tang of electricity Madame Marisol had first breathed in all those years ago when she and the House found each other.

The light from the entryway cast shadows on menacing shapes that rose up out of the darkness. Quintalion took one look at the blackness and pointedly ushered to Madame Marisol. 'After you,' he said, his voice tight.

'Don't you worry about them, dearie,' Madam Marisol said, and retrieved a long rushlight from a copper bracket and striking it against the wall. 'They can't hurt you. Come in, come in. I'll take you to this package of yours. Her name's Tuesday, by the way.'

They walked together with only the flickering rushlight to guide their way. Quintalion kept a step behind Madame Marisol and she could hear each breath, slow and deliberate.

Silence, but for their breathing and the *tap, tap, tap* of feet against cold marble. Tall shapes surrounded them, upright coffins and keeping-houses, each lit by a cold light coming from within and illuminating the faces of the occupants.

Quintalion moved in front of her and gaped up at one of them. 'They say this is where souls sleep,' he whispered.

Although no windows broke through the monotony of the darkened room, a slight breeze played about their faces. 'Oh, them?' Madame Marisol asked him, and lifted her rushlight to illuminate one of the sleeping forms.

A young girl spun gently, wreathed in the light that held her, her tiny unshod feet barely visible above the door of her keeping-house. Gold, glass and flowers encased her.

Quintalion leaned forward and studied an emblem picked out in swirling strokes. 'That's the House of Tantallon, isn't it?'

Madame Marisol nodded. 'That poor little thing is the older sister to the current Princess Regnant.'

'She looks like she's only sleeping,' he whispered reverently.

'In a way, she is.'

His eyes glinted and Madame Marisol couldn't tell whether horror or naked opportunity lay in wait behind those dark pupils. 'But to sleep all your life — to have never *known* life. What's it like when they're woken?'

Amused by the mixture of innocence and cunning in Quintalion's voice, Madame Marisol traced a gnarled finger over a carved flower: a goldenrod, if she recalled correctly. 'Oh, they could tell you what a cup of tea is and hold a decent conversation about the weather, but if you asked them what love feels like or what it's like to stare up at the night sky and see it staring back at you ...'

She paused and chose her next words carefully. 'They have no experiences, you see, my poor duckies, only possibilities.'

'Fascinating.' He reached out a hand, still half in his trance of contemplation, and — before she could stop him — cupped the sleeping girl's face.

It happened so suddenly it was all Madame Marisol could do to pull Quintalion back and out of harm's way. The skin his hand had touched began to sizzle. A crack opened up on the delicate cheek — and then another, and another, radiating out from the first.

The little girl's eyelids fluttered. She opened eyes of palest blue and smiled down at them, and then a fissure split her lip in two and the smile became a soundless scream.

Madame Marisol turned Quintalion away and took out a gold pocket watch. Her gaze resolutely came to rest on the ticking second hand as it began its journey around the watch-face, but all the determination in the nine countries couldn't blot out the screams and breathy sighs of the little girl cracking apart like a porcelain doll.

Madame Marisol stopped the watch, reached into her cardigan to produce a monogrammed handkerchief, and dabbed at her forehead. 'Seventeen seconds. At least it was quick.'

Quintalion's hands shook. He pressed them together, white against black. 'I don't ... what the hell just happened?'

She returned the handkerchief to its shadowy nook, and popped a toffee into her own mouth, chewing on it reflectively. 'You just found out what happens if the wrong person does the waking. I'll have to send a formal letter of apology to the royal family — most annoying.'

'But her eyes,' he gasped, '... the pain.' His knees gave out and he staggered, only stopping himself from falling by grasping the nearest keeping-house. Madame Marisol found herself wondering whether she would need to fetch the smelling salts.

Instead she decided to take a more direct approach and slapped him across the cheek.

'What? Why did you ...?' She could see him pulling himself back, but it wasn't enough. Men lost their minds in the room; men joined the very people they'd come to dispose of.

Gripping his shoulder to anchor him to the present, she moved further into the room. 'Considering what you just did to that little girl, well, I quite think you deserved it.'

He allowed her to lead him past row after row of keeping-houses, one hand still clutching at the pink mark on his cheek. 'But I don't understand *what* I did.'

Madame Marisol stopped and swung herself around to look into his face. 'Each person must be woken by the person who left them here in the first place. Did you surrender the princess into my care?'

'Of course not.'

'Then she paid the price of your stupidity and you would have too had you been fully mortal. You have your father to thank for the fact that you're still in one piece. Anyway, we're here.'

In front of them stood a plain keeping-house with only a small clock-face as decoration, the hour hand of which pointed to seven, and an inscription along the bottom that had long ago weathered and chipped until it was unreadable. 'Tuesday,' she said, pointing to the girl in the case. 'She's the one you've been waiting for.'

He studied her, leaning in to examine every curve and angle. 'But she's so ... ordinary. Is this a joke, old woman? Where's the warrior? The magician?'

Madame Marisol frowned at him, and thought, not for the first time, there must have been some inbreeding among his circles at some point in time. 'I made a vow to take care of this girl. To keep her safe until ... certain events necessitated her awakening.' A vein pulsed in her forehead. 'And now you tell me that the old ways are dying, leaving the Tempus free to pick each of us off one by one? And. You. Don't. Want. Her?'

Her breath came in great gasps, and she was dangerously close to losing her calm, blood pressure be damned. Quintalion stared at her, raised his index finger, opened his mouth, and then clearly thought better of it.

'Yes, lovey?' she said to him. 'I dearly hope that the next four words out of your mouth are *I've changed my mind* — for your sake.'

He paused and seemed to think his options over. Finally, he said, in a quiet and slightly hesitant voice, 'I've changed my mind?'

'Right answer, ducky.' Madame Marisol grinned. 'Now, you just go ahead and wake her up, like you did with the other one, and then wait for her outside. I won't have you frightening her when she wakes. She'll meet you when I decide she's ready and not a moment sooner.'

Quintalion muttered an affirmation and stared up at the girl before them. She had a plain, unremarkable face with a long, straight nose and small lips. Her hair, which reached just past her knees in shaggy, unwashed tendrils, was the colour of bark.

'Well, go on then,' Madame Marisol told him.

He raised his hand to touch her, but pulled back just before his fingers brushed her cheek, and pulled out a flesh-covered glove.

'What are you doing?' She eyed him suspiciously.

His forehead was slick with sweat. 'I saw what happened before. I'm not taking any chances.'

The glove was so thin, as delicate as a cobweb, that Quintalion was forced to wiggle his fingers into it one at a time with a barber-surgeon's precision. Barely breathing, he leaned in and, with the lightest touch, traced the hollow at the base of the girl's neck. Colour blossomed outwards, infusing her skin with a golden glow.

Madame Marisol nodded. 'You've done your job, now kindly leave this to me.'

He turned without a word and strolled towards the small square of light at the distant entrance of the room.

Madame Marisol watched him leave, making sure he didn't duck behind a keeping-house and cause more problems. When she was satisfied that he had, indeed, left the room and shut the door behind him, she turned her attention back to Tuesday. A strange humming surrounded the girl as the golden light zigzagged around her.

She waited to one side, tapping her foot impatiently. Some woke instantly and others, like Tuesday, took their time to venture into the world.

By now the light had enveloped the girl and she was held, for the briefest of moments, in its brilliance. Then she opened her eyes, looked around, and said, 'What …?'

And then she fainted.

'Welcome to existence, dear,' said Madame Marisol, with a slight smile. 'You'll get used to it.'

Kirilee Barker is a Brisbane-based writer. She holds a creative writing degree from Queensland University of Technology. Having written her first fantasy epic on the back of several Post-it notes at the age of six, she wonders whether fantasy is in her blood and, if so, whether that's entirely healthy.

Presented by Express Media, **The John Marsden Prize for Young Australian Writers** is open to poets, short fiction writers and novelists under twenty-five. It has been running since 2004 and is judged by John Marsden himself. All winners are published in *Voiceworks* or on the Express Media website, and share in a $5500 prize. The closing date is in August each year. For more information, visit *www.expressmedia.org.au*.

DENIS BASTION
Katharine Susannah Prichard Speculative Fiction Awards

Wolves, Sheep and I

The village women called Mary a witch, said her eyes were tinged red with Devil's blood and all who came across them were cursed. She couldn't do any magic, though she tried. But she saw what others didn't. The first time she'd met him, she saw through his guise. Squeezing her mother's rear with one hand, the other swinging a bottle of gin, he smiled at her, licking his lips. She didn't smile back; all she saw were his teeth, stained with blood.

*

I touch the hilts of the small blades, one hidden in my sleeve, the other in the folds of my skirt. Tonight, the air is hungry for blood. Thunder explodes in the night, the pagans gods are at war as rain falls grey over London. On the great city's edge, in the White Lady Inn, flagons of ale are passed among the unruly mob. Taxes, Napoleon and the latest hangings are put aside as old Widow Winifred, the inn's owner, spins a story about a creature called Death, a wolf, a man, a demon, who stalks the night looking for flesh.

Hood drawn low over my head in the shadows under the stairs, she still finds my eyes. She nods to a man at the far left. Drunk with all the right signs, eyes shifting without purpose, and more ale falling about him than into his coarse mouth. Charlie the Smith spends his money on gambling, and when he wins, which is rare, he spends it all on women. Every time he comes to me, I refuse. Not that his money is any less worthy but his is a kind sort of fool. He stares at me before struggling over. I tire at the aspect of refusing him again; he looks so happy to see me.

Thick lashes, scarlet lips — I know those vices, to smile with my eyes and taunt with my mouth. They say I work for the Devil, turning souls to darkness. Maybe I *did*. Mostly I just worked for myself.

'Scarlette—'

'Not again, Charlie—'

'But I have money—'

'Not enough,' I say as I always do to him.

'I've watched you.'

'Every man watches me.' Despite myself, I blush.

'You always look sad,' he whispers.

'This is a first. Men have said I look like a lot of things, but never sad.'

'They don't care to look deeper—'

'There is nothing deeper.' Another reason I refuse him; even drunk, he makes me nervous.

I glare at him but don't see that reaction on every other man's face whose business I make mine. No fear, no lust. Just kindness and sadness; the most noble of fools.

'Why do you treat me so? Like a common wife, instead of a common whore.'

'Nothing common about you, as a wife or a whore,' he smiles.

My refusal freezes in my throat; a warning churns in my belly. I may not see the sun hail the morrow. We can be fools together tonight. I can use a bit of kindness. 'But you'll have nothing left in your moneybag.' I squeeze the bulge in his pants.

'That's not my moneybag.'

I laugh, and with his arm firmly in my grasp I negotiate the throngs of wandering hands and lingering eyes towards the rear door. The Widow nods, continuing her tale.

I know the alleys like the lines on my hands and lead him back to his abode above the Smithery. His breath is ragged with anticipation as I light the oil lamp in his room. I take off my cloak. He gasps at such finery.

'You're right. I'm not common.' My laughter peals around the barren room.

My hands explore his thick, safe arms and strong, broad shoulders.

'A great man you've grown into, Charlie. Look at me.'

His eyes brighten as they meet mine, and his heart's burden reveals itself — everything that could make him my slave. If I wanted.

On his small bed, my fingers trace the grooves of his body; coarse lips, hard chest, thick thighs. In the dull light he looks more babe than man. But soon his snores fill the room.

I sigh.

Pulling my garments together I make sure the blades are in place. I look at the moneybag sitting on the floor among his dirty trousers. I hide it in a place he can only find when sober, lest he spend it all on drink when he wakes.

The air is biting cold; my breath forms a spectre before me as the laughter of shrouded souls echo through the streets. The clicking of my pattens against the cobblestone is barely audible amid the pattering of rain. I keep to the shadows.

*

Mary's mother was being more trouble than she was worth. That previous evening had been stormy, but thunder was not all that'd trembled the starless night. Yelling and screams echoed into the wee hours of morning.

At dawn, by the cock's crow, the girl woke up in the top of the barn. All was not right; she could see the truth of the day's promises shift in the freezing air. She found him on the house floor. Mama wasn't lying by the fire nor was she out feeding the chickens. She was gone.

Mary called out until her throat was sore. She ran the few miles to the village but the men laughed at her and the women made hexes and signs of the cross before scurrying away. Her legs ached as she ran home, hoping that maybe she'd just been silly and Mama had really gone to the neighbours. But her cries for help were met with stones. Bloody and terrified, she didn't know where her feet took her and could barely see through the tears.

'Mama,' Mary called until she found herself in the barn again.

He was there. His hands tangled snake-like around her, his stench and pungent breath made her dizzy. He pushed her to the ground.

'Little witch, little witch, I will have a piece of your magic this day, little witch,' he sang as he clawed her undergarments away.

She tried to scream but her face was shoved into the ground, and her mouth filled with straw and dirt. Then came the pain and wet trickling down her legs. She choked and gagged and prayed death would be a mercy for her. With a last thrust he howled into the air, before she was left bleeding on the floor.

'Just a common whore. No magic to be had after all,' he laughed, and walked out of the barn, barring the door behind him. In the darkness her tears stopped flowing and her heart slowed down to a gentle drum. Crawling around the barn, knowing its secret entrance behind the bails of straw, Mary escaped past the village and out onto the dirt road towards the city of forgotten pasts.

She woke up in the doorway of the White Lady Inn, ten and three years old. The boarding house had been full. She had nothing to pay for a little bread and soup, let alone a warm, dry bed. The door opened and a soft hand brushed her hair back. She'd always remember looking into those old eyes that burned red just like hers.

'Would you like me to turn her away, ma'am?' a voice called from inside.

'No,' the lady had called back, looking deep into her eyes. 'I've been waiting for her. Mary.'

'How do you know—?'

'I know things. Just like you.'

From then on Mary learnt to handle herself with the fineness of a court lady. The Widow Winifred taught her to spin the ribbon of lust and use her sight to unravel the hearts of men.

✳

The wind is cold and again I feel that unease creep into my belly. Every sound sends shivers down my spine. The moon hangs a gypsy's orb in the sky. I pass the church without a look, its gates forever closed to my kind.

'Hey, lassie,' yet another drunk slurs at me. 'Wha' a pretty young thing doin' out 'ere?'

He reaches for my hand as my other curls around the blade in the folds of my skirt. I stare into his eyes, and they widen with fear. Just a harmless drunk. He shrinks away as though burned before stumbling off into the dark.

I'm not out for business. I'm out for blood. I feel it. Something other than I stalks the night.

✳

Mary saw the first one just a few months after meeting the Widow Winifred. She'd been late from an errand, and the sun had given way to the wash-water colour of dusk. Then she saw one. His teeth weren't as long as the wolf who took her own innocence, but his claws looked deadly and his eyes were locked onto a little boy just a few steps ahead of him. The other souls on the road were none the wiser. Maybe they were blessed. Who'd want to see demons on every street?

Then the pair turned down an alley. As her heart threatened

to stop, she picked up a piece of a broken glass before plunging into the darkness. Careful not make any noise, she listened to the scurrying of mice and moving garbage.

The sounds changed. Ragged breathing. Soft cries. Behind a mound of waste she found them, the beast's back to her, bending over the still body of the child.

She crept behind the creature, plunged the glass into his neck then threw her bloodied cloak over the writhing beast. Dragging the boy from the place, she left him near a church before running back to the White Lady Inn.

Widow Winifred found her in the Inn's kitchen the next day, bloodied and exhausted. Instead of asking questions the widow set her a bath and gave her new clothes.

'I killed a man.'

'Nay, you killed a wolf. A demon. Sight is a blessing and curse. We see what no man wishes to acknowledge.'

'Surely the Church can help? Father Jacob—'

'Wolves don't betray their kind. Only we protect the innocent.'

The widow gave the girl a parcel wrapped in black velvet. Two silver blades, each one half of a broken heart.

'There'll always be wolves, just as there'll always be sheep. But then there'll also be us. We can choose not to be prey.'

✳

I *did* choose. I became Scarlette. It was a sacred duty, I'd long since convinced myself. With every kill I began to wonder, then long, for the moment when I'd see him. The thought terrified and excited me.

I think of Charlie and wonder: if I'd been born into another life, would I be at his side now? We could have been happy fools. But such thoughts are futile. The wolf is there on the other side of the lane, licking his lips, bottle of gin in one hand, talking to Juliet, the washing girl from the Inn. I could go to Charlie now. I could play the wife.

Instead I glide across the street. He seems to sense my presence and turns to face me. My hood shadows my face. His eyes linger on the curves of my corseted breasts.

'One day, I'll become an actress,' babbles Juliet.

'You already play the part of a sheep. Leave.' She throws me a hateful look before flouncing down the road towards the inn.

'What name have you?' he growls.

'Scarlette.'

'You bewitch the night with your beauty.'

'There is more magic to be had.' His breathing quickens. 'You lodge near by?'

'Aye, in town for,' he pauses with a smile, 'private business.'

'Take me.'

He licks his lips.

His room is more sumptuous than I would have thought. I set the oil lamp against the wall. 'May I leave my cloak on? The night is cold.'

'I don't mind my dinner wrapped in velvet.'

I position the blades within the folds of the cloak and make my way to bed. His coarse hands scrape against my skin while his lips taste my flesh. I slide a nail along my breast and drops of blood make their way down my belly. His tongue laps them up and makes its way to their source. My fingers curve around a hilt and with the other hand I lift my hood.

Light and dark dance in the room. Jagged and curved under furled lips, his teeth are poised ready to devour. My blood pumps. Like the others, he would presume it is fear.

By the light of the oil lamp, I glare into his eyes and they widen in recognition.

'Witch.'

But he is too late. My blade has already travelled along his neck and he has no choice but to go to the hell he came from. The gurgle of his blood is a welcome sound to my ears. I slip outside where the shadows welcome me into their midst.

I walk by a puddle and see my moonlit reflection. Haunting eyes, crimson lips smiling over long, curved teeth as white as snow. Wolves roam, sheep wander and I hunt.

Denis Bastion writes YA fiction and enjoys experimenting with short stories. Shortlisted for the John Marsden Prize in 2009, he won the 2010 Katharine Susannah Prichard Open Prize for Speculative Fiction. In 2011 he worked on his YA urban fantasy novel and on completing his BA in literature and history. He also hopes to study a Masters in education in 2012. Denis facilitated the Vermont Writing Group for two years, and remains a firm believer in community within the industry. He believes nothing can replace the magic of a good book, literature being a platform for inspiration, discussion, reflection and positive change.

The Katharine Susannah Prichard Writers' Centre is run under the auspices of the Katharine Susannah Prichard Foundation Inc. It is located in the Perth Hills, in the former home of Katharine Susannah Prichard, the internationally celebrated author of *Coonardoo*, *Working Bullocks* and many other novels, stories and plays. The centre encourages and facilitates services for writers at all levels of the craft. The **Katharine Susannah Prichard Speculative Fiction Awards** have two sections: the Open Awards, and the Mundaring National Young Writers Awards (for entrants twenty years old and under).
kspf.iinet.net.au

JENNY TOUNE

Rebelslam Poetry Competition

new&improved

our mythological wounds stir & thicken in
the language of our desolation
my tangible slashes spill fresh blood between
thighs already ruined by the chemical menstruation
of this year's cover girl

we're sculpting space, &
I'll stay for as long as it takes
to redefine my silence as kinesis
& my movement as protest, because
this year's model is already barren
& the CEOs of the new&improved
are birthing iconic playthings that sit
bloodied & abused on our overrated
pedestal of need

this year's dogma is already scorned —
pushed into the maw of the divine parasite
by the pseudo-intellectuals of
mentalgarbage.com

the virtual predator flashes titanium eyes
as she feeds on the dispersed remnants of age …
the virtual arbitrator cruises the beat
for more heirs to abandon
in post-Cambrian jungles …
the virtual boy-child procreates
recreates
masturbates
in a frenzy of pointless entropy …
& our mythological wounds stir & thicken
in the language
of our isolation

Jenny Toune graduated from the TAFE Advanced Diploma of Professional Writing program with the Outstanding Achievement Award in Poetry, and she has had short stories, poetry and arts reviews published in Australia and the USA for the past five years. She was also a South Australia State Poetry Slam Finalist in 2008 and 2010. She has written and performed a tap dance/spoken word show as a featured artist at Melbourne's Overload Festival 2009 and at Rebelslam, Murray Bridge 2010, and is currently torn between performing in her spoken word/dance shows and finishing her manuscript.

Friendly Street Poets (FSP) is Australia's longest-running community open-mic, uncensored poetry reading and publishing group in the Southern Hemisphere. Started on 11 November 1975 by Andrew Taylor, Richard Tipping and Ian Reid, FSP was Adelaide's first regular, open-to-all poetry reading. It has since achieved local, national and international recognition for its dedication to the nurturing, support and promotion of poetry.

Rebelslam is a registered International Poetry Slam event that began in 2008 and is held bi-monthly.

friendlystreetpoets.org.au

DAVID BLISSETT

Hawkesbury River Writers Prose Fiction Competition

Angel Burnt Orange

The Cedar Creek track is blocked and that's the royal flush. All escape routes are consumed. Isolation is total. Hours earlier, danger and options had staggered in on high-frequency static. Warning begot warning. All advice ignored. Now there is nothing. The ridge is an island, surrounded by the scald of hell, char-grilled limbs and oceans of rusted leaves. Baking winds herald an imminent end, and orange tongues flare and leap on westerlies topping fifty.

It'd all been foretold. The forecasts were unequivocal. Soil profiles, fuel loads, heat and humidity are all off the scale. Of course it's El Niño, the anointed boy, but bringer of only evil. His prophesies were dire: uncontrollable activity, crowning inevitable; just add ignition. Dry thunderheads rolled east from the Wollemi and a stray lightning bolt was all it took.

Now, as arrowheads thrust across the Deerubbun and into the light woodland on the western face of the range, demons take flight. Roaring wings beat across the gyrating crowns of the trees, blazing in orange, red and black. Dusk arrives hours before her time. Wild beasts thunder up the ridge, sending banshee tornados worrying off into the undergrowth, clawing the green-life like hungry talons. There is a roar beyond anything earthly. A devouring.

At the crown of the hill the air is chromatic and scarlet as even oxygen surrenders to the looming phoenix. Cinder flurries hatch flickering newborns that leap to maturity around the perimeter of a brown garden. Water pressure has failed. Electricity is a memory. The unbreakable pump refuses to start for the first time in history. And the newly spawned grow to take on invigorated lives. The windbreak to the south is soon ten feet high and alive. Every window blazes red. The world is a furnace. Teeth gnash. Fear and ashes. There is a fleeting moment; a breath for little more than hopeless prayer to the one who created this terror in the first place.

Death and time find themselves on common ground. The lance cuts afresh. Radiant heat stings and melts all but the air itself. The energy of the world seems focused on one small ridge, scorching and alone. There are screaming words, impossible to hear. Then, at the point where life itself seems set to concede, a thudding tremor shakes the earth and wailing turbines bade the living to hold on for just a little longer.

From out of the east she comes — angular, awkward, enormous. Is it Shania? Olga? Delilah? Who can tell. But it is her. Square, burnt orange steel, like another creature born of flames. She spins on her axis above the quivering slates, and sizes up the dimensions of the foe. Despite the overwhelming opposition, she refuses to leave. The angel. The angel.

Then a downdraft — warm and sugary, like breakfast syrup — heralding hope. A new hurricane blasts across the property, spawning rain out of dry, naked skies. The heavens open and an effervescent deluge of relief begins to cascade down, lush with life, and the power to save. Roofing floods and geysers churn out across flame-filled gardens. Life — where there was only the promise of death.

In seconds it's over. The orange lances pass and scorch east in search of fresh blood. A fragile island is left shimmering black and silver — ash and grateful steam, salvation, mercy and life — all impossible gifts from above. Perhaps no prayer is truly hopeless.

And the angel pivots thanklessly on her eternal grey wings and thunders off to her heavens once again.

David Blissett is a Sydney-based business writer for Mission Australia, and works as a volunteer writer for the Taronga Conservation Society and the Australian Home Education Association. He also writes novel-length and short-story fiction. His novel manuscript *Vertigo Gingko Fineto* was shortlisted in the 2008 New Holland Publishers and NSW Writers' Centre Genre Fiction Award. His short story achievements include winning the Bundaberg Writers Association Short Story Award in May 2010, winning the Hawkesbury River Writers Prose Competition in September 2010, and making the shortlist in the 2010 Alan Marshall Short Story competition.

The Hawkesbury River Writers meet at 7pm on the first Thursday of each month at the Mooney Mooney Club on the Hawkesbury. The **Hawksbury River Writers Prose Fiction Competition** is open to short stories of any theme and genre to a maximum of 1000 words. First prize is $100 and second prize is $50, with certificates of commendation awarded at the judges' discretion. For further information, contact Alan Michie: *alanmichie@gmail.com.*

JANINE MIKOSZA
My Brother Jack Literary Festival
— Sunflower Bookshop Short Story Award

Flight

Stella tilted her head to get a decent view of the bird between the bars on the window. She watched as it jumped from branch to branch with a twig in its beak. The bird bashed the twig vigorously against the tree trunk until it shattered, and picked up each piece carefully, tore out tiny strings of bark and layered them around the perimeter of the nest, building the walls of the fort. Its tiny eyes darted from side to side, on guard for the enemy.

She assumed the bird was female. It could be male, of course, one that shared the parenting role, or at the very least helped to build the nest. Harry may have told her this, but the only thing she really remembered him saying was that all brown, plain-looking birds were females with no other role but to nest and nurture. But then what did he know?

An insect buzzed about her ear and she cursed the lack of movement in her arms. She shook her head and tried to blow a stream of air in its direction. Fairy-floss clouds drifted past the window and the air felt a touch warmer than usual on her skin. It must be spring. *Of course,* Harry would have proclaimed, *birds lay their eggs in the spring.* She no longer knew how much time she'd spent in this room or how many seasons had passed since his death.

The bird was the colour of a coffee bean, with light beige

mottling on her chest and fawn feathers fluffy and delicate under her wings. Her beak was a muddy yellow, her eyes a deep brown, with feet darker still, almost black; but in the sunlight her feet were brown, not unlike an ageing black cat lying in the sunlight to reveal his ginger-brown undercoat to the world. The bird probably survived only because she had no remarkable features, and certainly none to separate her from others of her kind. Stella wondered if this species of bird was introduced or native to the country. What was her purpose? Apart from her task to find a mate and lay eggs, what use was she?

She didn't know what type of bird it was, scientific name or otherwise; Harry would have lectured her, but then he always told half-truths. He would inform her of the bird's title, its genus, breeding and feeding habits, and its sex. She recalled him telling her that a slip of the hand could change a chicken's sex. No, that was wrong. Surely, it couldn't be a chicken; it must be some other animal. Maybe it was a frog or another of those poor, slimy creatures he once dissected in front of his students.

The bird stopped work on the nest and sat still and quiet. She, plump and maternal with her feathers fluffed out, looked far nicer than Stella had during pregnancy, with her sausage legs, acres of sweaty, elephantine flesh and lumpy, red blotches on her puffer-fish face. The bird's eggs must be laid soon. How long would it take? Would they slide out of her or would she have to push them out? The babies that had been pulled from Stella took forever; *it's like running a marathon, which I do all the time,* the doctor had said, turning to share a laugh with Harry, who had stood there, nodding and guffawing in return. She lashed out and struck the doctor square on the ear with her fist and he had muttered *you bitch,* and she was sure he cut her a little more as punishment.

One morning, squawks came from the nest. Among the leaves and twigs Stella could make out two nude heads, ugly little things. Their beaks were orange and open like nail scissors, screeching for food. She watched the bird feed them worms and squirming bugs from her mouth. After the chicks had eaten, the mother bird tilted her head from side to side and stared at the strangers, these aliens that emerged from her belly.

The racket was incredible: high-pitched, almost unbearable. The babies flapped their naked wings and screamed: Mummy. *Mummy.* Feed me. *Feed me. Now. Now. Now.* During one of her twice-daily visits, Marjorie commented on the birdsong and how nice it was to have some life in the room. There were only a few quiet periods in between feeds, and the bird relaxed in those moments, fluffing herself up. At these times, Stella felt the stiffness leave her own limbs.

The chicks didn't seem to sleep but always calmed down when their mother sat beside them. Stella's children had been erratic sleepers. She recalled the sensation of waking from deep, dreamless sleep three, four, five times a night, month after month. She would grapple with their little bodies one at a time and attempt to stroke each one on the head or the back, but this would make them cry more; often she'd just leave them to it and sit in the corner until they were silenced by exhaustion. Harry would stay in bed, and she was certain he was always awake. How could he not be? At the time she wondered if he'd ever felt remorse for doing nothing to help. Years later, when she had confronted him, he pretended to remember nothing. Even in Harry's final days, when the boys were almost adults, when the simple task of washing dishes or making a bed was difficult, she was always doing, doing, doing. On the day fatigue took over, when she gave up, if only for a minute, and sat down on the dirty sofa, his silence was broken; he berated her for being a bad mother, for her inability to love, for her *uselessness.* His moods and fist ran that house. Only broken sleep allowed her slivers of respite.

The chicks grew bigger and squabbled with each other. Her boys once quarrelled over who wouldn't visit her. It was the first time they ever fought over *her*, in those deep, flat intonations of theirs. She heard the echo of their voices bounce off the concrete walls outside her window and pictured them at ten years old, silently wrestling in the grass. She would watch, arms crossed, leaning on the back door, while they pointed fingers and yelled and prodded at each other's small, white bodies. They made her head hurt. When they were silent, crumpled in the grass glaring at each other, she would whisper to herself: *Why are you here?*

Marjorie walked in the door, holding a tray of pills trapped in their miniature cups. There were only white tablets for a long time, but now she was forced to swallow the bitter red ones, too. Marjorie always entered the room with a booming voice, spouting rubbish about the weather or the price of a loaf of bread or how Mrs So-and-So down the hall was to be released soon. First thing every morning, Marjorie would move the bed upright so she could place the pills one by one into Stella's mouth. If she clamped her jaw shut, which happened only occasionally, Marjorie would gaze out the window and wait until she gave up and opened her mouth. She swallowed the tablets, hard and ragged in her throat, and closed her eyes so she could imagine the chicks taking food from their mother's mouth.

The pills helped her sleep but also gave her vivid dreams: images and smells of freshly baked bread, of soft fabrics and movement and touch, and warm human scents that made her jump in her sleep. She didn't know which pills gave her these dreams but suspected the red ones: they were the easiest to swallow. During the days, she ached for the aromas from her dreams. Often, before Marjorie unlocked the door and entered the room, a woody perfume preceded her. Stella closed her eyes and breathed it in, and would see wild roses in her garden from long ago, pungent moss under stones and the damp floor of a magical forest.

There were other dreams of running — anywhere, it didn't matter. Often she would race through the streets of a grey, deserted city, or across a meadow of soft grass and yellow flowers, or along the beach, sand between her toes and salty air on her face. She was a racehorse who refused to stop after the finish line. Sometimes she ran around a track and could feel the muscles in her legs, warm and flexible from their work. Her body was fluid, gliding above the ground, and a crowd cheered her on. Now and again, her dreams would be filled with dancing, of flying light-footed across the floor as if she were dancing on air.

But the recurrent dreams were of flight. The crisp brown bush and boxy concrete house of her adult life would give way to the forests of her childhood, wet and verdant. She breathed relief into the soft air, flying home through the birch and pine trees alive with small brown birds. From the air she inhaled the smells of her childhood and waved to her tiny friends, off to school with their plaited hair and coats drawn around them to ward off the cold. The dreams stayed with her every morning as she watched the wispy curtains trying to hold back the sunrise and listened to the incessant tweeting of the birds.

Marjorie liked the birds. While she wiped Stella down with a sponge, she laughed at the noise and spoke about the magpie that had dive-bombed her, pecking out a pea-sized lump of her scalp. She thought this was funny. Stella ignored her and watched the brown bird groom herself, sliding a taut feather through her beak and letting it go, following with a burst of melodious song.

One day Marjorie stared between the bars at the nest of babies now covered with patches of fawn and grey down, and began to sing, slowly and softly, a familiar song from long ago. As she left the room, Marjorie sang louder *when the pie was opened the birds began to sing*, and Stella heard her lumber down the hallway in time to the rhyme … *to set before the king.* Even though she sang it to the boys, it had always reminded her of Harry, with his dyed black hair and cruel mouth. That song had never sent the kids to sleep. Stella blinked away tears. They ran down her face and slid brine into her mouth.

On that same morning, humid and warm under an expansive blue sky, one of the baby birds, a teenager with its gangly legs and ungainly body, walked over to a branch and hopped up and down on the spot, flapping its wings. Then it was gone. Stella watched and waited for it to come up to the nest again; it never did. The other one flew off a day later, and she wondered if the pair was alive or not, if they'd been attacked by a cat, hopping desperately towards the tree hoping their mummy would save them. She wouldn't. The bird wouldn't care at all after they'd left the nest. Early one morning Stella heard the bird trilling *tink-tink-tink*, and it occurred to her that maybe the mother bird was fending off attackers of her own. Eventually something would get her — a sneaky cat, a desperate dog, perhaps a carelessly driven car or even someone taking a knife to the bird's chest, carving out her insides for no reason.

She wondered if the chicks would ever recognise their mother again. Would they have some kind of familial marker that each would recognise, possibly a pattern in the feathers or an idiosyncratic shape of the beak, invisible to human eyes? Harry once told her that birds always went their separate ways and never recognised each other again because they were too busy with the task of survival to notice one less of their kind. Once, long ago, she didn't believe him. But later, with the boys gone and Harry finally being put to good use in his beloved garden, Stella thought for once he might have spoken the truth.

The nest was empty. As soon as the boys finished school she had told them to leave the house, and they seemed relieved. Back then they didn't understand their father's sudden absence: now they understood everything.

Another bird would come along to the nest, she was sure of it. The nest was already built, so any old bird could take it over and make it her own. Stella would lie there and watch another do the hard work. In the meantime, she waited. At this time of day, it wouldn't be long. The restraints were uncomfortable but she closed her eyes and ignored the pain. With dusk creeping through her window, she would soon be in the silken air, soaring through her forest towards home.

Janine Mikosza is a Melbourne-based writer. 'Flight' won the My Brother Jack Literary Festival Sunflower Bookshop Short Story Award in 2010. Her short stories have appeared in *Etchings* and *Wet Ink*.

The **My Brother Jack Literary Awards** are run by the Glen Eira City Council with the support of Allen & Unwin, the Baha'i Community of Glen Eira, Eastend Booksellers, Hardie Grant Egmont, Ilura Press and Sunflower Bookshop. The Awards offer prizes in Primary (prep to grade six), Junior Secondary (years seven to nine), Senior Secondary (years ten to twelve) and Open categories, which are announced at an annual awards ceremony in October. It is open to people who live, work or study in the City of Glen Eira, and entries must be unpublished and not have previously won any awards. There is no theme, genre or style restriction for any category in the My Brother Jack awards.

KEVIN GILLAM
Reason-Brisbane Poetry Prize

the unwritten blue

remember, in that bruised light — we had dozed in
    the loft of the A-frame, woken
then walked — the tuarts browning skyward, warblers

    and wagtails flitting — you were talking about that book
Life of Pi — then the river, fat, white froth,
    moving left to right as if having been read.

I don't remember who noticed the dead bird first,
    one wing pointing skyward, the unglazed eye.
a bush parrot, burnt red and khaki plumage

    already being reclaimed by bracken. you went to touch it,
saw an ant, pulled away. we were silent then,
    hushed by fate and its casual cruelty,

late afternoon painting in charcoal around us.
    retracing our steps, a symphony of drips
and burps from rain and frogs, you on about

    slivered moons and life and fiction and
narrative's tidal pull. it was then,
    in that falter in your voice,

that staccato within legato, that you hinted
　　at some loss deeper than sense.
that night, in the warm cusp of the A-frame —

　　the tropical triangle we called it,
pot-belly below having been going all day —
　　you told me about your twin sister that

died at birth, how some days you saw her
　　as a bird, flying above and ahead, calls of
kinship or warning, other days as the sky,

　　how you'd noticed, out walking and looking up,
that while the gates and letterboxes and gardens stayed still,
　　the clouds and unwritten blue moved with you

Kevin Gillam is a West Australian poet with two books of poems published, *Other Gravities* (2003) and *Permitted to Fall* (2007), both by Sunline Press; and has a volume forthcoming with Fremantle Press in July 2011. He has also had poems published in numerous journals and anthologies, including *Best Australian Poems* and *The Best Australian Poetry*. He works as Director of Music at Christ Church Grammar School in Perth.

The **Reason-Brisbane Poetry Prize** was established in 2004 as part of the Words in Winter Celebrations that are held each August in towns across the Hepburn Shire in Victoria. It is named in honour of Len Reason and Jeff Brisbane, two local men who loved poetry and life.

In 2010, the competition, initially for Victorian residents only, was opened to all Australian residents. It is now one of the most lucrative poetry competitions in Australia. The prize is generously sponsored by Joy Brisbane, a published poet and author; her aim is to encourage and nurture the talent of both new and established poets.

LLYWELA WILLIAMS

Campbelltown Literary Awards

Water, Lily

She had awoken with a start, bathed in sweat, her heart thumping in her ears and her throat. Bolt upright, her breath staggered, eyes wide and unblinking, terror pulsating through every clammy pore of her skin. She could hear the thunder rolling over the tiles of her roof and the rain beating down.

She knew the front door was open; she could hear it banging against the frame. Her mind froze. The wind reeled through the house, bringing with it the smells of moistness having finally subdued the day's heat. She sprang to her feet and raced to her daughter's room. The bed was empty.

'Oh Christ!' She felt like being sick, purging herself, but she had no time. How long had she been gone? Her mind raced. She fumbled for keys, for her mobile, rushed her feet into gumboots, grabbed the torch at the front door, was gone.

She screamed into the howling rain. 'Lily!' Her words were caught by the wind. Sylvia knew where she would be, despite the darkness but because of the rain: at the river. It was her Lorelei calling her, although she was only eight years old. Soaked to the skin within minutes, her breath rasping at the back of her throat, breathless, voiceless. Maybe she could still catch her. The beam of light from her torch was growing weaker, flickering across the bike track with its tree-root bumps. The wind was catching her hair, and the torchlight was catching a million tiny raindrops and making them shine like diamonds. Over the O-Bahn bridge, down and around to the creek she ran. Its banks were surging. The water was torrential and eddying in raging swirls. She screamed out Lily's name. Nothing.

There was a flash of light in the dark as she flicked open her mobile phone and, with trembling fingers fumbled for zero, zero, zero, o, o, o, oh, oh, oh. Oh Christ.

'Who do I need?' A pause while she registered what was being asked. 'Everyone!'

'No. Fire brigade, police or ambulance?' patiently asked the operator.

'All three. My daughter, she's gone. She's in the river. I can't see her. Please, you have to help me.' The desperation in her voice was rising, her breath heaving, her eyes darting in the darkness for anything of her Lily.

'Okay, calm down, tell me where you are.' The disembodied voice, so practised in its calmness and evenness, was like a gentle hand on her arm.

'I'm at the river. Oh my God, where's she gone?' The terror, sheer panic was rising up in her. The operator was trying to prise information from her, get a location, trying to calm her. It was three in the morning: was she sure her daughter was at the river?

'There's no place else. She's autistic,' she screamed. 'She's obsessed with water. I'm always on my guard but she must have got the keys from under my pillow as I slept. She got out.' Silence while the operator began to understand, or at least tried.

'Someone will be with you soon. Stay on the line.'

'I can't. I have to look for her.' The phone clicked closed.

*

Many years ago, a close friend had invited Sylvia over to swim in her pool as the summer grew hotter and her belly larger and riper. She loved the weightlessness of the water, the buoyancy it gave her pregnant body and her thoughts. Sometimes she would lie there alone with her thoughts, floating aimlessly, listening to the tiny gurgling noises in her inner ear and trying to decipher the sounds of the world beyond — the cockatoos screeching overhead, the kids next door playing and laughing — but all slightly muffled and distorted. She imagined the sounds that her baby would hear through the filter of amniotic fluid: the gurgling of her digestion, the beating of her heart, a whole unheard symphony of chaotic, discordant sounds.

Sylvia would dive underneath, immersed in her thoughts, and, like a marine geographer, chart the depths. She watched the dancing, expanding wavelengths of light shimmer across the pool's floor, a mirror of the ripples on its surface. Her bubbles rose to the surface like a myriad of silver mercury spheres, incandescent in their beauty.

When her waters broke, Sylvia had already been balancing on the tightrope in her mind for several days. It was the normal anxiety of what to expect and how the birth would go. But Jasper would be with her, she reassured herself. They had rehearsed all their breathing exercises together, felt close in the last days of their waiting. The midwives ushered them through the labyrinth of corridors and rooms, and the deep bath was filled, waiting for Sylvia like an old friend. She submersed herself in its warmth and drifted with the contractions, breathing deeply, closing her eyes, focusing on the sensations of her body: the tightening, the tension, the reprieve. Hours passed like this, her skin wrinkling as if she were aging under time-lapse photography. *Jasper is here, everything will be okay* was her mantra. The warmth of the water calmed her and soothed her. Crescendos of pain ebbed through her and her moans grew more and more intense. There were reassuring words from the midwives, backrubs from Jasper. The swallowing blackness of pain and then, almost unexpected, the urge to push, like nothing she had ever felt before. She had read about this in all her pregnancy books but nothing could prepare her for how overwhelming the urge was, and how urgent. More unintelligible words from the midwives, from Jasper. A gasp of air as if she were about to dive and hold her breath forever. A tiny head crowning in an underwater world. A midwife supporting the baby in its first swim, an umbilical chord unfurling, still pulsating with blood, and then up to her mother to hold to take her first breath. And a scream as loud as blue murder.

✳

In the rain by the river there was the lazy flash of red and blue, circling silently, the siren on mute. Two policemen got out of the car, and headed towards her fading beam of light. One walked her back to the car, a blanket draped unceremoniously around her shoulders, her head lolled in her hands, teeth chattering, shivering. There was static across the radio, the mic held close to unknown lips, despatches of desperateness ricocheting across invisible airwaves. A blur of conversation: *who?*, *how?*, *when?* A strange clinical dogma to it. And always, *are you sure?* Reassurances for otherwise.

'Maybe she was just in another room. Did you look?'

'Well, no.' A spark of possibility. 'But why was the front door open then?'

There were more cars, more serious-looking men, a blankness sewn onto their faces. A whisper — 'Maybe she's that psych patient that went missing?' A raised eyebrow. 'Let's get you home.'

✳

She remembered their walks together down by the river, with Lily strapped into her pusher so she wouldn't run away. There would always be a lone ibis, with its curved beak and lost thoughts of Egyptian gods, standing solitary in the water. There were moorhens, with their flash of red-orange against shimmering black. There were the interloping willows among the magnificent gums. If Lily were tired she would restfully soak up the images and peacefulness, and Sylvia would breathe deep and unwind in the inner solitude of motherhood. The pusher would crunch through the bleached eucalypt leaves; their pale yellows curving, some like crescent moons, and a few completing full circles, looping in upon themselves. The leaves would be scattered across the water, interrupting the reflections of the gums and the unreachable sky. In places, a thin algal film blurred and obscured the mirror images of the trees.

On those walks by the river, Sylvia replayed in her head all the conversations about Lily. 'She will never talk, never make friends, never truly live in our world.' It felt like drowning in a sea of despair. The dreams of her daughter and her daughter's future were all being stolen by men in cold white rooms. How dare they dictate to her in this way. She would storm out from each prognosis determined to prove them wrong. But niggling doubts shadowed her. Lily didn't smile, she didn't look her in the eye, it was always through her and beyond her as if she could see an angel sitting on her mother's shoulder. The years of voicelessness spread. There was never a 'mama', that magical word that would make them belong to one another, just a distancing of space and emotion between them, a ravine of confusion and despair. The tantrums deepened; wild kicking, screaming. At those times Lily was like an injured animal, biting and scratching.

Not long after Lily had been diagnosed with autism, a speech therapist had suggested that she be taught sign language so as to help her communicate. Intensively, Sylvia had laboured with a blind sort of optimism. She plunged in feet-first, only ever coming up for short quick breaths of air, always just enough to sustain her until the next doctor's pessimism. In the quietness of night Sylvia and Jasper studied signs together and chose to focus on essentials, the ones that were easy and were everyday things. There was 'book':

two hands brought together as if in prayer and then opened, with soft palms facing up. 'To eat': fingers together and brought to the mouth as if with food. When sitting at the table for lunch, they would sign it over and over, reinforcing it with words: 'Look, Lily. Food, Lily. Time to eat, Lily.' Sometimes they would lean forward and shape her hand gently and help her sign. Weeks passed with no glimmer of recognition, just an endless pantomime in all its repetitive beauty.

'Water, Lily. Do you want some, water?' Sylvia stroked her cheek forwards with two gentle movements of her index finger as she said the word 'water'. And Lily signed it back. *Water. Water.* Two soft strokes on her baby-soft cheek. Sylvia sat motionless, an unbelieving stillness in her being.

'Water?' Sylvia said and signed simultaneously.

Water, water, Lily signed back, and grabbed for the bottle.

It was her first word.

Sylvia raced to her sign language books and looked up 'wet'. *Of course,* she scolded herself, *I should have used signs that were more meaningful to her.* She found the sign for 'wet': holding her palm upward and bringing her fingers together and releasing and then bringing them together again. She put Lily in the bath and signed it over and over again.

'You're all wet, Lily. All wet.' She signed with an urgency for proof. Lily signed back.

Sylvia breathed out as if she had been holding her breath for the past three years.

Jasper was no longer there when Lily signed 'rainbow', waving an arch with her hand. She had seen them in books and once for real in a sun-split sky, rain clouds dark and ominous being chased by a chasm of blue. The colours had dazzled even Sylvia. But Jasper had already gone, leaving amid a flurry of self-recriminations and contrite platitudes. He couldn't bear it any longer. Yes, he loved them, but he'd had enough. It was all too hard. Too messy. Too draining.

At the time Sylvia was holding Lily in her arms, trying to control her kicking and screaming. She slumped to the floor.

'What, right now, Jasper?' Hers was a look of wild disbelief.

'Yep.' There was a resolute firmness in his voice. 'It's like this every day, Sylvia, and I'm sick of it. And what for? To get through to her? Make a life for her? What about us, Syl! We've disappeared in this mess. There's no time for us. Lil doesn't go to bed till two in the morning, and she spends half the time scratching herself and screaming. You're just obsessed with her, making her better. It's not going to work, Syl. Just wake up.'

'But she's started to sign now, Jasper.' It was raw how she said it, like an accusation.

'Wow. "Water." Bit whoop.' A slammed door, the rush of wind was a slap to her face. Lily was still howling and thrashing like a fish thrown ashore.

Within weeks, there was the sign for 'rain', too, fingers mimicking the falling droplets of water.

✳

The policemen assigned to Sylvia at home checked all the cupboards and behind all the doors for the ghost of a red-haired girl who should have been there. A policewoman sat with her on the sofa, urging her to change into dry clothes, but Sylvia was limp with exhaustion and unresponsive. The storm slowly subsided and daylight crept in through the windows, like an intruder, stealthily and unnoticed. The policewoman took down a photo of Lily from the piano: a small child sat in the bathtub absorbed in play, pouring water from one brightly coloured cup to another. Her hair, the colour of autumn, was knotted and entangled. A swirling galaxy of freckles was sprinkled across her face. There was another of her dancing under a sprinkler at the golf course. She could almost hear the *tch, tch, tch*. The water arced around gracefully and beaded the grass with spherical jewels, momentary and ephemeral. The third photo was of Lily in Jasper's arms down by the river. Sylvia saw her looking at that one and remembered that evening with photographic clarity. It had been one of those scorching-hot days, and they had walked down there for the ritual of evening coolness among the gums. Late evening shadows stretched out across the grass. Lily had sat transfixed on the little wooden bridge, with Jasper holding her. In his embrace she was content to watch the ripples in the water, concentric certainties growing outward and then another random beginning elsewhere, bending and refracting reflections into a collage of irregularities. Sylvia looked up and saw the gnats dancing in the evening sunlight, catching the light like a million tiny cosmonauts, swirling on their grand, insignificant journeys. They were like specks of light dancing in haphazard paths, curling through the air. She looked back to Lily and Jasper, raised the camera to her eyes, pressed the button and captured the moment so that, in its perfection, it couldn't escape.

A police car pulled up outside. There were whispered words and lowered heads in understanding between the uniformed. Sylvia was still lost in the memory of that moment long ago, down by the river, and grasping at the idea that it would never happen again.

A gentle voice, a hand on her arm. 'They've found Lily,' said the policewoman. There was resignation in her voice, a note of defeat in every word. There was no need for any more words. All the rest was unspoken. Salty tears ran down Sylvia's face.

Llywela Williams was born in central Queensland and later moved to Melbourne, where she completed an arts/law degree and a PhD. During her studies she lived for lengthy periods of time in Germany and Russia, and is now happily ensconced in Adelaide with her German partner and three young children. She is currently trying to improve her piano playing, volunteers for several environmental organisations, and is eco-retrofitting their 1960s house. The Campbelltown Literary Award is the first short story competition she has entered.

The **Campbelltown Literary Awards** are run by the Campbelltown City Council and are open to previously unpublished pieces that have a specific reference to the City of Campbelltown, capturing its experiences and culture. Entry conditions and results are made available on the City of Campbelltown website. The theme for the 2010 awards was 'Reflections on Water'.

www.campbelltown.sa.gov.au/site/page.cfm?u=2000

ELAINE BARKER

Friendly Street Poets Satura Prize

Certainty

If I had told you
about the spider-web
which bridged the space
between two small branches
on the *Prunus pissardi*
I'd come upon
that cold morning
on the path across the garden
and if I'd spoken of its spare mystery,
the threads strung from its bridge line,
each silk strand spun with dewdrops,
each glistening sharp and fine,
that web would have drawn you in
and you would have marvelled
at its mathematical precision,
the clarity of design,
and would have pictured it
like an unspoken whisper
and carried it with you
as I have done.

An Adelaide poet, **Elaine Barker** has had two collections published: *The Windmill's Song* (Wakefield Press, 2003) and *The Day Lit by Memory* (Ginninderra Press, 2008). *High Heels and Tartan Slippers* will be published by Ginninderra at the end of the year.

Friendly Street Poets (FSP) is Australia's longest-running community open-mic, uncensored poetry reading and publishing group in the Southern Hemisphere. Started on 11 November 1975 by Andrew Taylor, Richard Tipping and Ian Reid, FSP was Adelaide's first regular, open-to-all poetry reading. It has since achieved local, national and international recognition for its dedication to the nurturing, support and promotion of poetry.

The 2010 **Satura Prize** was judged by highly acclaimed Dutch film director, writer and producer Rolf de Heer.

friendlystreetpoets.org.au

Hugh Kiernan

Cancer Council of Victoria Arts Awards Short Story Competition

A Spiral Staircase Going Nowhere

Outside the hospital I waver beside a suitcase of pills and pyjamas, pressing a leg against the charcoal fabric to balance myself. My suddenly expanded horizon is now framed by asphalt, roofs, trees and the occasional shrub. Colours struggle and dissipate beneath the watercolour wash of this June sunlight, pale as my skin. I turn to track the sun's path across the sky, searching for warmth. I twist at the neck. A faint brushstroke of radiant heat traces across my face.

Clouds and branches shield this warmth from me. I wait for shadows to pass, wondering whether my new sensitivity to sunburn is really such a danger. Today, I have no desire to protect my skin, being more concerned with hosting the poisoned circuitry that sits beneath its surface. As lazy air movements connect me to the sun, I breathe with the quiet limbs along the roadside. The drip bag of chemicals being empty, I am set free to stand on the street.

I see her smile, fluid through the glass as the car approaches. She is sharply in focus now, coming towards me out of a daily life I have lost contact with. I belong with her, in the space beside her. But I see an empty seat. I am not in it. I sense for the first time that I am changed.

I stand in the bathroom, holding a towel in front of my chest, dripping water onto the mat. After several minutes I become aware I have been staring at myself in the mirror. The person staring back is a bony, colourless impression of whom I think to be my real self. I doubt it is me, so I look again. More minutes pass.

My home caresses my eye. Angles are not ward regimented and occasional shadows fall easily across the carpet. Within the foreground of this more intimate perspective, I experience the freedom to move without having to push the drip bag along beside me. Like a jellyfish on a reef, I glide weightlessly through familiar surroundings.

I hold a mug of coffee and stand beside the dining room table, looking at the pile of letters. There must be twenty of them, neatly stacked with a slight twist; the start of a spiral staircase that goes nowhere. The same June light angles in across the table, highlighting the crisp fan of white envelopes. I sip the coffee and stare at them. I feel warm. I am wearing clothes for the first time in a month.

Making piles in front of me, I separate the paper into invoices and claim forms. The torn envelopes I push to one side. I recognise most of the names. Hospital, pathology, radiology, X-ray, CT scan, ambulance, specialist; all ask politely for my due attention. Apart from the logoed names, everything is written in a language I do not speak or understand. The codes and shorthand mean little to me. There is not one complete sentence in the whole lot. At the bottom it is clear what things mean. I have no idea how to go about paying for it all.

I try to complete a claim form and wonder what happened to May. The last I remember it was April. Two-way claims, in- and out-patient services, components of hospital and medical charges, out-of-pocket charges. And there are some invoices I do not recognise at all. I have never been to Monash Medical Centre. Why do I have a bill from them? And what is Southern Health? I put the pen down and sit back. The disconnect between how I feel being home again and how I feel sitting in front of thousands of dollars worth of bills is extreme. I leave the piles on the table and float away. Days will pass before I return to them. She seems to understand and says nothing.

I had left here when they fed me into an ambulance one night. There were three of them; careful, concerned and silhouetted on the dark street. We explained that the cancer may have something to do with the ribs giving way. It was all new and the words were still fresh to us. They listened and nodded. We were right to call them. If I had bent down and leaned back into our small sedan I would never have got up out of it. They held my weight, lowered me onto the stretcher and slid me into position behind the driver.

I went straight through Emergency on the trolley. A drip of painkillers started to settle me down. It was two in the morning and the doctor spoke quietly, asking questions, telling me what she knew and what she wanted to find out. She went away to phone a specialist, which impressed me but also scared me. When she returned she started at my left shoulder and worked her way down my left side, from bone to bone, gently feeling every section of my skeleton. She would slide her finger tips across my skin and occasionally press or squeeze. She stood at the foot of the bed, looking at me as she worked her way up and down the bones of each toe, from left foot to right foot. Then, up my right side it was the same. She was intent on finding and following the line of bones her training told her was there. The painkillers were working, so she pressed into my ribs. We both felt them wobble and shift each side of the breaks. There being no other damage, she ordered a morphine drip and left me. I gladly floated away.

I could not move for days. I lay there under the saline bag and prepared myself carefully before every breath. But most of them hurt anyway. Broken ribs are painful.

Then I could not move because of the morphine. I had a drip line and a bag of dreams. I could pump as much as I wanted into myself.

I had no reason to move. Bad news was waiting: kidney failure, spinal disintegration, chemotherapy, hair loss, gout, a stuffed immune system, and a few other things besides. All ready and waiting for when I returned to earth.

So I decided to stay away as long as I could. I would reach my hand out for the drip line and feel my way up the tube till I got to the plastic dial. It was like adjusting the electric blanket before lapsing into sleep. 'Lapsing' is not the right word, though. With morphine the fun was only just beginning.

That sensation of floating in slow-motion is just so good. You forget you cannot move. You transcend movement, levitate on the spot. And when you think you're about to land you suddenly take off again for another circuit, another frolic. Just for the fun of it. You have been high-jacked.

That seemed to go on for some time. In between flights it was not so pleasant. I felt a weight on my chest, pushing down, squeezing me into the mattress and constricting my breathing. I thought of the two miners trapped underground for two weeks in Tasmania, waiting to be rescued, with the rocks squeezing them and a dead body beside them.

I scared myself awake with these imaginings. I did not know when or how they would end. Would I be rescued from beneath these rocks? I'd reach out and feel for the tube again. The questions were always there, though. How do broken ribs heal? And if they heal, how do kidneys heal? And my spine that's made of Swiss cheese, how would that heal? And, anyway, how does cancer heal? *Does* it heal?

I lay there in the departure lounge thinking of these things. Thank God for the morphine.

Some days later I began working my spine sideways across the mattress, using my elbows as levers, until I could roll onto my left side. I wanted to stand up on my own and it was bound to hurt. Working my ankles up the centre of the bed, I forced my knees to flex and move forward towards the edge. Supporting my weight on my left elbow, which snuggled under the good ribs, I lifted my right shoulder upwards. I paused, knowing that as soon as I pushed off and tried to sit up my right side would feel it.

I pushed off my left elbow and let the shot of pain travel through me. My shoulders shook involuntarily but I kept pushing. In an upright position finally, I let both feet dangle beneath me. I sat still and waited. It was afternoon and quiet. Visitors stood in the corridor, meekly peering into rooms. I was not sure what day it was.

Another moment, another shot of pain, and I stood shakily in the middle of the room.

The question I had fended off for weeks asked itself yet again: 'What the hell just happened to my life?' This time, however, I spoke the words into the empty hospital air and made them real for the first time. A full, dopey minute later I had chosen a response.

'Okay, I start now learning to live with this.'

It was a compulsive thought, an instinctive thing. It was not informed by any philosophy, belief or other commitment. It was simply a statement of fact. Standing up was living with it. Breathing was living with it. I did not have to understand the totality of what had happened. I was surrounded by people who knew the science of it; the physics and the chemistry. I felt no urge to match them. They seemed to act in spite of me, anyway. I was a jelly to be moulded and fashioned in their harnesses. What I had to do was see life in the midst of all the paraphernalia. I told myself I must not forget that.

And so this jelly being of mine spawned a second self to stand beside me, circle around the dangers, deflect the conclusions of science and the pain of others. My real self could pass to him, for safekeeping, when the machines and the needles closed in. And when there were no answers in anyone's eyes I could absent myself, leaving behind a pyjama-clad and smiling self to perform the role of the sick.

She noticed quickly, of course. She said she loved me and she did. I woke up and she was there, again. But the turbulence of my exploratory flights could not be named or described. I sat there in pyjamas and drew what I could from her, knowing that was what I was doing. I had to find new ground before I signalled to her.

I sensed I had avoided being sucked into that single, poisoned dimension that, I had been told, was about to consume itself and be obliterated from space and time. Out of necessity I had created a second focal point, a new being, and left behind enough jelly substance to act as decoy. I made my escapes as seamless as possible and, once out of range, began to twist the kaleidoscope of daily life, looking for health in the distance. When the time came, I welcomed my discharge into illusory space. I had prepared myself for this.

And so, I allow myself to exist as a jelly fish, sensing vibrations and absorbing pressures. My smudged body passes through doorways and along corridors, tracing a passage against the jambs, walls and furniture. At first this feels like a public clumsiness, but looming impediments seem to make way as I approach. Seeing a specialist's name on a door I ease myself towards it with a watery stare.

I stand in a lift and watch myself press buttons. The door divides and so do I; two of me walk out. If one of us bumps into a door jamb, or another person, it does not matter. I retract, giving way to stronger energies as if they are just one more needle. I see a narrow opening ahead and calculate the odds, then allow my other self, my jelly shadow, to drift ahead of me, and I pass through an instant later, on my own.

This shadow self disappears ahead in the crowd, leaving me to fend for myself. Or he moves ahead in time as I flail against the past. I take a breath and hold on to the air a moment longer than usual. I buy time for reconnecting with him, for setting my bearings and proceeding. Sometimes I pretend to be busy for a little while, looking for my keys or an appointment card, taking a few more breaths until he slides back inside me and we move on together. And as we walk he interprets what is ahead. He grows out of me, but he does so at my will. He is not made of bad cells.

I eventually return to the dining room table and look again

at the collapsed pile of letters. I ring the health fund. A polite, friendly voice speaks to me from what seems a great distance away. I explain that I have just returned home from a month in hospital and have been confronted by a pile of bills. Could she help? My hand shakes as I hold the receiver up to my ear. I look at the papers on the table. They seem to have more substance than my own words, even the torn envelopes.

I hear sympathetic murmurings from a long way away. I wait. I breathe and feel for my other self. We inhabit each other and I feel the kaleidoscope twist inside me. I am in focus at last. Then I say it, 'I have cancer … just out of hospital … not a lot of energy … feeling a bit confused … don't know what … all this paperwork …'

I wait again. We wait again.

'Look, just sign a claim form and put the whole lot in the mail, attention to Carol. I'll be happy to do it for you. Is that okay? Now, go and have a good cup of tea, won't you.'

I place the phone down with a still-shaking hand. I sit down and listen to the silence. I am stunned by the sudden realisation that I am on my own at the commencement of this new game. And we are learning quickly.

Hugh Kiernan has been writing for over twenty years and has published pieces on childhood, school life, the workplace, sport, family life and illness. He has published a children's book on photography and co-edited an anthology of stories by writers in his local area at the time, the Yarra Valley. Hugh now lives in Melbourne, where he continues to write in the memoir genre.

The **Cancer Council of Victoria Arts Awards** is an uplifting program created as a means for people touched by cancer to share their experiences creatively through writing, art and film. It generates the hope that we will find a cure for cancer. Entrants include cancer patients, survivors, carers and those who have lost a relative or friend. In 2010 the theme for the competition was 'Lost and Found'.
www.artsawards.com.au

KATE GILBERT

Gum Leaves Short Story Competition

The First Dahlia

I watch my sister moving up the patchwork road verge at a chin-wobbling trot, mouth open and fat legs pumping. She climbs past houses stacked up the steep hill like a child's building blocks. Two deep-chested Rottweilers urge her on. A neighbour waves unheeded with his empty coffee mug.

I wait near the window. Patches of dew cling to grass in spite of a rising summer sun. Heat lies like a suffocation on the town, washed up against the side of the mountain, and the running woman.

One hand presses a large pink flower to her chest. The other holds her dressing gown clear of terry towelling scuffs. Her creased face is blotchy. Pieces of faded frizz stick to her temples as she leans into the hill. She gains the corner, executes an exact right angle turn and slaps along the concrete footpath, disappearing behind the high hedge.

✳

'Come and help me do the dahlias,' my sister commanded not long back. She lives two doors down. We shared a cuppa and I watched her plant the bulbs. Her tongue peeped from her mouth as she dug, and she was slow to rise to her feet. Her knees gave her trouble, the last few years.

'Enough left for that garden outside your front,' she announced, swiping snails from her bottom fence rail with the trowel.

'You can plant them,' I said, 'but I won't see the flowers.'

She ignored me with a slow blink and pressed her lips together.

'Mine'll be first,' she said. 'More sun.'

'You know I'll be gone by the time the first one blooms,' I persisted.

She patted my shoulder, her face blank. Only her grey eyes, crows' feet deepening, betrayed covert awareness.

'Oh, you won't know yourself, soon,' she said.

She ventured no closer to a goodbye. She helped me up the street, chatter punctuated by her throaty smoker's laugh — the same laugh I had heard after births, deaths and marriages for fifty or more years. An *ahh* of sympathy at the loss of a child, a stilted phone call when my business collapsed, stoic hard work sorting our parents' belongings — I had come to expect no more. But I watched through the window as she hunched home, bent and beaten.

*

Now I hear feet on the gravel as she rushes past my dahlias and their firm, nodding buds. A key scratches at the lock; her hand rattles the doorknob. It chips plaster from the wall with a bang and the flower she drops makes a vivid spot on the foyer tiles. I wait for the crumpled face, the *I love you*, the reaching out.

My sister runs past me, across the room to the empty wheelchair and kneels beside my fallen body on the cold floor. There is silence while she holds her breath. Then she expels it slowly with a jag midway. She picks up the bright knee-rug and folds it corner to corner, and places it on the seat.

Kate Gilbert lives in the Hawkesbury with too many relatives and animals, stealing time to work on short stories for children and adults, memoirs, and children's novels. Kate's stories have won awards and commendations in Australia and overseas. She has wanted to be a writer since learning to read, and has scribbled stories and poems ever since. She is a daydreamer and a night-owl who loves dusk, coffee, yakking with friends and walking on the beach. Kate Shelley is the name she uses when writing for children.

The Scribbli Gum website was set up in 2007 with the joint efforts of Ruth Strachan, Robyn Gosbell and other voluntary assistants, all commonly known as Twiggy Branch. They were looking for works that were cameos — small and fine, well-crafted — whether in prose or poetry. **Gum Leaves** is the prose section of this endeavour, closing annually on 31 October. It seeks works of fiction or nonfiction, of any theme, from 200 to 1000 words. Winning entries are published online and there is a small cash award. Other competition run by Scribbli Gum include Gum Nuts and Gum Blossoms, both of which are open to poetry. Details can be found at *scribbligum.com*.

CHRISTOPHER GREEN

Australian Horror Writers Association Short Story Competition

Letters of Love from the Once and Newly Dead

Thomas knows that the doors are already locked, but locking up has become a habit, and his habits are as near and dear to him as family. The sun is going down. He moves through the last of its light and checks that the latches are tight, the bars still strong. Nothing has ever tried to get in, but the lady on the nightly news will remind her audience to examine such things before they sleep, and Thomas doesn't want his sense of duty to be coloured by her chiding.

The house is silent, save for the clicks his arthritis and the floorboards conspire to create, and Thomas purses his lips and whistles something he remembers from somewhere. The rooms are too quiet otherwise, devoid of the commotion that comes with family — the pester of a child or the happy squabbles that had once meant everyone was getting settled in for a meal or a stretch of television watching.

Noise is to his liking, and he makes some more, swinging the heavy indoor shutters together too hard on their chunky, oiled hinges. Hinges like that used to be special-order, once upon a time, but now he sees them every time he goes into the hardware store, in a wide bin right up front where the girls who scanned your items and took your money used to stand, back when such things were safe.

There is a single chair in front of the television, and Thomas sits in it and turns on the news. People say the news is always the same, and in his experience those people are right — except for a couple of years ago, when they were wrong. Now that they've gone back to being right again, Thomas finds he isn't as glad of it as he feels he should be.

Eventually he gets up and heats up some food, listening to the anchor woman's voice from the other room. He can hear the way her words have to twist their way out of her smile.

He brings the food back and eats it in front of the television. When he's finished, he turns off the news and walks back through the dark of the house to the kitchen, where he washes his cup, his plate, his fork and knife. After the clamour of the news, the hollow sound of tap water in the sink and the wind against the house wears at him like a river. He is a rock, a pebble, once much more than he is now or will ever be, worn small and smooth and meaningless by the world as it goes by.

Thomas returns to the television, stands in front of it but doesn't turn it back on. It's always the same, after all, after all, and dusk is close.

He lives alone and can afford, now and then, to flick on the bare bulb fifteen minutes or so before it is absolutely necessary. The light shows him the empty walls and the polished floor. It makes his bent shadow tall, and Thomas tries to remember what it feels like to stand up straight, to open a beer with his bare hands and not a bottle opener. He looks down at his hands, at the knuckles gone bulbous and grotesque. His own grandfather had hands like that, and he remembers how they scared him.

He turns off the light and leaves the room. Lying in bed and waiting for sleep suddenly doesn't seem worse than this. Sometimes the light isn't as sweet a thing as he thinks it will be.

✳

He is awakened by the neighbours' dogs. They are dark, feral shadows, and they prowl their yards with a sense of purpose Thomas envies. From his window he can see them as they snap at the night, rattling chains that stretch from their necks to the stakes in the centre of the lawn.

Tonight, the dogs are furious. Something out there has got them baying, and the dogs that had been silent kick up as well. They settle in fits and starts, occasionally woofing deep in the back of their throats as if to clear them.

Thomas watches his own dogless yard even after the beasts grow silent, but there is nothing there aside from the little garden he dutifully began with the seeds they sent everyone in the mail.

Nothing and no-one. Nonetheless, he makes his way quietly down the stairs and rechecks the latches and locks, the bar on the door. Everything is as it should be, and Thomas returns to bed.

✳

The phone wakes him up.

He reaches for it in the dark. He has been dreaming, and in his dreams none of this is real, none of these shutters and bars and clasps and latches matter even in the slightest.

But the phone isn't there, hasn't been there for years. The ringing is downstairs, and he shuffles down the hall as fast as he can and descends the stairs. When he reaches the phone, he knocks it from the table in his haste. It clatters to the ground, and the noise is like a slap across the face. The dogs are silent. The house is dead and still. *Is there someone in here with me? Had the shutters held? Even now, somewhere in the house, was there a broken latch on the floor beside a muddy footprint?*

He picks the phone from the floor and puts it to his ear. 'Grace?'

No-one speaks. It isn't uncommon for people to ring one another and yet to not say anything. Thomas has done it himself, in his weaker moments. Everyone needs someone, even if they've dialled a number at random. If it was Grace she hadn't hung up, at least, and so he tried again.

'Gracie, is that you?'

He can hear breathing on the other end of the line. He knows it's her, knows it right to the marrow, just as surely as he knows he should spare her the guilt of having to hang up on him.

'Grace, I ...' And there it is. If he says it, his daughter will never call him again, even anonymously, even in the middle of the night. 'I'm glad you called,' he says instead.

She hangs up.

'Goodbye,' Thomas says into the receiver anyway. He puts the phone back on the hook and goes back up to bed. The wind is hypnotic. He knows he should go back downstairs and check the locks, test the doors and windows, but instead he closes his eyes and listens to the world breathe.

✳

He is awake before the sun falls across his face, but he cannot bring himself to rise until the world becomes brighter. One of the city's trucks is making the slow grind up the street outside and the dogs don't bark. They're used to such things. At last, he showers and shaves, then dresses and walks to the shops. There is a truck ahead of him, moving in the opposite direction. Thomas isn't sure if it's the same one that drove past his house. He isn't sure if it matters.

The city has many trucks.

Along the way, he stops counting the stares and pitiful looks he collects. Once, one of the trucks slows, and he raises a hand to the driver without looking. It should be enough, and it is. No-one the truck is looking for would wave, even if they could, and Thomas has. The truck gains speed and turns left at the next corner.

The store is self-serve. All of them are. There are two rows of cameras at the entrance, one facing in and one facing out.

Just inside the shop is a big metal door. It has no handle, not on this side, although Thomas has seen it open to disgorge security guards a time or two, and on those occasions he saw the monitors they watched inside.

The store is busy and almost soundless. No-one speaks. Thomas buys bread. He buys jam. He buys eggs and cheese and, to his surprise, spies a small bar of chocolate that has fallen behind a row of canned goods. He plucks it from the shelf and adds it to the things he carries.

It is brutally expensive, and Thomas finds he doesn't care. Once the machine accepts his money and dispenses his change, he leaves.

The walk from the house to the store feels longer every time. Before he attempts it, Thomas finds a park bench and takes a seat. He watches another of the city's trucks trundle past, this one so full that he can see the angle of arms, the splay of stacked legs through the open back. It drives no faster or slower than the other cars.

There is a woman and a man on the sidewalk, each of them holding a little girl's hand. *How brave*, Thomas thinks, and watches them. *How terribly brave.* The adult's eyes never stray towards one another; and when the girl raises her head to look at her father, her mother lets go of her hand and strikes her smoothly across the face.

Thomas gives them a polite nod and pretends not to look at their faces. They scowl anyway and drag their daughter along when she slows, and when they have gone by he hears the man slap the girl again, hard enough to make her cry. She does.

The traffic is slower. Down the street, back in the direction he will soon have to walk, a boy pushes his way out of the bushes and staggers into the road. His clothes are hanging off him, and he leaves one of his shoes in the gutter.

'Someone should call that in,' says the girl's father from beside Thomas. He sits down on the bench without waiting for a spot to be offered.

'I'm sure someone will,' Thomas says, 'but it won't be me.' He watches the boy, at the limit of his flagging vision. 'Did your wife send you over?'

The man flashes him the look one man shares with another when he's been sent on a fool's errand against his wishes. 'She wanted to know if you're okay out here, all by yourself.'

Thomas laughs. He can't help it. What kind of a question was that? 'Nothing wrong with being by yourself these days, according to most people. Right?'

The man shrugs, clearly nervous, and Thomas feels sorry for him.

'I'm Thomas.'

'Kyle.'

'Kyle,' Thomas says, and nods as if he's known the man's name all along, even though he's sure it's a false one. When a man of thirty-five or forty lies about his name, it hardly flows trippingly from the tongue. 'Kyle, your family has nothing to fear from me.'

'I'm not saying we do. It's just not every day we see a man willing to nod at us. It's ...'

Thomas sighs. 'Unusual?'

'I was going to say disconcerting.'

The boy up the road is trying to retreat into the bushes again. They're sharp, though, designed for defence, and they hamper his progress. A few cars have pulled over, and Thomas can picture their drivers, windows rolled up and doors locked tight, their phones pressed to their ears as they ring the city and ask for a truck.

Kyle clears his throat. 'Just leave my wife and daughter alone. Please.'

Thomas nods. 'I will, I promise.' The boy down the road stops, and for a breathless second Thomas thinks he may turn and come toward them. Eventually, he turns in the other direction and wanders up the street, becoming something else for Thomas to fear on the way home.

Kyle stands up, and Thomas reaches out and brushes his elbow. It is a gentle touch, light as a feather, and the man recoils from him as if burned.

'One thing, before you go,' Thomas says, ignoring Kyle's reaction. 'I bought some chocolate, on a whim. I don't eat it, normally. I'd much prefer your daughter to have it.'

Kyle's eyes can't hide the truth. The girl has never tasted such things. 'And where will I tell her I got it, when she asks? Who shall I say the gift is from?'

Thomas shrugs. Was the girl so starved for attention that this kindness would be one too many? 'Tell her you bought it last month, when the shops had an extra supply.'

Kyle's face darkens and Thomas sees that he's guessed wrong. The man isn't afraid his daughter would find some measure of affection for Thomas; he is afraid she'd find it for himself.

'Do you need anything or not?' Kyle asks, changing the topic. His eyes go past Thomas to the shop, where his family are waiting. 'Is there someone I should call for you?'

'No. No, thank you.'

'No-one?'

Thomas stands too, suddenly as eager for the conversation to be over as Kyle is. 'I'm fine, and rest easy. You needn't fear me.' He points at the shop. 'I'm known here. When the guards don't see me come to collect my groceries or the postman sees that I haven't collected yesterday's mail, the city knows to send a truck.'

Kyle's face goes red. 'I didn't mean ...'

But he did, and Thomas knows it. He offers the man his hand anyway, another of those old habits that die as hard as everything else does now. Thomas is unsurprised when the man ignores it and walks passed him, his wife and daughter.

Thomas turns in time to see Kyle strike the girl again, a clean, hard slap that she wasn't expecting. Thomas finds it hard to think worse of him for it.

It's for her own good, after all.

∗

That night, the anchorwoman assures him that the news remains the same. Thomas stays up after it's finished, rewashing the dishes, seeing to shutter repairs that aren't warranted or even necessary, pottering around, telling himself that he isn't waiting for the phone to ring.

When he finally locks up for the night and trudges up the stairs, he's bone-tired. The phone rings when he reaches the top and he rushes back down, cursing himself for not having a phone by his bed, knowing that they wouldn't have installed one even if he'd asked. Most people aren't strong enough to resist the temptation of a phone so near to them. They'd answer it if it rang, and perhaps the person on the line would speak as well. And something dangerous would blossom.

Four rings. Five. He grabs it before it can ring again. Will Grace wait? In that eternal half-second before he can lift the handset to his mouth, he tells himself, *Six rings. That's how many I'd have given it. After six I'd assume they weren't home, or, more likely, were asleep, at this hour. Six rings, please God, let her be there because it's only been five and I can't live without—*

'Mr Carter?' a man's voice asks.

His hand trembles and he resists the urge to hang up the phone. 'Yes?'

'Mr Carter, I've recently been assigned to your case. Have you got a few minutes that you wouldn't mind spending with me? Just a quick chat, that's all it'll be.'

'My case?' Thomas asks, but he knows what the man is talking about. It doesn't matter. For a long moment he contemplates simply not answering or, better, hanging up, but he knows what will happen if he does. The people who don't answer these calls from the city are paid a visit and, often, they're found locked inside their own homes, the wardens now prisoners.

'Yes, your case. I just thought I'd touch base with you, Mr Carter. Make sure you're alright.'

'Please, call me Thomas.'

The man is smiling, smiling at the old fool, the fossil who can't move with the times. Thomas can hear it in his voice. 'No, thank you, Mr Carter. You see, it's just that sort of thing that's bumped you up my call list tonight. The offer is a kind one, but wholly inappropriate. Some people in your area have expressed concern about your welfare.'

'Kyle.'

'Pardon?' ·

'It may not be his real name, but he's a man I met today at the store. He's most likely the man who called you about me.'

'You must know I can't tell you that.'

Thomas grits his teeth. 'Look, there's no law against sitting by yourself on a park bench and watching the world go by, and that's all that I was doing.'

'Did you make him an offer of chocolate?'

What nonsense. 'Yes, I did.'

'Then I'm sure you understand his concern.'

Thomas closes his eyes. *Understand* is such a loaded word. Sympathise, yes. Understand? Never.

'Mr Carter. I know you were just trying to help, that there's nothing malicious in your actions, but people are rightly afraid. I mean, a man of your age, on your own ...'

Thomas's grip tightens on the phone. Dollars to donuts the man doesn't have the guts to say it, so Thomas says it for him. 'I am not so empty that I will come back for the first person that shows me a kindness, sir.'

The man becomes quiet. *Cat got your tongue? Maybe we should send a truck by your place, then, and see if you're still sucking in wind.* Thomas listens to him as he starts to say something a couple of times, and when the words finally come down the line, they are, 'I wasn't implying otherwise, Mr Carter. Your daughter ...'

'Left. Afraid of what the world's become.'

'Then I'm sure you can understand this gentleman's concern. There may not be a law against sitting on park benches, but that doesn't mean the practice will win you friends.' Thomas doesn't say anything, and the man clearly takes his silence as agreement. 'Your wife, sir. It says here that she's passed away. When she did, did she …'

Thomas sits down and holds his head in his other hand. He's glad he didn't turn the light on, as the dark feels so much like home. 'She didn't come for me, no.'

'So …'

Thomas clears his throat. 'Someone down the street. She found him in his garage.'

The man on the phone is nodding. Thomas can hear the cord on the other end of the line bounce against something, a desk or a keyboard. 'Then you can see what we're afraid of, what everyone's so worried about. What if you, afterward, you go looking for one of these people you so innocently watch walk down the street? What then?'

Enough of this. 'You tell those bastards there's no chance of that. Write that in your little computer, too. Put it in whatever file you've got on me. None of them have any chance of finding a place in my heart, you hear me, because there isn't room. Not for any of you.'

'Mr Carter, please. I'm not trying to upset you. I'm only asking you to give some thought to your actions.'

Thomas hangs up the phone. It doesn't ring again.

✳

The night is still. The dogs are quiet. Thomas has been asleep, until something in the backyard awakens him. He lies in his bed and listens to the noise as it wafts up from the backyard: a soft rustle of fabric against wood. He gets up and goes to the window.

She's gorgeous, and he's never seen her before. She stands near the fence, her pale skin lit by the moon and the splash of unfocused spotlights a couple of houses over. The climb over the fence from next door to here has appled her cheeks, and she clutches something in one badly broken hand.

The news, always the same, is very clear about what to do in these situations. Do not approach, do not attempt to communicate with, call the police, and ask them to send one of the city trucks so the matter can be dealt with professionally.

Her eyes shine up at him. The woman and Thomas watch each other until he has the presence of mind to reach for the rifle leaning against the wall and go downstairs. Once there, Thomas opens the set of shutters that look out into the backyard. She's still against the fence, its shadow slicing across her body, across the sundress she'd selected this morning, the last dress she'd ever choose. Her blond hair is blood-soaked, and the side of her face has gone ragged with bone.

Car accident, a voice inside him says, and he unlocks and opens the side door and goes out into the backyard with her.

She doesn't move, and Thomas keeps the rifle steady and advances. The fence has a few bloody handprints near the top, and the palings have splintered where she's climbed over. He looks down, and sees that the thing she clutches is the collar of the neighbour's dog.

'Hello,' he says, just as gently as if she'd called him on the phone, as if he might scare her off if he is too loud. 'Hello.'

She hears him alright, but it doesn't seem to matter. He sheds the last stubborn splinter of hope now that he can see her clearly. He was right. He's never laid eyes on her before.

Thomas has been told, just as everyone else has. If you stay out of their way you won't become a target. They aren't back for you unless they are, and if they are you'll know. He's heard stories, of shop assistants and checkout girls and delivery men coming back to those they'd secretly loved, but Thomas lowers his rifle anyway. If this poor, broken thing has been unfortunate enough to somehow love him, so be it. He'd welcome it.

She still hasn't moved. She's staring at him, or so he thinks until he steps aside and sees that her gaze is actually fixed on the gate behind him.

The gate that leads to the rest of the world.

He goes to her, surprised at his courage. *Am I brave, or simply beyond caring?* He finds her letter in a pocket she's added to the dress herself. Everyone has pockets now. In case. The little slip of paper has been laminated.

'I shall return, my dear,' he tells her, and retreats to the house. Thomas is nothing if not a creature of habit, useless old habits made flesh, and he locks the door behind him, then turns on the light and sits down at the table.

The phone stares up at him like a skull with many eyes.

Dearest Victor,

My love, I pray that I found you. I pray that I did and that you stopped me, or that someone stopped me on the verge, the very verge, so that I can be close enough for you to know I sought you out and far enough away to not drag you down with me. I do love you. If you're reading this then you'll know that, without any doubts, and perhaps that's the best and last gift I can give.

Pray for me, Victor.
Your Melissa

Thomas reads her note a second time, then turns off the light and opens the side door again. She's still there, eyes on the gate, waiting for him. He's forgotten the rifle, left it inside somewhere, but it doesn't matter. He tucks the note back into her homemade pocket and turns away from her. The gate is locked and he unlocks it; swings it open and out of her way. She moves forward with a joy and determination that her face is barely capable of showing, but her eyes, her shining eyes, they thank him as she goes by. He thinks he sees her smile.

When Thomas goes back inside, he turns on the light once more and returns to his seat at the table. He has brought paper with him, and he uses it to compose a letter of his own. Everyone he loves is gone except for Grace, and she has kept herself and his grandson as far from him as possible since all of this began. He writes down everything he knows about the place she has gone, every clue, every background noise he heard back when she would speak to him when he called, every ambient sound when she'd called him that Christmas a couple of years ago from an unlisted number.

The list of things he knows about her new location is short, surely not enough for him to track her down. He doesn't know if it works like that, anyway. No-one does — or rather, everyone will eventually.

Still, there is a chance that he knows something he doesn't remember now, that when he stops this old habit of breathing he's clung on to for so long he'll simply stand back up and know exactly where she is.

He writes his letter. Now and then, as he crumples up a draft and tosses it aside, agonising about his handwriting and the impersonality of the typewriter in his study, the dogs outside let loose with a deep series of bounding barks. There's one less dog adding to the clamour, though. Thomas can tell even if the others can't.

Grace, he writes, *forgive me for finding you. The alternative is worse, though, far worse, to grow old and lock the windows and bar the doors against a threat you would gladly welcome and you know will never come. I'm too old and all of this has gone on too long for me to imagine some high school crush or tangled one-night stand placing me above the others she's met since me. Forgive me, Grace, but know that when I come for you, it's only love. Love. If I find you, forgive me. Don't let me hurt little Francis.*

Thomas folds the letter and places it into his wallet. Many such notes are laminated, as Melissa had done to hers, but he doesn't think his wallet will be opened and closed many more times before someone else reads what he's written.

He turns off the light and sits in the dark, listening to the wind as it picks up the rhythm of breath again, wondering if the phone will ring again, wondering who will be on the other end if it does.

Thomas takes the chocolate bar from his grocery bag and eats it. When it's gone, he sets the wrapper down beside the phone, walks to his doors and windows and, one by one, undoes the locks.

Christopher Green was born in the United States and moved to Australia at the age of twenty, after meeting his wife on the internet (she wasn't his wife at the time). His fiction has appeared in *Dreaming Again*, *Beneath Ceaseless Skies*, and *Abyss & Apex*, and has won an Aurealis Award and the Australian Horror Writers Association Short Story Competition. He lives in Geelong with his wife and their two perpetually muddy labradors. He is currently writing a zombie novel and posting one chapter every weekend at *www.arizonaafterwards.com*.

The **Australian Horror Writers Association (AHWA) Flash and Short Story Competition** started in 2005 and now runs every year. It is open to unpublished stories only. The judges look for well-written tales that make them think and give them goose bumps. The competition has two categories: Flash Fiction (1000 words or fewer) and Short Story (1001–8000 words), with the winner of each category receiving paid publication in *Midnight Echo*, the official magazine of the AHWA.

www.australianhorror.com

CECILIA MORRIS
Poetica Christi Press Annual Poetry Competition

Earthly Ending

I sit on the porch
palms bend ragged-ended
in tropical warm rain.
A small grey gecko darts
around the walls.
Tuckoo Tuckoo
The sound of fear or lust.
Succulent green vegetation
holds the franchise of the
World Pharmacy as you
lie in your hospital bed,
and the clear fluid drips
into the forked vein
of your right hand.
From your face
fragile pale eyes
reach a free hand
from the white coverlet,
that thing with feathers
races around the room.
White curtains billow like
small sails that hold your
last breath and will carry
the shell of you to a warm place.

Cecilia Morris is co-author of three published books on human relations, as well as two anthologies of poetry: one published by Poetry Monash, and another with her mother (also a poet) through grants from Bayside Council. She has had several poems published in journals including *Quadrant*, and won the Bayside Poetry Prize in 2009 with 'Everday Gardener' and first prize in the Poetica Christi Press competition this year with 'Earthly Ending'. She facilitates a group of poets in Bayside called Coastlines. Her poetry reflects her interest in nature, the sea and the ever-changing complexities of life.

Poetica Christi Press runs the **Poetica Christi Press Annual Poetry Competition** from 1 August till 31 October every year on a given topic. The entries are given to the judge who selects a winner and a runner-up, as well as another twenty-three entries to go into an anthology to be published the following year. Some of Poetica Christi's past anthologies have been commended in the FAW awards, and its 2009 bestselling coffee-table book *Reflecting on Melbourne*, which included colour photography and artwork alongside poetry, was shortlisted for the 2010 Caleb Prize.

www.poeticachristi.org.au

JOSEPHINE ROWE

Australian Book Review *Elizabeth Jolley Short Story Prize*
— *Readers' Choice Award*

Suitable for a Lampshade

I got the call when I was too far away to do anything about it. There was a pile of marking to get through that I knew I wouldn't get through, but that had been the case even before the call.

I'd rented a holiday house from a friend of a friend. And they'd probably bought it and all its contents from the children of an elderly deceased lady, or of one who had recently been moved to an aged-care facility, because the bookcases were still crammed with Reader's Digest omnibuses and craft books; *Advanced Macramé, Crocheted Endings*. Also the kitchen cupboards were stacked with earthenware plates and mismatched glassware and crockery, and these anodised aluminium cups that reminded me of the photographic version of my childhood, which is really nothing like the childhood I can actually remember.

The rent was only one hundred and twenty-five a week because I was a friend of a friend and because it was the middle of June. The wind came right off the Pacific to whine under the doorsills and through the gaps between the old weatherboards, and to rattle the windows in their poorly made frames.

I'd gone there to dry out, from you as much as anything else. Okay, from you and only you, because I was still drinking and I had no intention of drying that out. Straight vodka or watered whiskey out of the little blue anodised cups, which I considered taking with me when I left. It was inherited bric-a-brac, after all, and this friend of a friend hadn't had time to develop any real emotional attachment to any of it. So the cups, and to a lesser extent the books on crochet and macramé, and some sixties plastic swizzle sticks I'd found in the third kitchen drawer — I was already thinking of those things as mine.

I was trying not to think about you. I had all this work to do and I'd bought a pair of glasses with small lenses and thick frames so that only a limited amount of the world was in focus at any one time. I thought they might minimise peripheral distraction, help me keep my attention on what was in front of me. You probably know it didn't work out that way. But the glasses made me look like someone who drank Laphroaig instead of Jameson and worked from a typewriter instead of a laptop, and I liked that.

There was no good place to buy coffee near the house, so there was no good reason to leave it. I made drink ice in the freezer of the ancient Kelvinator and read most of a book on anaesthesia that was written in the forties, and if those things didn't keep me happy they at least kept me a reasonable and safe distance from unhappy. I'd say anaesthetised, but that would be too obvious and not entirely true. I played chess and Scrabble against myself, and the essays on Jeffers and Riding stayed unread and unmarked on the kitchen table.

In the weeks I was there, the sky never grew any lighter than the colour of bruised mushrooms, and if I drove to the ocean it was grey and hungry in the James Reeves sort of way. Maybe every second or third day I drove to the ocean and just sat in the driver's seat, watching the container ships crawling after each other so I could tell where the horizon was — though most days the sea was the same colour as the sky, and if not for the ships you wouldn't have known any difference between them.

Some afternoons there was a girl on the sand with her dog, a black wolfish mongrel she'd throw pieces of driftwood for.

He churned the wet grey sand up under his paws, chasing after whatever she threw.

Yeah, I thought. I know how that is. I know exactly how.

And down on the beach the wind pulled at them, made their hair and her loose clothing ripple. Like the two of them were only shapes cut from cloth.

Cloth girl with her cloth dog. My fingers would always creep to the door handle but wouldn't push it down.

Yes, it was because she looked like you. There are worse reasons for wanting to talk to someone. Because they look like they have money, or they're beautiful or they look like somebody famous — those are worse reasons.

Anyway, it was because she reminded me of you that I finally got out of the car and went down to the beach to ask her about her dog, or whether she lived nearby or something similar. Maybe I asked if she knew a good place to get coffee. I don't remember what I asked because, whatever it was, she didn't answer it. She just pushed her hair off her face and asked if I was the one driving that blue Skyline. All her clothes were shapeless and only the wind whipping the fabric up close to her skin brought any kind of definition.

When I nodded she said, Yeah, I thought so, and threw a stick for the dog. Nobody just watches the ocean. Not in this weather.

I'm just watching the ocean, I said. The dog came back with the stick. Why, what are you doing in this weather?

I'm just walking my dog, she said. He doesn't give a damn about the weather. Sweet, stupid thing, and she threw the stick again. Then she smiled and looked at me from behind her wind-whipped hair. Maybe, she said. Maybe you're just watching the ocean.

And I was still trying not to think about you, or the holiday house I'd once rented with you; its own mismatched glassware, or how we'd made love against kitchen benches and spat gin into each other's mouths. Carrying everything back out to the car on the morning we left, your tired grin above a box of groceries we hadn't managed to get through, or the carton of bottles that we had.

But it was no good and I remembered everything. The arguments, the ugly carpet. The way the sound of the hot water system found its way into our dreams and we dreamed of the same things for six nights. How the firewood had been cut from old railway sleepers, and the bolts glowed red hot among the embers. Sleeping in the car at the side of the highway on the way home. The trucks shuddering by and your breath clouding the window, the early light cold, almost blue, and oh god — if I could have kept things just like that. If I could have stopped time at the side of the Hume with you sleeping and your hair across your face and me just watching you sleeping, the trucks shuddering past. Well, you know I would have.

I think maybe the girl knew this. Maybe even knew that she reminded me of you, but she was good about it. Or she didn't have to be good about it, because she didn't care either way. Her dog lay on the wooden decking outside with his legs stretched out ahead of him, and when I said that he could come in she said, No, he can't, and he stayed out there, looking woeful. It seems strange to me now that I never learned the dog's name. It could have been Samson or Solomon, something biblical. The girl shook the rain out of her coat and left it by the door.

Then when the call came through, she was asleep on her stomach, her long legs still slightly parted and the damp sheet pulled up across the backs of her knees. I stumbled naked to the front room with the phone, not wanting to wake her, tripping over a powerboard, a lone shoe. When I answered, my voice sounded thin and hostile. I stood looking out the window. The sky had grown dark and the dog had fallen asleep out on the decking. There was the pile of paperwork that had never left its manila folder, and your mother on the line asking why I hadn't answered the home phone or the work phone, why I hadn't returned any of her damn messages.

Three days, she said, and as she kept talking and all I could think about was how I should have gotten out of the car that morning. I should have walked along the highway and thumbed a ride back to Melbourne with one of the truck drivers. Then you would still be asleep in the passenger seat. The light would still be almost blue, your hair just-so across your face, and this little cluttered house with its storm and its sleeping dog and its anodised aluminium cups would be a dream you were having. I would be standing naked at the window of the dream, watching the sky grow dark. There would be a box of groceries on your back seat, and you would be okay. You would be safe.

Your mother said *sudden*. She said *collapse*, she said *supermarket fucking car park*, and I don't remember how I answered any of that. I don't remember what I said before hanging up. Just that after I'd hung up, I pulled a book down from the shelf and turned to Chapter Three: Suitable for a lampshade, or a handkerchief. And how I just stood there with the book open at page sixty-two, waiting for those words to mean something.

Josephine Rowe is a writer, editor and semioccasional teacher. Her poetry, fiction and nonfiction have been published in *Best Australian Stories*, *Best Australian Poems*, *The Griffith Review*, *Overland*, *Island*, *HEAT*, *Dumbo Feather*, *The Lifted Brow* and *The Age*. Her collection of short stories, *How a Moth Becomes a Boat*, was published in 2010 by Hunter Publishers.

She is a participant in the 2011 International Writing Program at the University of Iowa and is currently working on a new short story collection, to be published by UQP in 2012. For more, please visit *josephinerowe.com*.

The *Australian Book Review*'s **Elizabeth Jolley Short Story Prize** honours the late Australian writer Elizabeth Jolley. Entries should be single-authored stories of between 2000 and 5000 words, written by Australian citizens or permanent residents. Results are announced in October, and the winning story will be published in the October (Fiction) issue of *ABR*. First prize is $5000, and three shortlisted stories each receive $1000 and a copy of the publication.

The guidelines and entry form are available from *www.australianbookreview.com.au/prizes/elizabeth-jolley-story-prize*.

Louise D'Arcy

Australian Literature Review *May Short Story Competition*

The Second Wife and the Cat

Marietta killed Will's cat while he was out. She was supposed to have been writing — one thousand words a night, that was the goal. After dinner, when Will had finally left for his CFA meeting, she'd sat down at the computer and sighed.

The cat arrived while she was fiddling with fonts. He demanded to be let out through the window. When Marietta ignored him he jumped onto her desk and laid a warning paw on her hand. She shook it off.

'Bugger off, cat,' she said, waving the hand at it. He flattened his ears.

They glared at each other and Marietta felt a certain relief — battle had been declared; the cold war was over. For a few silent seconds Marietta acknowledged his prior ownership of Will but counter-argued her own efforts to ingratiate herself through toy mice and unexpected cat treats. Then she shook her head at him.

'I'm going to win, you know,' she said.

The cat looked away, but only to lick its flank. Marietta made to pick him up and found herself holding a limp furry sack. Holding it out in front of her, she made her way to the kitchen. She wedged him against her hip and opened the door.

When the cat scratched her, a long calculated gash down her forearm, she dropped him in surprise. Wild with fury and pain, she screamed and kicked him. Even as her foot swung back she knew she'd regret it. The cat streaked off yowling over the fence into the neighbour's garden.

'No!' she yelled. 'Come back!'

At first there was no sound, and she sent up a silent plea: let Buster the Foxy be chained up, or baring his tiny shark's teeth impotently through the kitchen window. Then the snarling came, and the yelling,

'Buster! Leave! LEAVE!'

They brought the cat round half an hour later, thankfully before Will got back. She took him, concealed in his Coles carrier bag, and buried him at the bottom of the compost heap under a summer's worth of tomato plants and overripe bananas. She washed her hands over and over but she couldn't shift the smell.

The cat, Will's first wife's treasure, had been the sentinel, guarding the door to Will's house from the very first day she moved in. She'd stepped round the cat, gingerly, respectfully at first, then with increasing resentment at his assumption of seniority in the household. 'I get fed first,' he would declare, causing Will to leave her tea bag stewing in the cup.

And the smell of his food turned her stomach, with its almost appetisingness. As did the noise the cat made as he crouched before the bowl and worked his way methodically through the claggy mound. It was the sticky clicky sound of lovers kissing on the television. After that she tried to kiss Will silently and he turned from her, hurt at her lack of passion.

Will wanted them to be friends and told her the cat was taking to her. *He never normally does that,* he'd say, over and over, as the cat brushed an indolent haunch against her leg in passing or sprawled along the back of the coach, so she could feel his breath on the back of her neck. Once, the cat had sat for a whole evening on her lap, flexing his claws through the fabric of her skirt just a millimetre short of pain. When she undressed that night she'd seen the Morse code on her thighs and got the message. Will never wondered if *she* was taking to the cat.

At night the marble eyes drilled into her from the chair on Will's side of the bed. She feigned asthma, the cat feigned friendship, finding her clothes and nesting in them, reaching a paw into open drawers and hooking out jumpers. She told herself that this way led to paranoia, never an attractive thing in a new wife. A new old wife, one who should be past foolish fantasies. But still she shut the bedroom door against Will's objections and almost felt her heart soften at the pathetic siren song that kept Will awake and fretful.

She would never share with Will her fear that his first wife, dead and therefore unimpeachable, was watching her through those cold eyes, judging and finding her lacking.

Will's first wife had had the cat from infancy. He was an orphan kitten, his mother flattened by a garbage truck. Fed on egg yolk and sunflower seeds from birth, he had a coat that gleamed like a conker. He'd pined when she, his second mother, died, also at the hands of a hasty driver. In the weeks that followed her death his coat had dulled and stared, and only careful handling had brought him back to health. *What else could I do?* asked Will, as if Marietta had queried, *I couldn't let him die.*

She wondered at the restricted options Will gave himself, and wondered, too, if the same limited range had led to his proposal, one afternoon in the botanic gardens beneath her favourite gingko tree, just when she had begun to despair of their relationship going anywhere. But it wasn't a question you could ask.

When Will got back she told him. Straight away. It was the best way with things like this, she'd learned. Get it all out in the open, expose it thoroughly to the air and let the cooling-down process begin. But instead, Will cried.

'I'm sorry,' was all she could think of to say, rather than 'Why aren't you mad at me?' which was what she'd wanted to say.

'It's not your fault,' he said, when he was able to get the words out.

Having her guilt taken away made things worse, but how could she say 'Well, it *was* my fault, actually'? And this made her want to lash out, rather like the cat had done.

'He hated me, you know. He always had it in for me,' she said.

Will looked down at his wet hands lying in his lap and said nothing.

'For God's sake, Will! It was only a cat!'

Why not tell him to get a life while you're at it, she thought. *What a bitch!*

They both studied his hands for a bit longer.

'I'm sorry,' she said again, and heard how she'd devalued the word.

After Will went to bed she sat at the computer. The one thousand words wrote themselves.

Louise D'Arcy is a writer based in Yackandandah, north-east Victoria. She has been writing for fifteen years and has had more than thirty stories published. In 2005 her first novel, *Harry Gets a Life*, was shortlisted for the HarperCollins Varuna Publication Award, and in 2007 she was shortlisted in the Canadian '3-Day Novel' competition for her novel *The Weekend*. In 2009 she won the Albury City Library Short Story competition for the second time with 'Happy Birthday', and in 2010 she won *The Age* Short Story Competition with 'Flat Daddy'.

The *Australian Literature Review* (*AusLit*) runs short story competitions throughout the year. The *AusLit* **May Short Story Competition** was part of a round of three competitions run in March, April and May: Best March Short Story (theme: suspense), Best April Short Story (theme: teen/young adult) and Best May Short Story (theme: troubled family relationship). As winner of the May Short Story Competition, Louise D'Arcy received feedback on her story from authors Michael White, Rebecca James and Bernadette Kelly, along with a Kindle eReader. *www.auslit.net*

LIZ WINFIELD
Norma and Colin Knight Poetry Award

Morpheus

The cat has settled into my softness,
slung herself over my arm
watching the wind
in the trees, grass, umbrella —
the world is in her eye.

She tucks her head under my arm,
and purrs herself a lullaby.
Whiskers to heaven,
she is a cat-prayer
holding the world
safe beneath her lids.

When she dreams no-one dies
except for cartoon deaths.
It is a world without suffering,
without pain, without tears.
She dreams her life into my belly like a god.
She makes a sun from my love
and keeps us warm.

Liz Winfield's poetry has been published in journals and literary magazines in Australia, the UK and Ireland. Her first collection, *Too Much Happens*, was published by Cornford Press in 2003 and was written with the assistance of a grant from Arts Tasmania in 2000. Her second collection is the chapbook *Catalogue of Love*, published in 2006 by Walleah Press. Liz coordinates the Republic Readings, Hobart's monthly poetry reading, and teaches creative writing.

The **Norma and Colin Knight Award** is an annual competition run by FAW Tasmania and open to all FAW members. The name of the award honours past members who have made a significant contribution to FAW Tasmania. Poems of up to 40 lines are eligible.

Amanda J. Spedding

Shades of Sentience *Steampunk Short Story Competition*

Shovel-Man Joe

Carmody missed the metropolis. The incessant buzz of motorised balloons, the hydraulic gait of carriage horses along cobblestone; horns and sirens, alarms and bullhorns, the ticking of a thousand clocks. The volume of a city in perpetual motion — loud and honest.

The silence of this landscape was secretive.

Golden plains, barren and unforgiving, stretched seamlessly around the train station. No town spawned from the depot — ghost or otherwise — it sat alone in the emptiness, exiled.

'The Last Outpost,' she whispered. Where you paid to cheat death for a chance to stare into The Pit. Ride the train, beat the Shovel-Man.

Steel tracks cut past the oversized platform and swooped into the desert, warping as they disappeared into the heat of the horizon, non-stop to the Edge of the World.

Carmody picked at the struts of the rusted water tank and watched the triumphant passengers from afar. Jostling for hierarchy of the platform, smug smiles on their faces, they waved their tickets high, so assured in their right to chase the next thrill in their idle, wasted lives.

She'd scrimped and saved every penny for a seat on the train; only the highest bidders got to ride. But even with Nate's money she'd been outbid, put back in her place.

'*Scrap Rats is what we are, what we's always gonna be.*' Her mother's voice, weary from a lifetime of disappointment, stoked Carmody's anger. '*More ain't for the likes of us. You'll see.*'

Carmody slapped sand from her best trousers; the pinstripe was bright from years of meticulous care, the brass buckles down the sides, gleaming. Chic, once upon a time, she'd heard them snigger.

All her life she'd watched them pass overhead in their motorised balloons, bestowing a wave like it were gold; listened to them haggle for the mechanisms her family scavenged as they screamed poor in their Angora coats and calf-skin boots—

'*Crack!* The whip struck Shovel-Man Joe! Back slashed red, blood and sweat flowed!'

Carmody snapped her head up at the voice. An Aeronaut, commanding attention from the station's roof. His brown leathers, worn thin at the shoulders, sagged on his angular frame.

'Piled high at his feet were limbs and entrails! The shovel scraped loudly; the fire inhaled!'

The goggles atop his aviator cap glinted in the sun and Carmody shielded her eyes against the glare.

'The throttle released with a hiss and a groan! The engine chugged forward on pistons of bone!'

Carmody watched the Aeronaut parade, transfixed. This was the reason they were here, to challenge the fabled warning to all pioneers that there are some things best left undiscovered; but she'd never heard the tale told quite like this.

'First Class hurrah'd and raised glasses high!'

A cheer broke out from the crowd, and they slapped each other's backs in feigned camaraderie. The Aeronaut saluted then leaned forward as if to impart a secret. The passengers responded in kind, craning their necks, eager for wisdom.

'The whore settled back, spread wide with a sigh!'

Women recoiled; men shouted: 'Scoundrel!'

The storyteller wouldn't be silenced. He crouched, beckoned them back.

'Listen well, listen well, one warning you'll get.' Though loud, there was an intimacy that hushed the crowd. 'The fire must be fed.' He scanned those below. 'Who among you will be paying the debt?'

The Station Master blew his whistle — three short bursts and the Aeronaut flinched. Carmody got to her feet as the pilot leapt to his. She wanted to hear the end of the butchered legend.

'Whispers in the halls. Scratching in the walls.' With exaggerated tiptoe he danced along the roof. 'One by one you will surely fall.'

An awkward laugh floated from the passengers. 'Bollocks,' Lord Hemsley shouted in false bravado, his hired brute glowering at the rooftop antics.

'Beware the Shovel-Man's ire!' The Aeronaut cackled like an old witch. 'Feed the fire! Feed the fire!'

Carmody's skin prickled.

'All aboard! All aboard! Fresh meat, the fire roared!'

A train-whistle shrieked.

She scanned the tracks. A fuzzy, black stain in the distance. Closing fast.

'He comes! Can you hear?' He pointed to the milling crowd. 'Who is the first to disappear?'

The passengers glanced at one another, asking themselves the same question before shaking it off. This performance was surely part of the adventure.

'Ride the train, it was writ! Be the first to The Pit!' He danced across the roof, the wooden slats keeping a steady beat. 'But who can tell me this …?' He stopped suddenly and looked over the passengers. 'Who has returned and spoken of it?'

Carmody ventured from the shade, her eyes locked to the Aeronaut.

Eyes closed, he lifted his arms, beseeching the sky. 'Ride the train if you dare …' His eyes snapped open and he spun his face to Carmody. Eyes, black as coal, locked to hers. 'You must all pay the fare.'

He yanked off his cap, exposing a scalp puckered thick with burns.

The looming train seemed to shriek in horror. Its black engine glistened. A red glow sat low in the windows.

Carmody's gaze flicked between the Aeronaut and the train. Both were charging toward the platform.

A scream.

The train bore down on the station like an angry bull.

The Aeronaut leapt.

Metal screeched. Sparks flew.

His flight was graceful. Arms aloft, eyes closed, he didn't once look at the train. He'd timed the jump beautifully.

The train-whistle blared, drowning out the Aeronaut's last words, but he mouthed them clearly. *Pay the fare.*

A woman swooned, delicate hand to head.

Carmody closed her eyes.

The crunch was wet. The screams distant.

The heat of the engine singed past Carmody and she counted to ten before opening her eyes. The desert shimmered, her vision swam. *Shade.* She stumbled back to the shelter of the water tank and slumped on her travelling trunk. Mouth dry, heart racing, she closed her eyes. Was that her fate? Would madness claim her if she couldn't ride the train? There was no going back.

Raised voices and soft sobs drifted toward her.

'Miss? Miss? Are you all right?' This voice was close, soft and gentle.

Carmody forced her eyes open. The face before her was blurred around the edges, smudged in the centre. *Dark hair.* She blinked until her vision cleared. His hair wasn't dark; it was blonde beneath a dark blue cap. The same dark blue as his eyes.

He proffered a flask in his white-gloved hand. 'Water.'

The flask trembled in her fingers as she raised it to her lips.

Cool liquid swirled down her throat, soothing. She sighed, tipped a little water into her hand and splashed her face.

'Better?'

'Much. Thank you, sir.'

He waved her off. 'It is just water.'

'It was a kindness. Thank you.'

'You are welcome.' His knee joints cracked when he rose. His boots were spit-polished brilliance, his pants perfectly starched. Red letters emblazoned his wool jacket: *Abaddon Rail.*

Was he her chance for a seat on the train? 'You work at the depot?' she asked, hope rising with her as she pushed to her feet.

Teeth white as sun-bleached bone crowded his smile. 'No, miss.' He pointed to the train. 'I am the Engineer,' he proclaimed, his shoulders held proud. 'I drive The Beast.'

Carmody frowned.

His eyes darkened, seemed more alive. 'Primitive, loud and hungry.'

'Hungry?'

This time his smile was more smirk. 'She is not the magnetised trains of your city. Steam power must come from somewhere, miss …'

'Boone. Carmody Boone.'

Before she could ask his name, or for his help, he tipped the brim of his cap. 'It has been a pleasure, Miss Boone.' He dipped his head. 'Safe journey.'

With military precision he turned on his heel and strode into the sunshine.

No. 'I can't make the journey,' she called after him.

He stopped but didn't turn around. 'Anyone can make the journey, Miss Boone.'

'Not true,' she said, taking a step towards him. 'The train is the property of the rich, the elite. It's their playground. Those of us who seek passage only are priced out of seats.'

He pulled at the cuffs of his jacket then dusted the sleeves. 'The train belongs to those whose desire for the destination outweighs all else.'

Carmody took another step, stopping at the edge of the shade. She wouldn't make her confession in front of the other passengers. 'All the seats are taken and they laughed off my offers of purchase. I know the rules. No ticket, no ride.' She took a breath. 'I'll sell anything I have for the journey.'

He kept his back to her, silent.

'Please.' She regurgitated the word and the shame that came with its use.

He adjusted his cap, straightened his shoulders. 'Where there is a will, there is a way, Miss Boone.' He still refused to face her. 'It comes down to how much you want to ride the train, nothing else.' He dipped his head again. 'Now, if you will excuse me, I must avail myself of a mop and bucket.'

He marched to the platform, the passengers parting like the Red Sea before him.

Carmody stood alone. Stranded. An outcast again. She pulled the timepiece from her vest pocket; it was all she had left of her brother.

The internal mechanism whirred as the clock-face rose, flipped, then settled back into place. The green needle pointed due east. *'Green always points home, Carm, so you never get lost again.'* Nate had made it for her when she was five and wandered out of the junkyard after a stray puppy. He'd been the only one who'd looked for her.

She ran her thumb over the brass casing. A year had passed since he'd died detaching a timer from a gas bottle.

Her father hadn't smoked since.

She tucked the timepiece away and went after the Engineer.

✳

'Where there's a will, there's a way,' Carmody murmured.

The view through the carriage window never changed. Four days on the train, four days of endless desert and empty sky. The monotony of visual nothingness, the rhythmic rocking of the train and lack of sleep conspired to sedate Carmody, and she sank deeper into the leather wing-back.

She'd tried to stay awake last night, had fought sleep hard, but she was alone when her eyes had snapped open at dawn. The man — Simon — was gone, but she could still feel the cold caress of his metal hand. 'Be honoured,' he'd told her; his motorised limb was one of a kind.

'Not a Scrap Rat anymore.' The bitterness in her voice, so like her mother's, was directed at no-one but herself. She'd made her decision. The timepiece was heavy around her neck, but it was safe.

The train jolted her gaze to the door and her heart stuttered. *Had she locked it?* She hurried across the compartment, sighed in relief. Resting her head against the mahogany, she closed her eyes.

'*... beware ...*'

Her eyes snapped open. A child's voice.

'*... one more ...*'

The whisper sounded like it was just on the other side of the door. So close.

'*... Godspeed, Ssssssimon ...*'

Carmody flinched.

That name. Hissed like steam.

A shadow flitted beneath the door. '*... whore ...*'

Branded again, the word flicked a switch inside her. The names, the insults, the superiority they believed protected them and made her sport had her lunge for the door. She twisted the key and threw the door wide.

No-one.

Heart hammering, she glanced into the corridor. Empty. The clanking of the tracks and coughing of the steam engine the only noise. She stepped tentatively from her room and scanned the doors to the other compartments. Closed. Locked, too, she was sure.

She lingered in the doorway; the windows opposite framed the same desolate view as her room. *'See the world,'* Nate had begged as his life pumped from the stump where his arm had been. She'd promised him better; she'd go to the edge of it. Death had tested them time and again as children, and finally claimed her brother. She wanted to know why.

She put her fingers to the timepiece again; she'd stopped looking at it four days ago, the morning the whispers started. Four names had drifted past her door as if on a breeze. Two she knew.

At breakfast, the Dining Carriage had been abuzz with gossip and speculation. Two couples gone, and rumour had it passengers in the lower-priced seats were also missing. The excited murmurings, their bravado as it dawned they were living the legend, playing the game, hadn't sat right with Carmody. When they raised their glasses to the Shovel-Man, she'd left, their sniggers following her.

Another gone at lunch, two more at dinner, and the furtive glances in her direction gained momentum. They knew where Lord Hemsley had spent the afternoon. He'd heard the scratching before she had. 'Rats,' he'd told her, spitting the word out like it were poison.

Carmody knew better; she felt the intent behind it. Sometimes, secretive scrapes from the corner of her room tormented her for hours; other times they struck hard and fast, screeching like fingernails clawing down a chalkboard. They'd been warned.

No-one spoke of it. Just as they no longer spoke of the dwindling passengers. But their glares let her know what they believed. She'd been dragged into the legend by their fear and suspicion.

She'd barricaded herself in when the whispers told her. Now, no-one left their room. Food was scarce, sleep too frightening to entertain.

'Help!'

Carmody yelped as the door to the first compartment burst open.

The widow Danforth stumbled from her room. Eyes wide with

fear, her greying hair whipped about her face as she sobbed. 'She's gone! I fell asleep and she's gone!'

Carmody slammed and locked her door.

Fists pounded the other side. 'You did this!'

Carmody backed away. Widow Danforth had started that rumour, had spat at her feet when Lord Hemsley had disappeared. 'Open up!' The handle shook, wood rattled in its frame. 'Open up, you whore!'

Carmody slid down the wall.

The train-whistle shrieked. So did the widow.

Scratch. Scratch.

Carmody scuttled from the wall and the train jerked violently, throwing her to the floor. A mirror shattered. Fists kept pounding. The engine wouldn't stop screaming. She crawled to the centre of the compartment, pushed to her knees, and the train shrieked to silence.

No fists pounded the door. The handle was still.

The train rocked gently on its tracks.

'*One by one you will surely fall.*' The Aeronaut's words haunted the room, scratches taunted through the walls. She looked to the door.

'... *Boone* ...'

'No ...' She shook her head. Every name whispered past her door took its owner with it. But she'd paid more for her fare than *any* of the others. She unlocked the door and pocketed the key.

She'd *paid.*

The corridor was empty. The compartment doors were all open. She was alone.

The horizon was aflame with oranges and pinks. Dusk. To her right, the curtain covering the door leading to the Dining Carriage was drawn. It never was. Heart racing, her fingers trembled as she pushed the velvet aside.

Endless desert, empty sky.

'Who is the last to disappear?'

Carmody spun to the voice.

His face was in shadow. Uniform tattered, the red letters glistened like blood on his jacket. 'Miss Boone.'

She backed against the door, grabbed the handle.

'Locked, of course.' He motioned to the window. 'Where would you go?'

'Where is everyone?'

'Come now, Miss Boone,' he clucked his tongue.

She shook her head.

'We have been travelling a week without stopping for—'

'No. Four days,' she countered, like that made all the difference.

He dismissed her argument with a wave of his white-gloved hand. 'The days tend to blur together out here.'

She edged towards her room.

'Your fate is sealed, Miss Boone.'

'No.'

He leaned into the fading light. Blackened skin sloughed from his cheeks; his ears were melted against his skull. Lips gone, his teeth shone in a perpetual smile. 'Pay the fare.'

She was closer to her room than he, but he moved as fast as his train and blocked the doorway.

'I paid!' she yelled. 'More than *anyone* else!'

'Which is why you were saved until last. The others threw money, valuables, things they would not miss. Token payments. But you ...' He ran a blistered tongue along his teeth. 'You sold everything to ride the train.'

The timepiece burned hot against her skin.

'All aboard!'

He leapt, slamming her against the carriage door. She raked her fingernails down his face, ripping large strips of flesh from his cheek. He howled, backhanded her.

Knocking her to the ground was a mistake. She'd grown up fighting her way to her feet. She punched into the side of his knee with all her might and he buckled, the snap of his tendon like music to her ears.

She scrambled to her feet, but he grabbed her ankle, tripping her. She bounced off the wall and he roared as she raced up the corridor toward the engine room. He'd left the door unlocked. He hadn't expected any resistance from her. She flung it wide. Hot wind buffeted her, the couplings clattered. She hesitated; the engine room was enclosed but there was nowhere else to go.

She fished the key from her pocket, took a step onto the buffer, and her hair was yanked from behind, a hand closing around her throat.

'You can only enter in pieces.' His breath was hot against her ear. 'Joe only feeds the fire.' He laughed softly, and Carmody twisted her head, swung her arm up and rammed the key into his eye. Nate had taught her everything was a weapon.

He shrieked, stumbled back. Carmody wrenched free, yelling as her hair ripped out in his fist. She ran to the engine room door. Unlocked. He was as arrogant as the others. She slammed the door shut and slid the bolt as the Engineer crashed into the other side.

She spun, looking for a weapon.

Shovel-Man Joe.

The legend was real.

His back, criss-crossed with scars old and new, glistened with sweat. Blood sluiced down his skin, staining his denim pants.

Veins bulged in his shoulders as he shovelled widow Danforth's head into the firebox.

The Engineer screamed for Joe, but the Shovel-Man was fixated on the fuel at his feet.

A liver-spotted hand tumbled from the slop of red, pink and white sizzling on the engine room floor.

Carmody spotted the whip and snatched it up.

The shovel scraped, empty, against the floor.

Carmody gripped the whip tight. The sun was almost set but she was determined to see dawn. She'd come too far, lost too much to stop now.

Joe turned. The skin of his face was filled with pustules, his lips like two strips of leather. Flames danced in the blacks of his eyes. He struck the floor with his shovel. 'Feed the fire.'

The train jolted, but Shovel-Man Joe knew his Beast and rocked in perfect time with her.

His gaze flicked from Carmody, to the fire, to the tracks stretched ahead. *Her. Fire. Tracks.*

The flames began to dwindle.

Her. Fire. Tracks.

The Engineer yelled for Joe to attack, but … Carmody cocked her head. *Joe only feeds the fire.*

Hate burned deep in her chest. There wasn't enough 'fuel'. All of this. *All* of it, was for nothing.

The shovel clattered to the floor.

Fire.

Joe's left foot went in first. Embers flickered. He grabbed the firebox. Skin sizzled. Right leg; the fire crackled. Joe peeled his hands from the scorching metal, leaving flesh behind as he manoeuvred his body deeper into the pyre.

The train jolted, picked up speed.

Flames surged up his back, eating at his shoulders as he squeezed them into the furnace.

Shovel-Man Joe turned, smiled.

The pustules burst. Skin melted from his face, his lips peeled back and he sank into his fire.

Fists pounded on the window behind her.

Carmody's gaze flicked from the fire to the tracks to the shovel. *Fire. Tracks. Shovel.*

The wooden handle seared her flesh and she looked through the window to the tracks beyond. As the sun dipped below the horizon, her reflection rose. Eyes as black as coal stared back at her.

She pulled the timepiece from the chain around her neck, turned and smiled at the Engineer.

'Feed the fire …'

Amanda J. Spedding's stories explore the darkness of the human soul. Her fiction has been published in *Andromeda Spaceways Inflight Magazine (ASIM)*, *Shades of Sentience*, Tasmaniac Publications and Pill Hill Press. She is a freelance editor and proofreader, Committee Member for the Australian Horror Writers Association (AHWA), and Field Correspondent for Innsmouth Free Press. Amanda lives in Sydney with her amazingly supportive husband and two very cool kids.

Shades of Sentience explores our world and all the different levels of perception and experience with which it is perceived, presenting articles and fiction that sees beyond what is expected to reveal all the strange, beautiful oddities of existence.

The **Shades of Sentience Steampunk Short Story Competition** was open to residents of Australia and New Zealand, and offered $200 in prize money and the chance to be published in *Shades of Sentience*. It is the first step in a battle of the two great punk genres, with 'Cyberpunk' as the theme for next year's competition.

sentientonline.net

ELEANOR MARNEY

Scarlet Stiletto Awards

Tallow

Dear Tunney and Peter,

I've been in such conundrums about this letter. I didn't know when to give it to you, or if I should give it to you at all. I considered enclosing it with my will, but finally decided that would be unfair. The posthumous surprise is the coward's way out, I believe. I didn't want you to feel like I was sidestepping the fallout from all this. I didn't want it to be that way.

So I've written this to be given to you both on the twenty-fifth anniversary of our aloneness. I should apologise before I begin — this is not a happy story, but I must tell it anyway. James pressed me not to do it; he thinks you will contact the police. Maybe you will. I will have to trust you both. Whatever happens, I will have to bear it.

A part of me wants to ask your pardon, beg your forgiveness, but another part of me stands resolutely beyond that. I did what I did for you both, and I have a dogged feeling about it: that things happened as they did, and I can't change them now in any case.

I don't have regrets. Which isn't to say that I don't still have nightmares ...

This is how you make a candle.

Cut your tallow into pieces, then place the pieces into a large double-boiler over water that is already gently bubbling. Stir the tallow until it reaches 71 degrees Celsius, and is completely melted.

Add the colour chips or scent to the melted medium — this is really a matter of personal taste. Keep in mind that anything added will affect the way the candle burns. But raw tallow can have a meaty smell, and you might not fancy the amber greasy look, like yellowing teeth or tobacco-stained fingers.

Cut the wicks to the desired length of the candle plus five inches, and tie the wicks to the iron broach. Check that the temperature of the tallow is still 71 degrees Celsius, then dip the wicks in the tallow for a few seconds. Lift back out, and allow the candles to cool between dippings for about a minute or so. Once the weight of the tallow stiffens and straightens the wicks, things will get easier. Make sure the wet candles aren't touching each other.

Continue dipping and cooling. Repeat the process until the candles have reached the desired thickness, or forever, until your back and shoulders ache, and you wonder if this whole terrifying ghastly business will ever end —

Flora's cards are labelled 'Tallow', just the creamy square of 240 gsm with the secretive dark script, her name and the contact for the shop, very much like an exclusive club, a health spa maybe. The products *are* exclusive, you know it's a good way to make something popular — people usually desire the things they think they'll never attain. Flora recognises that yearning, but she doesn't feel it any more. She has Douglas, and Tunney and Peter, to assuage it. She mines it only as a plank for the business now, working it into a recipe for commercial success. People desire, they desire candles and soap, even though candles and soap are really just fat and lye mixed together in the right proportions.

… standing there in your gown, smiling your Hellos *and* Thank you for coming to my weddings, *when Bev Dingle comes up, clutching her Winnie Blues, already half-pissed before the reception has properly started. Heedless of Douglas's tall morning-suited bulk, she squeezes your arm. Oh Flo, she sozzles out, Oh Flo, yer mum would be so proud, I dunno how ya snagged him, but ya snagged a bewdy there, Flo, ya lucky girl, and then the press of the queue is pushing her down the reception line. You and Douglas exchange quick grins before you straighten, three more hours to go and you smile, stretch your face —*

The soap is cut with a butcher's knife from immense pale-grained blocks. She only sells by weight.

The candles are not for the faint-hearted. They are *big*, bigger around than Flora's own thigh, and some as tall as herself. She likes the *scale* of them, an art form. She never uses colour, keeps the ice-white, or honey-gold, or brown-pear tones as the focus. Natural is very in, like recycled wood panelling or free-range eggs.

… Dad only lived long enough to see the twins arrive — the podling pair he called them — and he never liked you talking with that Melbourne accent, but the twins, weren't they something, jus bewdiful, jus' what the doctor ordered, right before he had his stroke —

Tunney and Peter like to slide their fingers down the sides of wax mountains. Press their hands against a soap block, and then sniff the lavender on their skin. Flora likes to stand at the entrance to the shop and look at the graduating heights of the cold, white pillars, the golden draped waterfall of dangling hand-dipped tapers, the massive chunks of soap, like something she's chipped off a glacier. The sense of personal accomplishment is fantastic. You can't buy that.

... but that was after Mum died. She was always into crafty things, making do, making soap, sewing her own clothes, the big Vacola jars labelled 'Peaches' and 'Stewed Tomatoes'; you can still remember the peaches, melting in your mouth after all these years ...

The shop is entirely neat and pragmatic, like Flora herself, a stylish amalgam that friends term 'Quaker modern' — elderly gentrified industrial location and Flora's old-fashioned wares in combination with glass, white paint, pale wood. She revels in it. It is like a present, a gift to herself, after years of dutiful marriage and the shepherding of her twin lambs through gestation and infancy and now school-readiness.

Actually, the shop is a present from Douglas, a reward or an apology. Compensation for all the business trips and late-night meetings and the isolation of solo parenting, all wrapped up in an old façade rejuvenated by lime-wash and varnished pine.

'I think it's more like a present from James,' Douglas says as he curls an arm around her. She leans into his embrace.

'Oh, *James*,' she says, rolling her eyes.

A year after Douglas introduces him she finally nails the accent. Since he talks about himself so little, she waits until Douglas is getting beers from the fridge.

'Afrikaner,' she says.

'What's that?'

'Your accent. It is, isn't it?'

He smiles, not looking at her. 'Most Australians wouldn't know an Afrikaans accent if it bit them on the rear,' he says.

She notices he doesn't agree or deny.

'I remember. From my father's cricket Saturdays. The radio broadcasts.'

'Very clever,' he says approvingly.

She still doesn't know if it's the truth.

James Fisk is their accountant. Douglas has known James for years, years before he knew Flora. That Douglas and James now work in the same firm is like a kind of inevitability. James comes for dinner, stays to talk business with Douglas. He's part of the furniture of their lives, ordering the nature of it to some extent. Now's a good time to take a holiday, James says, before capital expenditure comes due. You should negative gear the rental property. You've been wanting that industrial tankage unit for the workshop, haven't you? James says. You should buy it.

'Really?' Flora smiles, sipping her wine.

'Seriously.'

'You said yourself it'll make things easier,' Douglas prompts with a grin. 'Increased productivity.'

'No, seriously,' James says. 'And then I can claim on it for you in July.'

The use of tallow or lard was the catalyst for the Indian Mutiny of 1857. To load the Enfield Rifle, the sepoys had to bite the cartridge open. It was believed that the paper cartridges were greased with lard, which was considered unclean by Muslims, or with tallow, regarded as sacred to Hindus.

Later, Douglas finishes the last of the red while Flora tidies up.

'We should pay him a retainer, I think sometimes,' Flora says, wiping the benchtop.

Douglas frowns.

'Don't say that. He'd be insulted.'

'Do you think he's content?' she wonders absently.

'Do I think he's what?'

'I mean, he lives alone, he's obsessed with work, he's so … *contained.*' Flora has a sudden mental image of straw-haired James, loosening his tie by one degree as he sits, whiskey in hand. 'I wonder if it makes him happy …'

'I think James's interests are in other things,' Douglas confides.

'What, he's not interested in happiness? I know he's not gay, so maybe, I don't know, having a family, or at least a partner—'

'You sound like my Aunty Vi,' Douglas grins. 'Not everyone wants a family, Flo. James' loyalties lie elsewhere.'

'Elsewhere? What are his loyalties, then?'

'Pecuniary,' Douglas says. It rolls off his tongue, like he's tasting the word. 'Leave him be. He has his own code.'

Flora leans on the benchtop.

'It sounds a bit cold, I think. A bit mercenary.'

Douglas drains the glass, looks at the ceiling.

'Does it?'

The story of soap was first told in 1000 BC. Women rinsing clothes in the river, below the place where animal sacrifices were conducted, discovered that clothes became cleaner in contact with the soapy clay oozing there, where the rendered animal fat soaked through the wood ashes and into the river water.

... so my hand is shaking even as I write this. It was Wednesday evening, I remember, because Wednesday and Thursday were the days I didn't open for business or do any preparation work. My midweek weekend, Douglas used to say ... He said he'd take the Sydney meetings from Wednesday to Friday. I wasn't expecting him back until Friday evening. He undoubtedly wasn't expecting me to enter the shop.

But we stopped there early on Wednesday evening because, oh Tunney, you had left Bear upstairs from the shop. Do you remember Thread Bear, dearest? We called him that because—

I'm stalling, I'm sorry. We entered the shop, and walked through the familiar dark colonnade, past the counter, toward the staircase. I remember wondering why I could see light under the workshop door, feeling that mixture of exasperation (*it must've been me, I've left something on*) and alarm (*is anybody there?*). When I slid the workshop door across, the rollers hissed, and you were both clinging to my pants' legs, and I saw your father ...

Douglas is standing near the centre of the workshop, in his business shirt and trousers. Flora's hands remember holding the iron over that shirt; now she is only holding her keys. Douglas is holding a small blowtorch, a kitchen one, like you use to glaze crème caramel, like the one Flora uses in the workshop. It *is* the one she uses in the workshop — she recognises this somehow. In his other hand, Douglas holds a short-bladed Bowie knife.

Tied to a wooden chair in front of him is a man in a singlet and a pair of dark trousers. He has bare feet. Flora can see only the back view — the man's sweaty black hair, his limp hands secured at the wrists, the bow of his shoulders. The floor beneath the chair, beneath Douglas's feet, is covered in thick clear industrial plastic, and there are puddles of dark red ooze spattered onto it. To the right of the chair is a blue shopping bag filled with bundles of paper money: yellow, blue, grey, more cash than Flora has ever seen in its raw form.

The whole scene is aglow, stark and bluish, lit up from the side like a diorama in the halo of the workshop desk lamp. It looks staged, filmic somehow. It is unreal. It can't be real.

'Rendering' converts waste animal tissue into stable, value-added materials, and refers to any processing of animal by-products, or more narrowly to the rendering of whole animal fatty tissue into purified fats (lard or tallow). Rendering can be done on an industrial, farm or kitchen scale ...

Flora is arrested there in the doorway, her expression frozen. She stares at her husband, at the whole scene, all at once, as though her eyes have widened so much that she can see everything in panorama, there's no need for the eye to flit from detail to detail; her view is omniscient.

Douglas is not wearing his tie. His face is ruddy, a bit sweaty, energised — it is rather like the way his face looks after sex. This pulls Flora back: the way Douglas's expression and *déshabillé* convey the sense of adultery, only this is not adultery. This is something else. Flora returns to her body in a rush, feels the press of the children's warmness against her leg. She blinks at her husband.

'*Flora.*'

Douglas breathes out her name. He is shocked, yes. Then his face changes, becomes paler, more still. His lips come together as he swallows. Flora recognises this: this is Douglas, composing himself. Possibly it is this tiny thing that tips her off, that clues her in. Douglas is composing his face for her. Only seconds after he says her name, he regains himself. He releases a switch on the blowtorch with his thumb. There is a *zup* as the blue flame goes out.

Flora feels realisation ignite as the blowtorch is extinguished. Perhaps it is the absurdity of it. How is it possible to put a composed face on this? But really, it is the speed of it, the rapidity of the transition in Douglas's face. This is not a singular act. This is something he does a lot. He can change his face, alter his expression at will; he can control his emotions quickly, to cope with sudden changes in circumstance. This is not the reaction of an ordinary loving husband, devoted father, corporate businessman. This is not the reaction of an ordinary person.

Flora understands.

> ... but please believe me when I tell you it wasn't an easy thing to do. On any level. Physically, it went on and on, all night. Mentally and emotionally ... I loved your father, loved him deeply. What he did doesn't really take that away. And what I did —
>
> I could say that I reacted on instinct. But in a way, he did too ...

She takes her eyes off Douglas only long enough to glance down at the child nearest her right hand.

'Peter,' she says in a low voice, 'you and Tunney go upstairs and find Bear, please.'

Something, the frisson of energy in the scene they don't understand, communicates itself to the children, like when Flora and Douglas argue. The children don't complain or query. Peter takes Tunney's hand, and says 'Come on, Tun,' and they head for the staircase together. Tunney has her thumb in her mouth.

Flora does not let herself think that she is frightened. She takes the one step down into the workshop automatically, relying on reflex, with her eyes back on Douglas. She rolls the door closed behind her. She keeps her face very blank, as blank as can be.

The most significant problem when rendering fat for tallow is the smell. Chandlers and soap boilers were often relegated to the industrial section of townships on account of noisome odours, an unavoidable by-product of large-scale boiling of animal carcasses.

Keeping her expression blank, getting the children out of the way — it's a miscalculation, she realises. It reveals something about her to Douglas. It reveals that she understands the situation, but what else could she do? When Douglas speaks again, she only starts because the tone of his voice is so familiar, so unnatural in this time and place.

'I wasn't expecting you,' Douglas says quietly.

It sounds so domestic.

And she should say something, she should say *Clearly*, or something like that. She doesn't say anything.

Her breath is starting to come back in, short and tight. She mustn't hyperventilate. She mustn't scream, screaming is what you do when you have nothing left. She forces herself to just stand, hands at her sides.

Check the tankage unit at 10.15pm, she's wiping sweat off her lip as she watches James prepare the buckets. She wishes her hands would stop shaking.

Oh God, I need a fag, I wish I had a fag, she whispers, and she hasn't said 'fag' for 'cigarette' in about fifteen years, but she's almost crying now she wants one so bad. It's like an ache in her chest, and James offers her a swig from his silver flask which helps some but —

With her omniscient eye, Flora observes the scene between the two players. The man in the chair is unmoving. She and Douglas are the players. The looks they direct at each other indicate that they have assessed each other correctly. All that remains is to act.

Douglas begins, he sets his face grimly and says, 'Flora, I'm sorry you had to see this.' Flora still can't trust herself to speak so she just nods her head quickly, but before she's finished the action she's wondering what he means. When Douglas takes a brisk, purposeful step towards her with the knife in his hand, she comprehends. He is apologising for what he's about to do.

He moves fast and she can't stumble back; there is nowhere to go. She makes a garbled cry, cringes as he swipes with the knife; she raises her hand automatically. She is still holding her keys. The knife clashes onto them with a sound like teeth clicking together — by some miracle none of her fingers is severed — and the force of the blow telescopes up her arm, sending her reeling off the step.

She bounces off the edge of the work table to her right, jarring her hip, twisting to see her husband. His face is unreachable, single-minded, and he has turned the knife to allow him to thrust down, make a clean plunge into her breast. She is half-sprawled over the table, pressed into the corner, and her left hand rakes the wall. She knows she is trapped completely and she feels her face, mouth stretched in horror, eyes gasping wide.

Flora's left hand hits something leaning in the corner, something hard. She grabs for it as Douglas steps in. She rams forward with the hard heavy broach-handle. The broach is made of cast-iron and shaped like a broom. At the base, where the broom's bristled head should be, there are twelve five-inch metal tines.

The broach-handle slams into Douglas's face with a ghastly thud, blood exploding from his nose. For a moment his robotic expression is cross-eyed, confused, and Flora almost makes a hysterical laugh. She pulls on the handle; as it comes away she can see the impression it has made in Douglas's skin, in his skull. He stumbles back, raising a hand drunkenly to the indentation in his forehead. He looks alien and slow, so Flora almost lets her guard down. Then he lifts his eyes, and she only has time to swing the broach-base up when he makes a lurching thrust forward, knife arcing high. She puts her whole weight into bracing, head hunkered down, shoulders hunched. The collision knocks her off the table, so by the time it's over she's semi-crouched over the handle of the broach, kneeling squeezed between table and wall, gasping, staring up into the ruined face of her impaled dead husband.

'Why did you call me?'

'Douglas always called you. In emergencies.' She exhales, feeling white and shocky.

'Yes, he did.'

'This is one. An emergency.'

'Yes, it is.' James still looks confused. 'And ... you trust me?'

'I can do better than trust you,' she says. 'I can pay you.'

She stays like that for a minute, blowing hard, then the demands of gravity kick in. She sinks forward, lets the broach, with Douglas's body decorating the end, crump to the floor. Douglas is half-on, half-off the step. His expression is one of total surprise. The tines of the broach have pierced him in four places across the heart-line of his chest, and in one place on his right bicep, snagging the muscle there cruelly.

Flora's arms are sore and shaking, but she uses them to climb her way up to the tabletop then she uses the tabletop to support herself as she steps over the broach and the body, stumbling onto the clear floor area beside the man in the chair. She'd forgotten about him.

She stands, holding the table and shivering like she has hypothermia, then her knees give way and she sinks in a shambolic fashion onto her bottom. Her arms flop, her breath is blowing in and out; she feels something building up inside her, the scream she couldn't afford to let out before. But she can't afford to let it out now either — she drags her hands up to her face, pushes them hard against her mouth, so that the only noise escaping is the 'ung-ungh-ungh' sob of air, wheezing in and out of her nose.

She closes her eyes. Slowly her breathing comes back under control until she's just going 'mmm … mmm …' behind her hand. Then she can take her hand away, open her eyes, just sit for a moment. Her eyes move around: the scene, the bodies, the plastic she's puddled on. Minutes pass. Then something clicks inside her and she heaves to her feet, staggers over to Douglas. Roots in one trouser pocket before pulling on his hips to access the other. She pulls out the mobile phone. Hesitates. Her fingers shake so she almost drops the phone, but she's got it open, thumbing the speed-dial clumsily. In the pause, she takes two deep levelling breaths, so when she speaks her voice hardly trembles at all.

'No. This is Flora,' she says, like her own name tastes odd in her mouth. 'That's alright … I'm at the shop. There's a, a bit of a mess here, James. Could you come over? … Ten minutes. Alright. Come in through the back. Thanks.'

She closes the phone carefully and puts it in her pants pocket. Then she looks down and pats herself over, like pressing down creases. She rakes at her hair, takes another deep breath, steps over Douglas's waist to get up onto the step, the door sliding, so she can go upstairs and put the children to bed.

... regarding the case of such absent (Missing/Lost) spouse, inasmuch as it has been satisfactorily established through evidence of circumstances approved by the court, that the 'presumption of death' rule may be applied, thus allowing the State to grant probate and obtain an adjudication of the issue ...

He enters through the backyard into the workshop; he must have parked around the corner. He seems very calm, hair sticking up like he's just showered, casual jeans, and he closes the door before turning around. She sees the way he stands still, looks. He's not shocked. She doesn't find this surprising. His eyes move over everything, his face serious and without emotion, just assessing. She stands on the step holding one arm across her body with the other arm, her shoulders still throbbing.

The time she spent settling the children has made regular programming resume somewhat, and she feels a flare of panic. Suddenly she doesn't know what possessed her to call him, or what he's going to do.

Then he meets her gaze and holds it.

'Okay,' he says. He closes his eyes, opens them. 'Okay.'

'... so if you're thinking four hours for the tankage unit, we'll—'

'Shut up for a minute, I'm trying to estimate poundage,' she snaps, and then she presses her lips. 'Sorry. Sorry, I'm—'

'It's all right.'

'It's not. I ...I'm very sorry.'

'Flora,' he says.

She looks at the floor, rubs her fingers. He clears his throat.

'Pounds. So it's, what, the American unit—'

'Yes. That's right.'

'So you just halve the weight. Is that right?'

She blows out a breath. 'Yeah. Yes, I think it is.'

He starts moving immediately. Walks over and puts two fingers on the neck of chair-man, seems satisfied, goes through chairman's pockets until he gets the phone, takes out his own phone, holds out his hand for Douglas's. She gives it to him.

He cracks them all open, takes out the SIM cards, pockets them, groups the phones on the workbench. He talks as he works.

'You walked in unexpectedly.'

'Yes.'

'The kids?'

'Yes. Upstairs. I've put them to bed.'

'Think they'll stay asleep?'

'Yes.'

'Okay,' he says. 'Do you have a baby monitor, or—'

'I've put it on.'

'Oh. Okay.'

He stands for a moment, considering her.

'You have very fast reflexes,' he says finally.

This is like a compliment, like telling her she was clever that time. She doesn't know what to say to this.

'I need garbage bags,' he says, 'gloves, buckets, bleach, cleaning gear. I need to get some things from my car.'

He is so efficient. He doesn't offer comfort, but this efficiency is comforting. She thinks of saying this, doesn't.

He rolls up his sleeves.

… only the steady grumming chew of the meat saw, which is really getting harder to bear every moment, second only to the noises when he finishes a section and then empties the full bucket of pieces into the tankage unit. The plop *and* squelch. *She goes alright for a while, keeps cleaning, but then on the last one she can't help it, rushes over to the rag bucket and retches, her stomach grinding painfully, her eyes scrunched shut —*

His equipment and her supplies, gathered in a neat pile off the edge of the plastic, and he's already put the money in a garbage bag. She watches as he unties chair-man, tips him onto the floor, the body lying at an odd stiff angle.

'So, this is … What do we do now?' she asks, a little wild-eyed.

'To get rid of them. I mean, isn't that what we have to do?'

'Yes,' he says shortly. Then he volunteers, 'I can get rid of this one okay. It's Douglas we have to worry about.'

'Oh. Okay. So what, we, we burn off their fingerprints or something?'

James's face twists.

'Bloody hell, Flora, this isn't the movies—' He stops suddenly, looks at her. 'Hang on.'

… wanted you to remember the good things about him, too. The way he read to you both before bedtime, the hugs he gave you, the love. It was never just a lie, or a cover story; it was real — the love was real. You have his dark eyes, Peter; and Tunney, you have his dry, deprecating humour. Something of him lives in both of you, and makes me love you even more each day. It's what got me through the —

They stop and sit together on the floor, backs to the workbench cupboards, sharing his hip flask. She feels washed out. She thinks they both look washed out, exhausted. There's hours to go.

'So are you going to tell me about it?'

'You mean Douglas.'

'Yes.'

'You want me to tell you about Douglas.'

'Yes,' she insists.

'Do I need to?' He passes her the flask. 'You're not an idiot, Flora.'

'How about I tell you what I think, and you just answer yes or no.'

'Just talk,' he sighs.

Flora nods, then begins.

'He'd been doing this for a long time.'

'Yes.'

'Longer than ... No, forget that.'

James says nothing.

'And not a ... what-you-call-it, an official government—'

'No.' He shakes his head. 'Independent contractor.'

'Oh. And is that what you are, too? An independent—'

'No.' He returns her stare. 'I mean, not anymore, no. I'm just ... I'm just an accountant, Flora.'

'Oh. So this ...' She flicks a hand out, to the scene. 'This is normal? For an independent contractor?'

James shakes his head emphatically.

'No, this is ... horribly, horribly sloppy. Unprofessional. Not at all what I would have expected from Douglas.'

'Sloppy,' she repeats. She sucks on her teeth.

'Yes. I'm sorry, you—'

'No,' Flora says. She closes her eyes. 'Don't apologise.'

'... *reassure you, Mrs Ernst, that we're still looking into it. Your husband's disappearance is still important to us, whether it's six months or six years—*'

'*Thank you, Detective.*'

'*Thank you, for being so understanding,*' *he says, looks around.* '*It's good you've kept up with your business.*'

'*Well, it keeps me occupied ... Would you like a candle, Detective, or maybe a block of soap? Here, these tapers are nice—*'

'*Oh, I couldn't—*'

'*No, please,*' *she says.* '*I insist.*'

It's 4.40am. She skims off the solid chilled fat from the aspic by just upending the buckets, like making sandcastles, and slicing the hard top white layer away from the jelly. James bags the aspic and takes it out to the car, with the other remains, for disposal.

Flora's hands are greasy, from stacking the blocks. She's anticipating a few hours' sleep beside her children until she has to get up and make them breakfast before kinder, before returning to the longer work of dipping the tapers and mixing the soap. James comes back for his gear as she's wiping her hands, closing the fridge.

'I've cleaned the U-bend in the sink. I'll do it again after you've finished,' he says. 'Remember to bag the rags, anything else touching ...'

'I know,' she says tiredly. 'I will.'

'I'm going now,' he says, hesitates. 'Flora ...'

She looks at him.

'Thank you, James,' she says. 'For everything.'

He moves, can't seem to decide whether to shake her hand or give her a kiss on the cheek, finally settles for squeezing her shoulder. His eyes seem slightly lost, hollow.

Then he nods, and leaves.

... maybe asking too much, but I wanted you to know the whole story. All stories contain a spectrum from light to dark. This one contains much darkness, but a candle emits 13 lumens of visible light, so I think of your father, and the love that produced you both, when I touch flame to wick. That love still burns. It will see us through.

Forever,
your mother,
Flora

Eleanor Marney was born in Brisbane, and has lived in Indonesia, Singapore and India. She has been awarded for her adult short stories, and her work has been published in *Award Winning Australian Writing 2009* (Melbourne Books), and in the upcoming horror anthology *Box of Delights* (Aeon Press). At the moment, between parenting, she is working on teaching high school students, writing the second book in a junior adventure series, and completing a YA crime thriller. She lives on ten acres near Castlemaine, Victoria, with her partner, four young sons, an excess of chickens, and a dog.

Australia's only crime writing competition for women, Sisters in Crime's **Scarlet Stiletto Awards** are Australia's most lucrative crime-writing competition for either gender. Top prize is the HarperCollins first prize of $750 plus the coveted trophy, a scarlet stiletto shoe with a steel stiletto heel plunging into a perspex mount. The 2010 competition attracted 145 entries, and Nadine Garner, star of *City Homicide*, presented the awards with Dr Sue Turnbull of La Trobe University. Submissions close in late August each year, with an entry fee of $10.

'Tallow' was originally published in *Scarlet Stiletto: The Second Cut* (Clan Destine Press, 2011). The book was launched by Tara Moss as part of the 2011 SheKilda Again – Australian Women Crime Writers' Convention, celebrating Sisters in Crime's twentieth anniversary.

www.sistersincrime.org.au

K. A. NELSON

Overland *Judith Wright Poetry Prize for New and Emerging Poets*

Chorus of Crows

When she saw Top Camp
(humpies made of corrugated iron/slabs of bark
people and dogs living together
children   discharge running from nostrils/ears
like sewage seeping from the broken pipes next door)
she didn't wince.
She learnt to overlook the rubbish
caught on broken fences
blown by westerlies that brought the dust
and the haunting sound of crows through
every crack.

When she met Topsy
(her husband used a star picket
punished her tribal way even though everyone knew
thatwhitefella contractor got the better of her)
she didn't faint.
It wasn't the first time she'd seen human flesh
open to the bone or held the hand of a woman
being stitched up.
Outside the clinic the crows seemed to sing
that white man
long gone.

When the Land Council mob
said no to a drink in the back bar
(the publican would only lace
their beer with Worcestershire Sauce
customers would stare/whisper behind cupped hands)
she bought a carton.
They sat in the yard yarning and laughing
at the crows as they burnt their beaks
scavenging for scraps
on the barbecue
hot plate.

When she walked across the Harbour Bridge
arm in arm with friends
(*black/white and brindle*
as her Nana used to say)
mothers pushed babies in their strollers
fathers shouldered children waving flags
people carried placards
and a breeze billowed out
that 'sorry' word above the crowd for hours.
Not a crow in sight!

Well into the New Millennium
it wasn't the daily press releases
of suicides/sniffing/stoushes
or claims the ATSIC experiment
had failed (miserably)
but another order from a minister
and a mandarin
carried out by men in overalls
that did her in.

When they took the dotted/cross hatched worlds
    off all the office walls to hoard them
in a secret storeroom somewhere
    (Mitchell, Fyshwick/Tuggeranong?)
when each piece of art and artefact was placed
    (without bubble wrap or due regard)
in Woolworths shopping trolleys
    that lurched along the corridors
their wobbly wheels protesting to the last
    when workers sat transfixed to telephones
and screens (like crows on a carcass pecking
    pecking unperturbed by passing cars)
she hurried to the women's toilet
    locked the door/flushed
and wept.

Later she stared at her blank wall
where Rover's *Universe* used to hang.
Without him she felt so far removed
from Top Camp
Topsy and the mob
from the fly speck she said she was
in a far- flung corner of his print
near one of five gold dots
(or sacred sites)
and as she stared
she thought she heard him say
Gardiya might like 'em*
might learn 'em
might read 'em right way
one day.

But beyond the blank space/concrete wall/double glass
it seemed to her the crows guffawed
(as if they foresaw
the NT Intervention).

---

* *Gardiya*: whitefella

K. A. Nelson is a former public servant and adult educator who lives in Canberra. She grew up in country New South Wales, has a BA in English literature and drama from UNE, spent ten years living and working in the Northern Territory (last century), and writes part-time.

The *Overland* **Judith Wright Poetry Prize for New and Emerging Poets**, sponsored by the Malcolm Robertson Foundation, is Australia's most prestigious award for emerging poets. It offers annually a major prize of $5000 and publication in *Overland* magazine, plus two smaller prizes. The award is open to Australian poets who have not yet had a collection of work commercially published — that is, by a publishing house with a commercial distribution. The prize usually opens for entries in September and closes in mid-November — but check *www.overland.org.au* for specific details.

The Fields of Early Sorrow

We encountered our first swarm of locusts on the flat, fertile plains approaching West Wyalong. Although the locusts splattered against the windscreen with great velocity, their demise was soundless. I was scarcely able to discern the white markings of the Newell Highway through the mass of smeared membranes. Acting on the advice of a cadet journalist who was raised in the region — in Bundaburrah, to be precise — I had secured aluminium mesh over the radiator. Katie sat sedately in the passenger seat while she watched the locusts come to grief.

Once the threat of locusts had subsided, Katie wound the window down and lighted a cigarette (I had purchased her a carton of Marlboros before we left). She tilted her head out the window while she smoked. It was only a small concession, but it filled my heart with warmth. Her dyed hair floated freely around her pale face. I caught sight of her auburn roots, which gleamed in the sun. Her complexion remained youthful, especially the salient splash of her blue eyes. Her arms looked as slender as I could remember them looking since our adolescence.

Katie finished her cigarette and drew a large pair of designer sunglasses over her eyes. It was difficult to tell whether she was still awake. She had barely spoken all day. My wife, Pollyanna, had warned me that Katie might inexplicably lose her temper. She had also warned me not to invest too much faith in Katie's displays of good humour or kindness. It seemed strange to receive such solemn counsel regarding my younger sister, as though she was a criminal mastermind whom I had been charged with extraditing.

I followed the highway past quiet rural townships, rows of grapevines, fields of blue lavender, native orchids, vast seeding machines, timber cattle yards and inviting weatherboard homesteads. The countryside looked resplendent in the afternoon sunlight. There wasn't a person in sight. For a fleeting moment I forgot the circumstances of our journey and felt truly happy sitting behind the wheel. In the ensuing minutes I reached the conclusion that all happiness was fleeting, although the same couldn't be said for sorrow.

I was forced to wait at a railway crossing on the outskirts of Forbes while a freight train approached. My gaze settled on a barren plateau to the left of the highway, which had been subdivided into paddocks. A flock of sheep were grazing the rich, volcanic soil in one of the paddocks. I wanted to awaken Katie so that she could share the view with me. But we weren't there to marvel at the landscape. It was this seemingly trivial act of suppression that caused me to feel disheartened for the first time all afternoon.

We had several hours to drive before reaching Dubbo. Pollyanna and I decided that it was best to avoid stopping overnight in Sydney because there would be too many distractions. We were due to drive another ten hours the following day before reaching The Buttery; a clinic situated on three acres among the rainforests and macadamia nut plantations in the shire of Lismore. Katie had been on the waiting list for the past six months. I was surprised she had made it.

I had taken one week of annual leave from my post as the editor-in-chief of *The Bendigo Advertiser*. I wondered whether the time would have been better spent taking my wife and my daughter to a beach resort on the north coast of the country. Having worked diligently for the majority of my life — I slept four hours per night on average — it seemed unfair to sacrifice a rare allotment of pleasure. I knew I couldn't burden Katie with my feelings. She already harboured enough guilt. Besides, driving her to The Buttery seemed like one of the few tasks that I had no right to delegate.

I frequently took note of Katie's flaccid features. She reminded me of my daughter, Ursula. While I was loading Katie's belongings into the car that morning Ursula ran into the street. She was wearing pink pyjamas. I had told Ursula that her aunty was taking a seven-month holiday because she was feeling unwell. Ursula grabbed Katie by the waist and refused to loosen her grip. She said she hoped Katie would feel better when she arrived home so that they could hold tea parties in her cubbyhouse. Ursula didn't even drink tea. Katie blinked repeatedly. She wrapped her arms around Ursula's shoulders and kissed the child's flaxen hair.

✳

Katie cast her eyes around the desolate bistro at the Parkes Leagues Club. Her pupils looked dilated in the bright lights. A small group of young men were shooting pool and drinking beer at one of the nearby tables. I had noticed one of the men eyeing Katie off when we first entered the building. She let out a high-pitched laugh.

'What's so funny?' I asked.

'I bet when we were children you never imagined you would wind up in a place like this, guarding your kid sister like a prison warden.'

I didn't enjoy being likened to a prison warden. I felt that I had been quite good-natured about my responsibilities.

'You're right, it never crossed my mind.'

'Mine either,' she said.

A crowd of elderly people appeared at the counter, drowning the bistro out with genial murmur.

'But here we are,' said Katie.

'Yes, here we are.'

'And nothing in the world could persuade you to turn back.'

It was difficult to gauge whether she was making a statement or asking a question.

'Nothing in the whole wide world,' I said.

Katie cast a sardonic smile at me. It was the kind of smile that a person never wishes to behold in the eyes of a sibling.

'This must be very different to the hustle and bustle of a newsroom,' said Katie. She seemed to place great emphasis on the words 'hustle' and 'bustle', as though they exemplified the difference between us, the thin metaphysical line between affliction and normality, or success.

'Obviously,' I said, trying to produce a smile. 'I take solace in the fact that I don't have to worry about split infinitives in your presence.'

A waitress who walked with a sizeable limp brought our meals to the table. I thanked her by name (I remembered her name from the receipt). She inquired as to whether we were passing through town.

'Yes,' I said. 'We are heading north.'

'Oh goodie,' she said, clasping her hands together. She smiled heartily at Katie and turned to address me. 'Keep your eyes peeled for the radio telescope 20 kilometres out of town. It's on the right side of the highway. The telescope was used to transmit man's first steps on the moon to the rest of the world.'

'We won't miss it,' I said.

Katie thanked the waitress with a kindliness that sounded rather condescending.

I wasted no time in devouring my meal. It was a charred rib-eye steak with an assortment of farmhouse vegetables. I hadn't realised how insatiable my appetite had become. We had only stopped three times all day: twice to fill up on petrol and once to purchase sandwiches from a roadhouse in Deniliquin.

Katie barely touched her meal. I had ordered her a bowl of chicken and leek soup — one of the blackboard specials — without consulting her. No-one had counselled me on what cuisine she might find appetising.

'Are you ashamed of me?' she asked.

I was surprised that she posed the question in a public setting. She had had all day to ask it while we were driving.

'No, I'm not ashamed of you.'

'Are you sure?'

'None of us are ashamed of you.'

Katie dabbed her spoon into her soup and watched the condensed liquid spill back into the bowl.

'Polly is ashamed of me,' she said. 'I can see it in the way she looks at me.'

'You're reading too much into everything. Pollyanna loves you the same as I do, the same as Ursula does. We all love you unconditionally. We just want you to get well again.'

'It's not that simple.'

'I know.'

Katie pushed her bowl into the middle of the table. She continued to clutch her spoon in a bid to prevent her hand from shaking.

*

We found the Westview Caravan Park five kilometres out of Dubbo along the Mitchell Highway. Just prior to the turn-off I noticed an abandoned drive-in that was bordered by a barbed-wire fence and rows of cactuses. We were greeted by a slim, affable man at the reception desk. He had slicked-back silver hair and he wore a red flannelette shirt. I asked him how long it had been since the drive-in was open.

'Must be almost twenty years,' he said, sucking on his bloodless lower lip. 'A man named Rex used to manage it. The crowds stopped coming so I guess old Rex figured he ought to cut his losses. A man's got to read the signs. Most of the drive-ins in this country closed around that time. From memory the nearest one left is in the Hunter Valley. Awful pity, if you ask me. Mind you, Rex had fourteen good years.'

The man smiled at the ceiling and located our booking in a hard-covered manual. He gave us directions to our cabin, told us where the amenities block and the swimming pool were located, and asked us politely to return the key to his wife at reception by ten o'clock the next morning. I was relieved he didn't ask why we were passing through town.

We located our cabin in a sparsely-populated site in the heart of the caravan park. It was stifling inside the cabin. The blinds were drawn and the kitchenette had an acerbic odour. I insisted that we both sleep on a bunk in a diminutive bedroom that was adjacent to the bathroom. I put my backpack on the bottom bed. I unloaded a packet of breakfast cereal and a carton of milk that I had purchased from a supermarket in town. Katie sat sullenly on a leather bench beside the fridge. She rubbed her shoes against the stained linoleum and complained that she was feeling nauseous.

Five minutes later I was reclining on a deckchair beside the swimming pool, enjoying the shade of a grey gum tree. I read a copy of *The Daily Liberal* — a newspaper covering Dubbo and the surrounding district — which I had picked up at the reception desk. There was a picture of a local wheat farmer on the front cover. He had won the second division prize in the national lottery. In spite of the six-figure windfall, he vowed to continue working on the family farm.

Katie removed her jeans and her blouse. She didn't have any bathers, so she swam in her underwear. Three young children — two boys and a girl who was wearing floating devices on her arms — were already playing in the shallow end of the pool. I guessed from their brazen formality that they were siblings. The two boys temporarily ceased teasing the girl when Katie entered the pool. She waded to the deep end and turned onto her back so that she could stare at the cloudless sky.

While I watched Katie float I became acutely aware that the allotment of time represented something vastly different to her. This time next week, her wellbeing would no longer fall within my jurisdiction. She would be in the hands of strangers, people well-versed in the realm of affliction. It must have been a frightening prospect. This time next week I would be sitting on a revolving chair in a newsroom, cross-checking citations, responding to readers' complaints and composing editorials, as though the scene at the swimming pool had never taken place.

Once more I began to contemplate the thin line between the poplars of an east-coast clinic and the brimming desks, the air-conditioning vents and the stark white lights of a newsroom. How had I managed to land on one side of the line while my sister landed on the other? Could the children playing in the swimming pool, splashing carelessly, conceive that their lives might take such a tumultuous course? Or was their bliss contingent upon the ignorance that such a course was possible?

＊

The swimming pool was empty when I awakened. I returned to our cabin, expecting to find Katie coiled on the large mattress in the double bedroom. She wasn't there. I followed a wide paved road and ended up walking a frantic circuit of the caravan park. I searched in the brick amenities block, even taking the liberty of calling Katie's name out loud in the female toilets. No one answered. I approached a man who was filleting snapper in the communal barbecue area and asked if he had seen anyone matching Katie's description. He pointed towards the Mitchell Highway.

I left the caravan park and walked along the highway in the direction of town. I was unsure why I had elected to walk in that direction. It didn't occur to me to take the car. There was no protocol to follow. The surrounding fields of canola burst into dazzling displays of yellow. Several grain trucks rattled past. I estimated that there was less than an hour of daylight remaining. I knew the search would be hopeless once the sun set. After following the highway for fifteen minutes I decided to turn back.

When I had almost reached the caravan park I caught sight of a dim figure sitting in the middle of the abandoned drive-in. It was difficult to gain access to the property because of the rows of cactuses and the barbed-wire fence. I hurried past a rusted yellow and grey sign that read 'WESTVIEW DRIVE-IN'. Vegetation enveloped the old ticketing booth in the far corner of the property. I reached a side fence and called Katie's name out loud. The figure looked in my direction, but made no obvious attempt to reply.

I removed my trousers and placed them over the barbed wire fence to aid my leap. I was surprised by the virility of my movements. I put my trousers back on and ran through the knee-high rye grass. When I drew nearer to the figure, I realised that it was Katie. She was sitting facing the giant white screen. A flock of goats were grazing the grass no more than 20 metres from where she was sitting. They didn't seem to mind her presence, nor mine.

Katie's hands were smeared with blood. It was emanating from a circular stain just below the ruptured knee of her jeans. Her face looked frightfully pale.

'Do you think they'll give me something to dull the pain at the hospital?' she asked.

I tried not to smile.

Katie rolled her jeans up and inspected the wound on her right leg. It was deeper than I had expected. A crust of torn flesh was seeping out of a long slit in her bloodied shin.

'Do you remember the first time we visited the drive-in?' she asked.

'You might have to refresh my memory.'

'Dad took us to see *The Conformist* by Bertolucci.'

'Now I remember,' I said, lowering myself gingerly to the soil. 'You were adamant that you were going to marry the lead actor. What was his name again?'

'Jean-Louis Trintignant.'

'Yes, you were rather smitten, as I recall.'

'Do you think I still stand a chance?'

Crimson ripples bled into the distant sun, which had begun its descent behind the dark mountains on the horizon.

'Does your leg hurt?' I asked.

'I'll live,' said Katie. She ripped a wildflower from the soil and placed it behind her ear. 'Although I'm not sure how I feel about that.'

'You won't be able to poach Trintignant from beyond the grave,' I said, attempting to be funny, which, according to my wife and daughter, had never been my strong suit.

'The main image I have of the film is that beautiful shot of the leaves rippling in the wind. I can't remember the last time I felt so excited.'

I still experienced excitement on a daily basis — at the sight of Ursula wearing her pink pyjamas in the morning, for instance.

'Do you honestly think I'll experience it again?'

'It's not for me to say.'

'If I'm not going to experience it again, what's the point in any of this? I've endured enough shame for one lifetime. This constant despair feels like the absolute truth. Even the small moments of happiness I can remember seem futile compared to the density of this feeling. You don't understand. There's no respite, not for me.'

I considered hugging Katie, but I suspected that the gesture would be insufficient.

'When you arrive home I'd like you to do me a favour.'

'Anything,' I said.

Katie inspected her right leg. Blood continued to trickle along her shin, staining her socks.

'I'd like you to tell Ursula the truth.'

'She won't understand.'

'That's not important.'

A warm northerly swept across the rye grass. Tall ironbarks twitched in the distance. My gaze settled on the towering blank screen. I noticed that white paint was beginning to peel away from its surface.

Murray Middleton is a 27-year-old writer who lives in Melbourne. He recently won *The Age* Short Story Competition and is reputed to have wept upon learning the news. He has also been published in *Verandah*. He currently works at Debney Park Secondary College with high-functioning autistic children. An autistic student recently described him as 'one of those humour people'. He weighs 64 kilograms and has always put writing before sustenance. Despite his moderate success with the critics and failed sales, Murray persists, almost on a Sisyphean scale; the battler as writer if ever there was one.

By entering *The Age* **Short Story Competition**, you'll raise the profile of your work, attract critical attention, and move closer to being published. The competition is run in conjunction with the international writers' association PEN. The first-, second- and third-place winners each receive $3000, $2000 and $1000 respectively, and are published in the *A2*. They are published on *theage.com.au* along with all highly commended entries.

For further information, contact Jason Steger on *jsteger@theage.com.au*.

GILLIAN ESSEX

Panton Hill 'On the Hill' Short Story Competition

Marge and the Night-man

The house where Marge had grown up was tiny, and often cold. You could see daylight where the weatherboards were broken and the plaster had fallen away in chunks. It had a large kitchen, a small front room, two tiny bedrooms — one each for Marge and her mother — and a dunny out the back. A small path led from the dunny to a gate that gave the night-man access to collect the waste. The pan was never full. Marge and her mother didn't starve but there was never much to eat.

The kitchen was Marge's favourite place. It had a blackened brick chimney, over a wood-fired stove of green enamel with white and grey flecks. In the middle of the kitchen was a rough wooden table. It had drawers underneath where her mother kept the special pie-making things.

On Sundays, they got up early and lit the stove they'd filled with wood the night before. They moved the table aside and carried in the old iron bathtub from the small shed out the back. They filled it with pots of water heated on the stove and then bathed and dried themselves with the scratchy white towels that her mother always boiled in the copper on Mondays. Sometimes, as they bathed, the water splashed onto the lino and formed beads that rolled into the cracks in the lino and seeped into the musty floorboards below.

Afterwards, they dressed in their Sunday clothes and went to church to cleanse their souls. Marge loved listening to the sermon — especially when it was about miracles.

When they got home, they changed into their everyday clothes and carried the bathtub back to the shed, being careful not to touch anything dirty. Then, they pushed the table back into the middle of the kitchen and it was here that the Marge's own miracle began. Her mother always managed to make something special out of the cheap cuts of meat and other bits and pieces she'd scrounged from somewhere.

Marge's mother would roll back the cheerful red chequered cloth that usually covered the table and open the drawer that had been hidden underneath. She would get out her wooden rolling pin, her pastry brush, her pie tin and all the other implements she needed, and lay them out neatly on the tabletop, like a surgeon before an operation. For Marge, the anticipation of the pie was almost as good as eating it.

Her mother's pies always had golden, flaky crusts, and the filling was warm and rich. Marge tried to make herself eat slowly, to savour every mouthful, but the pie was always so delicious she couldn't help scoffing. When she finished, she watched her mother elegantly slicing small pieces of her own portion on her plate and delicately chewing each mouthful and wished she could learn the art of restraint to make the whole experience last longer.

✳

On Marge's tenth birthday, her mother gave her seconds as a special treat. But Marge's belly wasn't used to so much food, and that night nature took its course. She lit a candle and reluctantly went out into the cold night air, down the pathway, to the dunny. She pulled up her thin cotton nightie and sat on the hard wooden seat, hoping there were no spiders lurking under the rim. The candle threw menacing shadows on the dunny walls.

Marge was only halfway through her business when she heard the crunch of heavy boots in the lane outside, and next door's latch rattling. She remembered it was Thursday — the day the night-man came. She strained as hard as she could, trying to get the job done quickly, and grabbed at the pieces of torn-up newspaper they used for wiping. Her face was burning with shame. She heard the unmistakable clang of next door's can being changed over, and then more footsteps — closer now — but her body refused to go faster. Then, she remembered her mother's advice: 'Whistle if you hear him coming.'

Marge pursed her lips and blew, but her mouth was no more co-operative than her other end. All that came out was a tiny popping sound. She heard the creak of the hinge as next door's gate swung open and then a bang, as it hit the fence. Perhaps she could sing instead? She needed to think of a tune, and quickly. She thought it might be blasphemous to pray for inspiration under the circumstances, but her situation was desperate so she pushed aside her qualms.

Almost immediately, a hymn tune, *When the Burden Bearer Came*, popped into her head. She started to sing — softly at first — but panic strengthened her resolve, and by the time she got to 'all my sins he rolled away' she was in full flight. At one point, she had to stop for breath. Initially she was relieved to hear that all was silent outside, but then she thought she heard a soft, deep chuckle coming from the direction of the gate.

By the end of the hymn, Marge had mercifully completed her other performance as well. She blew out the candle, pulled her nightie down over her knees and crept back to the house, feeling the way with her feet and launching into *Onward Christian Soldiers* because it always made her feel brave. She heard the rattle of the gate behind her and was grateful that the moon was obscured by clouds.

Once Marge was inside, she listened from behind the back door. She heard the clang of the cans as the night-man swapped the half-full can with a new one, a thwack as he fastened the clip of the lid, and then a grunt as he hoisted it onto his shoulder. Then, she heard a rich, baritone voice:

> In the dark of the midnight,
> Have I oft hid my face;
> While the storm howls above me,
> And there's no hiding place ...

Marge smiled. She would never be afraid of the night-man again.

Gillian Essex completed a Diploma of Professional Writing and Editing in 2009, and now works as a freelance writer and editor. She has been published in *Best Australian Stories 2010* and *Award Winning Australian Writing 2010*. She also writes nonfiction and poetry. Her work has appeared in the travel section of *The Age* and in the literary magazine *21D*.

'On the Hill' is an annual one-day festival that celebrates the delights of life in Panton Hill. It features live music, food and loads of entertainment. The **Panton Hill 'On the Hill' Short Story Competition** is an open competition accepting entries of no more than 1000 words.

JOHN BIGGS

Jacqueline Cooke Short Story Award

She's Late

Today's the day! And it'll happen right here in St David's Park. I'll wait for the right moment and then *wham*: I'll pop the question! Nah, she won't be surprised. I'll just bet she'll be expectin' it. And after that, we'll have a slap-up dinner at Hadley's. Somewhere posh for a change.

Nervous? I'm not nervous! I know she'll say yes. But I have to say, her mum worries me. She don't hold with her daughter doin' a line with a wharfie, let alone marryin' one. But, well, she'll just have to lump it, won't she? It'll put Betty in an awkward position but. She ain't used to defyin' her mum, just like her mum ain't used to bein' defied. I reckon her mum could send Pig Iron Bob on his way. Not that she'd be likely to. She idolises Menzies, the smarmy bastard. But back to me and Betty — love will out in the end. That's what they say, or somethin' like that.

The GPO clock's just struck twelve. Betty said she'd be here by now. She said she'd try to get her dinner hour a bit earlier but then you never know with bosses like her boss, that Mr Martin. He loves to stick by the rules. I reckon he does that just to punish his employees, but Betty don't agree. 'You play fair by him,' she said, 'and he'll play fair by you.' Yeah, well, doesn't look like it, does it, seein' as how she ain't here yet

But in another sense it don't matter. I've got the day off thanks to the shop steward. He called a strike over a couple of Mick scabs, father and son, who wouldn't pay their union dues. Frank Hurley was one of them. Suits me … oh no, no, no. *Hursey*, that was the name, not the photographer bloke. Anyway, suits me, as I was sayin'. Gave me all mornin' to work things out. Like what I say, type of thing, then what she says. Bet that'll be about her mum. So what do I say to that? Never you mind, I've got it all worked out.

Might as well have a bit of a puff while I'm waitin'. Should've bought some tailor-mades for today of all days. Oh well, it'll just have to be the makings. I'll roll one and sit 'ere and take an eyeful of the Hobart docks. They look bonzer, as always. 'Specially now me mates ain't slavin' away.

Yeah, now I look round me, I see the Park's cleaner than what it used to be. Fewer graves too. Goodo by me. It used to look like a bloody cemetery.

Betty. Oh gawd how I long to marry her! We met at the Belvedere Ballroom, that's where everyone goes who wants to pick up a sheila. That was three months ago. I took one quick look at 'er across the dance floor and I knew she was the one. Don't much believe in God, but it was just like he whispered in me ear: 'That one, Alf me old cobber, that one with the blue taffeta frock. I made her for you, you know.' Good on ya, God.

She was sittin' with a couple of friends. I crossed the room as fast as I could while tryin' to look casual. I tarted me voice up a bit. 'Please may I 'ave this dahnce?' I said.

She smiled and nodded. A slow waltz it was, 'My heart sighs for you'. Bloody oath it did. Still does only more so. 'Alf's the name,' I said. 'What's yours?'

'Betty Hopkins,' she said.

'Oh yeah, course, silly me. Alf *Thomas*.' I laughed at myself for not sayin' me full name like she did. She smiled like she thought it was funny too.

In fact, she smiled and nodded a lot. So I asked if I could take her home after the dance.

She smiled and nodded.

We caught the Dynnyrne trolley-bus. We got out at the Waterworks Road stop. Her house was just up from the corner. I was nervous by then, I c'n tell you! She was classy, not your everyday slag. Do I kiss her, like on our first night out, type of thing?

We stood at her gate, my hand around her slim waist, one good hug and she'd snap I reckoned. She seemed so fragile and that made me feel strong. That really excited me. But then the cat had got me tongue. I couldn't think of a blind thing to say now we were where we were and the Big Moment had arrived. *Jigger this up, Alfie boy,* I said to myself, *and you've lost her.* Finally I said, 'Oh well, suppose I'd better be goin'. Thanks for a lovely night ...'

She smiled and nodded. And she turned her cheek. She wanted me to kiss her! So I did. Just a light peck, of course.

She turned to hurry inside. She stopped at the front door, after she'd opened it with the key she'd been fiddlin' with in the bus. She smiled again, givin' me a quick little wave. I would have missed it if I hadn't been standin' there, stock still, watchin' her for as long as I could.

I ran home all the way to Battery Point, my heart runnin' a few steps in front of me and about six feet higher. 'Alfie, you've done it,' my heart shouted, 'You've got yerself the best little sheila in Hobart!'

After that, things between me and Betty went real bonzer. We went back to the Belvedere Saturday nights, to the pictures Wednesday nights — that's when I wasn't on shift — and lunch right here in the Park two or three times a week when likewise. When I wasn't on shift, I mean. I'd get some 'couta and chips from the wharf and wait for her for right where I'm waitin' now. We loved that, especially on those autumn days when the sun was still warm and the trees were on the turn. Real' pretty, they looked. Just like my Betty.

She talked a lot more now she felt comfortable with me. We kissed proper, on the lips, then we French-kissed (that's Number

Four, if you don't know the Points System we lairs went by). Then Number Five, then Number Six — and at that 'point' I disgraced myself in my excitement. But it was dark and she didn't notice. At least, I hope to gawd she didn't!

I was a goner after that. I thought about my Betty all day, every day and all night, whether I was awake or asleep. The sight of her bare tit (Number Six) made me drunker than grog ever did. I'd gone out with a couple of sheilas before Betty but it was nothin' like this. Nothin' at all.

Then she said: 'Mum wants to meet you, Alfie. She says it's about time, seein' as how you're my steady. Pick me up an hour early next Saturday and I'll introduce you.'

Of course it had to be, but I tell you what, I nearly shat myself on the way there!

Betty was her mother's daughter as far as looks went: the same strawberry-blond hair, the same small nose. But there the resemblance ended. Her mum was a fierce bloody lioness that had given birth to a sweet kitten (that's my Betty). Her dad was a nice easygoin' cove — when we met he seemed almost as nervous as me! He smiled like he was the one on display as we shook hands. He asked what I thought of the Seagulls' win at the North Hobart Oval this arvo. Then he took out a pack of Craven A and offered me one. 'No thanks, Mr Hopkins, I don't smoke,' I said. Which goes to show how strung-up I was, how eager to please. In point of fact I was *dyin'* for a fag.

I caught Betty's eye. She was tryin' not to laugh but she was lettin' me know I'd said the right thing.

I'd already had tea, but her mum had made some tiny little white sandwiches with no crusts, cocktail sausages and cream puffs. She wheeled all this stuff into the sittin' room on a dumb-waiter. She poured tea into china cups as thin as eggshells. We perched on the edge of our chairs (at least I did) while I force-fed myself to be polite. Soon as I'd put my plate down, she fired off her questions.

What school did I go to?

'Albuera Street.' That made her nose wrinkle a bit.

What did I think of that nice Mr Menzies?

'I like the way he talks,' I lied. Her nose unwrinkled.

Do I have any brothers and sisters?

'Two brothers.'

Then the haymaker: 'And what do you do for a living, Alfred?'

'I work on the wharves.'

'Oh,' was all she said.

Mr Hopkins broke the silence. 'Alf, how do you reckon the Seagulls will go against the Magpies next week, eh?'

We left soon after. Betty was as pissed off as I was about her mother, but it sorta brought us closer together. She and I, shoulder to shoulder against a cruel world, type of thing.

That was only last week.

The GPO's just struck one. I'm gettin' uneasy. Betty shouldn't be *this* late. Funny, too, I haven't heard any trams along Sandy Bay Road ever since I been sittin' here ... Trammies must be on strike, too, like us wharfies. Good luck to 'em, say I.

The GPO dongs again. It's tellin' me it's quarter past! She's really late. Like really bloody late. I'm worried.

I stand up and walk around. Maybe she's waitin' somewhere else ...

Ah, *here* we are! A strawberry blonde is walkin' towards me at a fast clip. Hang on a sec! She's put on a lot of weight all of a sudden and she's dressed like a drac. Oh cripes, don't tell me — it's her blasted mother! Why on earth did Betty tell *her* we had a date, today of all days?

She charges up to me, eyes flashin'. I brace myself. Betty and I are goin' to get hitched, no matter what this old bag says.

I say as calmly as I can: 'Why, what a *surprise*, Mrs Hopkins. How ya doin'? Where's Betty then?'

'We've been lookin' for you all over, ya crafty old bugger,' the woman says with a put-on smile. 'Just what are we gonna do with you, Dad?'

John Biggs, a fifth-generation Tasmanian, spent much of his professional life in Hong Kong, which gives his writing a Sino-Tasmanian flavour. He has published several award-winning short stories and four novels: *The Girl in the Golden House*, a love story complicated by the politics of post-Tiananmen Hong Kong; *Project Integrens*, a sci-fi that won an award in the Jacobyte Fiction Competition; *Disguises*, in which an Australian-born Chinese girl clashes with her traditional parents; and *Tin Dragons*, which enters the Chinese mining camps in nineteenth-century Tasmania.

The **Jacqueline Cooke Short Story Award** is an annual competition run by FAW Tasmania and is open to all FAW members. The name of the award honours the the significant contributions made by Jacqueline Cooke, a former president and newsletter editor of FAW Tasmania. Short stories of up to 2500 words are eligible.

LUKE CARMAN

ZineWest *Short Story Competition*

My Time

M y mother sent me a message that said, 'Come and see me for
lunch,' so I drove toward the west and wondered aloud if I
was wasting my time. Then I remembered my Buddhist training,
specifically the time we were sitting in my master's study, which
looked like the inside of a very simple portaloo, and he leant into
a downward-facing dog.

I said, 'Master, I feel that this training is an expensive waste of
time.'

He replied, 'Luke, you're my worst student. You never remember
anything I tell you, and you hardly ever pay me. But I want you to
remember this always: time is an infinite quantity.' He later died
of an overdose of Zoloft.

As all the world is a distraction perhaps, I drove on toward my
mother, in my master's light, saying 'Que sera' to myself as I drove
on toward the west.

The roads were straight and narrow; the day was wide and
bright. I shuddered off the M4 and onto Church Street. Parramatta
was full of its midday rumble, and Silverwater trucks clogged
the main roads as business folk crowded the cafes and homeless
troupes congregated about on the streets, all sweating in the heat
and looking forlorn. I parked illegally and negotiated through the
populace.

Mum was waiting for me in an empty coffee shop, her cup empty too but for a trace of chocolate-coloured froth. She looked sad and her face was gentle as I kissed her. Her fingers touched my cheek and the wild blond of her hair radiated light like a halo.

She said, 'I dreamt about Grandma again. She warned me someone is trying to get in touch with her, trying to be with her on the other side — that I need to tell them not to.'

I ordered a coffee and my mother sent a text message to my brother.

'Who's the person, Luke? Is it you? Are you thinking of killing yourself again?' She asked me with her voice calm and her age heavy under burning blue eyes.

I said, 'It's hot in here, we should have sat outside.' She nodded her head and my coffee was placed on the table by a man with tattooed forearms. I didn't see his face. One tattoo read *Cry now, laugh later.*

My mother was sweating. She said, 'Your aunt went into surgery the other night. They saved her life. Her throat was clogged with tumours and they hurt. Now it's clogged with scars and it still hurts. I thought maybe it would be her that wanted to die. But I wasn't convinced. I needed to ask you, and your brother.'

I drank and sighed and said, 'Do you remember last Mother's Day, we went to Grandma's grave, and Adam looked at her headstone and said, "So that's all you get out of eighty-nine years." And then you went, "I wish we could all just climb in with her, and go to sleep." And all three of us agreed without a word that life is a meaningless war of deep delusions and that death is the only salve?'

She thought about it for a moment and said, 'No.' But of course she was lying.

I drank my coffee down. We watched the people go by for almost an hour. Then, wiping my eyes, I kissed her goodbye, waved a few times and drove back to my home in St Peters. I sat in the courtyard of the house, reading my death letter over again. I said to myself, 'Time is an infinite pain,' and closed my eyes for a while.

Luke Carman self-identifies as an anti-folk monologist with epigrammatical tendencies. His work has been described as 'published' by several close friends, and his current project focuses on whatever gets him through the night. Working closely with Professor Ivor Indyk of the University of Western Sydney, Luke hopes to enter a state of semi-isolation in order to produce something slightly more entertaining than the Colossus of Rhodes. His work has haunted the journals *HEAT*, *Westside* and *Cultural Studies Review*.

ZineWest is an annual zine for new Western Sydney writers published by the New Writers' Group Incorporated, a group committed to promoting writing in Western Sydney. The editors seek short submissions from a range of genres: short story, poetry, drama, memoir, lyrics, comic and cartoon. The co-sponsor of the ***ZineWest* Short Story Competition** is the Writing and Society Research Group of the University of Western Sydney, led by Professor Ivor Indyk (*HEAT* Magazine, Giramondo Press). The Research Group appoints a judge to name prize winners from the entries selected for publication by *ZineWest* editors. The first edition appeared in 2007.

Louisa John-Krol

C. J. Dennis Literary Awards

Twenty Ways to Greet a Tiger

I. Timidity

No need to simper, cringe or grin; yet in this age of extroversion, shyness is the charm.

II. Temerity

Will you remember this kind of freedom? Relish it while it lasts!

III. Taciturnity

Those who know do not speak. Those who speak do not know.

IV. Tenacity

Your adversary surely respects this.

V. Talaria

You'll need these, the winged sandals that Hermes wore.

VI. Tamasha

If your flight fails, be sure to put on a grand show.
As they do in India, preferably with dancing.

VII. Thanatos

No palimpsest of slander, nor embalmer's eye in amber.
Only this mask of inscrutable power tempts you.

VIII. Tarboosh

The tassel on your felt fez cap, being red,
is likely to madden your foe. But why not tempt your fate?
I dare you!

IX. Tamarind

Should you fail to entertain, be sure your flesh is flavoured
for the feast of a king.

X. Teetotum

This small spinning top with letters on each of its four sides,
spun with the fingers, will determine who wins or loses.

XI. Tantivy

This running gallop, used as a hunting cry, might be worth a try.

XII. Temperance

Your eyes plead for moderation and mercy you never showed,
nor ever shall know.

XIII. Trepidation

Don't let anyone say that you were predictable.

XIV. Tachycardia

The beating of your heart is swifter than winds of the great Jinn,
who whirl constellations from one galaxy to another.

XV. Tartufo

This edible fungus will not save you,
but there are worse things
than enjoying a truffle on your way toward death.

XVI. Temporality

Your appointment with time is now.

XVII. Tenure

Yours has expired.

XVIII. Terror

Go on, you cannot help it.

XIX. Transcendence

You are a sleeper, more awake than ghosts.

XX. Tact

There is nothing a tiger values more highly.
You are asking: 'Why did I not share this with you immediately?'
Life often keeps her best secrets till last —
in your case, too late.

Louisa John-Krol is a recording artist and published writer, with internationally acclaimed albums (mostly on the French ethereal label Prikosnovenie) inspired by mythology, literature and faerylore. Born in 1966 and raised in Bendigo's bushland, she gained qualifications at the University of Melbourne. Her experience includes teaching, storytelling and singing in such festivals as the Royal Melbourne Show, Trolls et Legendes (Belgium) and Faerieworlds (USA). She recently completed a fantasy novel, *The Legend of Elderbrook,* set to carry music. Her poem 'Twenty Ways to Greet a Tiger' won South Australia's 2010 C. J. Dennis Poetry Prize.

The winners of the **C. J. Dennis Literary Awards** are announced during the C. J. Dennis Festival, held annually in Auburn, South Australia, on the second weekend in September. The winners of each category receive $200 and a certificate. The theme for the 2010 competition was 'The Year of the Tiger', commemorating the Chinese Lunar Year and celebrating the tiger as a symbol of greatness. The awards are organised by Peter Lane, who can be contacted on *peter.lane4@bigpond.com.*

FIONA BRITTON
Shoalhaven Literary Award

Gulliver

He fell
as a lightning-blighted oak might fall:
legs a riven trunk
out from under him.
His hands did a wild dance
when the net descended
but the ropes held fast.
My darling's head was sore for days
(so heavy was it, with its freight of brain)
I crawled close,
sheltered in the whorl of his ear and called —
such sweet *chansons*,
honeyed as a harp, he said.
But please, could I speak up?

My obtuse, ill-mannered oaf,
my beloved
spared me the worst of his temper.
Though he was a tethered beast
his appetite was vast,
as if devouring was his only wish.
His words,
when rarely he spoke
(Oh! Listen!)
tumbled out
like big ball bearings
rolling in a china dish.
I pressed my face to his splendid throat
— his beard a hedge of ragged bramble —
to feel that ardent rumble.

I fed him:
figs with leavened bread
to inflate a flattened spirit;
saffron for epiphanies;
cheese from my own goat, tied
with a waxed plait
of my own hair.
But these were specks to him.
I bade my sisters hasten,
hitch the wine barrel to the mule
and go,
to satisfy our unquenched guest.
By moonlight I slit the throat of a pig,
licked sticky fingers
to taste the sanguine stuff.

At night I went to him alone.
His voice was valley and summit
and all between.
He said, such things live abroad:
talking birds,
with blue plumes long as a mare's tail —
they do Death's business.
Magic, too,
in slips of folded paper;
stars, my love,
that nightly explode in the sky.
I sat in the cup of his palm
and cried for the handfed sparrows
who attend my window
— my plain parliament —
whose brown had seemed so fine.

Fiona Britton is a Sydney writer. She was a 2009 recipient of an Australian Society of Authors mentorship to develop her fiction work. She has had a poem shortlisted in the Blake Poetry Prize and she was the 2010 winner of the Shoalhaven Literary Award.

The aims of the **Shoalhaven Literary Award**, which began in 1999, continues to be the recognition of literary excellence and the enhancement of the image of Shoalhaven as a place of strong cultural development. The competition is open to all residents of Australia aged eighteen and over. It is sponsored by The Shoalhaven City Council Arts Board, FAW Shoalhaven Regional, and Bundanon Trust. The judge for 2010 was Kate Llewellyn, author of the bestselling *The Waterlily: A Blue Mountains Journal* and *Playing With Water: A Story of a Garden*, and co-editor of *The Penguin Book of Australian Women Poets*.

JENNIFER SHAPCOTT

Marjorie Graber-McInnis Short Story Award

Acts of Kindness

It should have been paradise. We were drinking shiraz and sitting on a green lawn sloping down to the river while the sun splashed gold on the eucalyptus trees. But since I'd arrived, Matt and Monica had been squabbling like a pair of monkeys and now Matt was rehashing an ambulance case.

'Poor bastard,' said Matt, refilling his glass. 'After everything that'd happened to him—'

'Charles doesn't know who you're talking about,' Monica cut in.

'Frank was a local character round here,' said Matt, taking a sip of wine. 'First his wife left him—'

'Because she couldn't stand him yacking all day.'

'No, there was more to it than that—'

'Let's face it, he was a bloody interfering old stick. On Sundays he'd pick up our newspaper off the lawn and fling it onto the verandah. No-one asked him to. Woke me up every time, made me cranky as hell.'

'You're always cranky.'

'What happened to Frank?' I asked.

'Tell him, Matt. But tell the story straight. Don't go adding bits.'

'I'll tell the story how I want to, or not at all,' Matt replied, glaring at her and lighting a cigarette. He shifted in his deckchair, then leaned back, as if settling in to tell the story. 'Frank was one of those older blokes you see around town, white stubble, old-style work boots and trouser braces. He worked as a foreman at the sawmill, used to sort out blues in the timber yard and help the apprentices. Then he got retrenched and everything changed.'

'What happened?'

'Well, first, his wife Dorothy got fed up with him being round the house all day. Her dream was to travel and take a cruise to Alaska—'

'When all he wanted to do was to ride his bike round town and talk to anybody who'd listen,' interrupted Monica.

'What did he talk about?' I asked.

'Everything. He had an opinion on everything,' said Monica. 'One day he buttonholed me and rabbited on about the granite in the school hall, how it came from the quarry they used for the pylons on the Harbour Bridge. He reckoned I should be teaching more local history at school. When I told him I had to go but I'd google it, he looked crestfallen, like a dog when you stop throwing a stick.'

'In the end he realised people couldn't be bothered listening to him. That's why he let someone swing an axe at him,' said Matt.

'Someone swung an axe at him?'

'Tell Charles what happened.'

'He set off on his bike one morning—' Matt began.

'Like the local vicar doing his parish rounds.'

'Monica, can I tell this story without you chipping in?'

'Okay,' she replied, her eyes narrowing. 'I promise not to interrupt, if you don't go adding bits, like what people are thinking.'

Matt didn't reply but from the fury in his eyes I knew he was going to tell the story exactly the way he wanted.

✳

As soon as Frank walked into the kitchen carrying a pile of wood,

Dorothy swore at him for wearing boots in the house. She was tapping at a computer on the table where her friends Maud and Agnes sat drinking tea. Frank noticed that both Dorothy and Maude were wearing pink tracksuits, their bus tour outfits, but Agnes wasn't.

'Would ya like anythin' from the shop, Dot?' he asked, stacking the wood against the stove. 'I thought I'd pop down the road now the weather's cleared.'

Dorothy looked up from the computer with eyes as hard as stones on an empty riverbed.

'Fish fingers for tea tonight,' she barked as Maude spluttered over her tea. 'And don't interrupt again. I'm doing me futures trading.'

'Off to help the local citizens are we, Frank?' asked Agnes.

'Yeah, as only Frank knows how,' sighed Dorothy.

'Why don't you call round at my place sometime?' asked Agnes with a wink. 'The lock on my bedroom door's broken.'

A warm breeze brushed against Frank's face as he cycled down the street and tried to erase the memory of Agnes's wink from his mind. He braked when he saw something hanging out of Mrs Applecross's letterbox, pulled out a parcel and left it on her front step. He hopped back on his bike and tried to brush away the image of a face at a window and a hand closing the curtains.

Next stop was Norm's servo to help fill up petrol tanks. The old biddies needed to brush up on their driving skills, he reckoned, the way they hit the accelerator as soon as he tapped on the car window for a chat. They'd have to do without him soon. Norm was selling up. Everything would go — the marigolds in the white painted tyres, the bowsers, the workshop — all replaced by a billboard promising a lifestyle for the over-50s.

He parked his bike outside the Leagues Club and bounded up the stairs, his eyes slowly adjusting to the dark interior and the carpet with red and green swirls that greeted him along with the jingle-jangle of the pokies.

'How ya goin', Frank?' asked Tom, sipping a scotch and coke.

'Same as yesterday. How are you, Tom, and don't say not bad,' replied Frank, before realising it was no good talking. Tom had switched off, eyes glued to the giant screen, watching *Wheel of Fortune*. Frank downed his beer and got up to leave.

'Ya not goin' now, are ya?' asked Tom. 'They're goin' to announce the raffle for the Honda Accord any minute.'

'They're always announcin' somethin'. Every hour of the day from the minute ya walk in. I'd rather gamble on the dish lickers—'

'If ya goin' to put a dollar on the doggies,' interrupted Tom, 'can ya lay a bet on Bold Explosion, Race 5, Maitland?'

'I wasn't, but I will.'

After calling in at the TAB, it was off to the boat ramp. Always something going on there — usually a nipper about to be run over by someone forgetting to check the rear-vision mirror. And yesterday the couple driving their boat away with the biminy still up. The husband had said, 'Thanks, mate. We hadn't forgotten. It's on the checklist,' brandishing a laptop like a shield. 'We always take it down last.'

'Like hell you do,' Frank had thought, but propped up for a chat anyway just before they sped away.

Cycling towards the general store, Frank shook his head at the loafers with their noses in newspapers, sipping coffee under black umbrellas outside the shop. Used to be a friendly place but no-one bothered to say hello anymore. Unbelievable, it was, Buddhist statues on the lawn, and the glass and crystal baubles hitting his face when he walked in — and all he wanted was a packet of fish fingers.

The woman with the red hair streaked silver down the middle shook her head. Awaiting deliveries, come back in half an hour and do you mind, that's my mobile ringing. To fill in the time, he wandered down to the river and opened oyster shells with his pocketknife. The breeze had grown stronger, and he clutched his hat with one hand as he rode back to the store. He was cycling across the car park when he caught sight of a man with a ponytail and sunglasses. He was walking with his head down, studying a piece of paper.

'Can I help ya, mate?' asked Frank.

'Nah, I'm right.'

'Where ya goin'?'

The man looked at him with bloodshot eyes. Fleshy face, lip ring and metal bolt through his nose. 'To a mate's house,' he replied.

Frank peered over his shoulder at the diagram. 'If ya turn ya map around so it's facin' the river—' he said, taking the piece of paper.

'Shit,' yelled the man as the wind blew the paper out of Frank's hand and swept it down the river where it floated like a white rag out to sea.

'Ya bloody idiot.'

'Can't ya ring ya mate?'

'His phone number was on that piece of paper, ya moron.'

'What's his name?'

'None of ya business.'

'We could drop round to the police station. Dan knows where everyone lives round here. No point in ringin' him, though, every time I call, a machine comes on.'

'Police station? Forget it, man. I'm out of here.' He began walking away just as a four-wheel drive swung into the car park. A man in sports trousers and a polo-neck shirt opened the car door and strode towards them carrying a sawed off .22-calibre rifle. He was followed by a man in tracksuit pants and singlet, buffed up like he'd come from the gym.

'You didn't show up, Zac,' said the first man.

'The bloody map blew away because this old geezer stopped me and—'

'Pathetic. Absolutely pathetic. Next you'll tell me he's a plainclothes copper.'

'Rhys, please. I wasn't leaving town. I was just getting away from this stupid old bastard.'

Frank slipped behind a bush as Rhys fired at Zac, who dived for cover behind a tree. Zac pulled out a handgun and fired back. When Zac stopped to reload, Rhys raced back to the car and turned into the main road, the car screeching and careering as it hit the gutters. Frank ran to the phone box at the edge of the car park.

'Yeah, I know. Leave a message at the tone. Dan, it's me, Frank. Can ya come down to the car park near the jetty? There's been a bit of trouble. Out-of-towners stirrin' things up. They're still shootin' at each other. Got to skedaddle. Dorothy wants fish fingers for tea tonight.'

From the phone box, Frank watched Zac reload while the man in the tracksuit pants fired from behind a garbage bin. Frank rode off in the opposite direction and let out a sigh of satisfaction. Trouble had come to town and he'd been the first to spot it. He bought a packet of fish fingers and cycled home with a light heart.

The house was dead quiet, curtains closed and the TV switched off.

Then he found the note on the coffee table:

Me and Maude are going away on a cruise. Agnes says she's happy to keep you company if you get lonely.

Dorothy

He turned as he heard the back door swing open. He walked slowly down the hall, jumping each time the floorboards creaked. When he pushed open the kitchen door, a man with a ponytail stood in front of him with an axe.

The neighbours heard a scream that chilled their bones.

✳

Matt stopped talking and took a deep breath.

'Did Frank survive?' I asked.

'Yeah.'

'How was he? Did he stay the same, I mean, did he go on helping people?'

'Yeah, he stayed the same. I visited him in hospital and we had a chat in the garden near the river. He was sitting on a bench, sharing his sandwiches with the seagulls.'

'To be honest, I miss the thud of the newspaper on our verandah. It was the only thing that got me going on Sunday mornings—' said Monica.

'Frank didn't get back on his bike in the end,' said Matt, seeing the startled look on my face. 'After he got out of hospital, he walked down to the heads one morning and spotted a couple of young kids struggling in the water. They were caught in the rip, panicking and screaming for help. Frank swam out and brought one girl in then turned round to rescue the other. But she'd been swept out too far — he couldn't reach her. He saw the lifesavers' row-out but then he got caught in the rip.' Matt paused and lit up a cigarette. Monica was staring at the river, her grey eyes growing thoughtful while we waited for Matt to continue.

'Frank was calm as he was dragged out to sea,' he said, after a few minutes. 'Maybe the boat would reach him, maybe not, he thought, looking up at the dome of blue sky. He'd saved one kid and raised the alarm for the other. That was enough. The sea could claim him now. Shuffling round a nursing home, shoved in front of daytime soaps, that wasn't going to happen to him. He was going out the way he wanted.'

Matt sat back in his chair and sipped his wine. I stole a look at Monica and noticed her face had softened.

'Poor Frank,' she said quietly before rousing herself and sitting up in her chair.

'You did it again, Matt.'

'What?'

'You added bits to the story. You said what Frank was thinking.'

'Yes — to help Charles understand the story.'

I waited for her retort but she was silent. She was staring at him. The sharpness had returned to her face, but when I looked more closely I thought I saw the glint of admiration in her eyes.

Jennifer Shapcott is the author of the novel *The Art of Resistance*, published in 2010. She grew up in Melbourne and studied Japanese history in Canberra and Tokyo. Her short stories have received several awards. She is currently working on her second novel and a collection of short stories. She lives in Canberra.

The **Marjorie Graber-McInnis Short Story Award** was established by Don McInnis to commemorate the life of his wife, a short story writer who lived in Canberra and passed away on 25 September 1997. The award is administered by the ACT Writers' Centre and closes each year on the anniversary of Marjorie's passing. First prize is $600 and publication in the ACT Writers' Centre magazine, *ACTWrite*. The 2010 competition marked the award's thirteenth year.

www.actwriters.org.au

A Favourite Sky

He's mostly been in bed since Easter. He's up for a while at night, though; I hear him stoke the fire and shuffle through paperwork. He sighs a lot. Sometimes he cries, a low moan of shallow sobs that I try to pretend is the dog whimpering against the cold. Mum must hear him, too, because she gets up and talks softly to him and the floorboards creak as they go back to bed together.

He's always back asleep when I leave for school so we leave notes for each other in a diary on the kitchen table. It was his idea. It's a black day-to-a-page one and he leaves it open for me with the skinny red tassel draped across today's message. His writing is a bit shakier than it used to be, but still much neater than mine. Every morning I read his message over and over while I crunch through my cereal and think what to write. I flick back through the pages; we've been at it for months now. Back when we started I had to write small just to make my news fit.

Good news — Johnno got his P's yesterday!! Modern history assessment due today, have to give a presentation — can't wait till it's over. Charles Sturt Open Day coming up in a fortnight, I'd like to go and have a look — what do you think? Hope your appointment goes OK today.
Love,
Tim

There just seemed so much more to say back then.

Hope your presentation went well, better you than me! Uni Open Day sounds good. Doc says I am doing all the right things and will be back to my old self before too long. Sooner I hope. Might pop in to the sale yards today, just to keep an eye on the old blokes.

Love,

Dad

The words have thinned out and dried up and now we're down to a daily effortful sentence. Reading it is like swallowing a tablet; writing it, even more so. I move the red tassel to see today's message.

Monday:

Good luck with your cross-country.

Dad

I want to scrawl *I'M SO BLOODY OVER THIS!* across the double page in thick red texta like a graffiti artist. I spin the blue biro he's left for me around my thumb and force out a reply in my usual printing.

Thanks.

Tim

I don't know why we write our names after our messages, it's not like anyone else is going to write in it. Mum knows it's just for us. I hammer her with questions on the way to the bus.

How long is this going to go on for? Can't the doc give him something stronger? Can't he at least TRY getting up?

As she drives down our steep driveway, the orchard rushing past behind her, I notice new lines crinkling out from her eyes.

He's sick, love, and it's going to take time, longer than we thought. He doesn't want to be like this. He's got another review next week.

As I climb out she catches my hand in hers and looks straight at me, her eyes a mix of fear and hope. *Don't give up on him.* I feel like she's X-rayed my mind.

Tuesday:

How'd you go?
Dad

Came 3rd. Johnno 1st (new school record) & Steve Mc 2nd. Zone is August 10th in Benalla. Maybe you can come?
Tim

Wednesday:

Well done. Maybe.
Dad

Thanks.
Tim

Thursday:

Not too good today,
Dad

I stare at the page and try to swallow the gritty desert-dryness out of my mouth. My stomach folds in on itself so I slop my cornflakes into the dog's bowl. I inch Dad's door open slowly. The curtains are drawn but I make out his shape: he's coiled up on his side, facing the middle of the bed. Mum's put some daffodils on the bedside table, next to his tablets, a glass of water and last Saturday's paper, still neatly folded. Part of me wants to stay at the door — I haven't been in my parents' room for years — but I pad in slowly, pull back the doona and tuck my long runner-bean legs into Mum's side. He opens his eyes, focuses on me, and we both manage something like a slight smile. Our knees touch lightly. We stay like that, cocooned together, in the half-light silence for a long time. Tears leak onto his pillow. Eventually Mum calls, *Tim! Bus!* Back at the door I stare at his thin, lifeless form and wish I knew what to say. I pause again over the page on my way out.

I miss you.
Love,
Tim

Friday:

Bit better. Got some fencing on tomorrow. Can you give me a hand?
Dad

Love to — ha ha! I'll grab Johnno too, he's owes me!
Tim

I wake as soon as the sun hits my window like a torch. I drizzle a thick river of honey through the volcanic porridge bubbles, leaving his to warm on the stove. I wonder when he'll be up and how long he'll last. Maybe he can sit on the camping chair in the sun and watch me and Johnno have a go at the fencing. That'd have to be better for him than another day in bed. I fill the thermos with coffee and throw some ham and cheese sandwiches in the backpack.

The diary isn't on the table. I hunt around in the neat pile of papers near the phone but can't see it. I don't really know where else to look. I throw a chunk of red gum into the wood burner just as Mum flings open the kitchen door. She hasn't brushed her hair and her eyes are wide. Her words chase each other out of her mouth in a breathless high pitch. *I can't find him anywhere. He was gone when I woke up.*

I jump up, knocking the backpack off the table. The frosty air stings my arms and face but I don't feel the stones cutting in to the soles of my feet. The ute is still out the back. I am running — *Dad!* — the morning light and the dust start to spin together and I hear a God-awful fear in my voice. *Dad! Dad! DAD!* Mum is racing, too, back through the house, down to the dam, across to the chooks; she's got the phone in her hand now. I wrench at the handle on the shed door, *Dad?* but it doesn't move. It's locked from the inside. I feel the blood swish around my body. *God, no. Please, please, please, no.* I slam my body against the door over and over. It rattles and clatters against me but stays wedged shut. When I stop my desperate crashing there is nothing, just my own rasping sobs and the soft whimper of the dog from inside.

✳

The house is brimming with locals, drinking cups of tea, elbow to elbow, and talking quietly. Big, rough farmer hands wrap around delicate floral teacups that jangle against saucers. Nobody needs introducing. Lemon slice gets offered around on a sagging paper plate. The phone never stops ringing. They come and go in a slow-moving wave; it's a haphazard car park out the front. We run out of milk and sugar and somebody reappears with more.

Casseroles in pyrex dishes start to pile up on the kitchen bench, with yellow Post-it notes stuck to the lids, *20 mins at 180. Can be frozen.* The fridge is jammed full of barbecued chickens and lasagnes and ice-cream containers full of soup. Mum gets me to hook up the spare chest freezer on the verandah and watches me rearrange the stream of offerings to make room for more. She smiles wryly — *shame we're not hungry.* She doesn't look as tall. She pulls her polar fleece around her sunken frame instead of zipping it up. *I'm freezing,* she says.

Even my principal drops in. He's younger than everybody else there and he looks kind of out of place with his pointy boots and gelled hair. When he shakes my hand and says *I liked your dad a lot* I feel something inside my chest start to splinter. I bite hard on my lip while I get him a coffee. Out by his car he tells me not to worry about my assessments.

Anybody from school been around?

Just Johnno so far.

There's um, he stares hard at the fuzz of yellow wattle down the drive then looks out longways across the valley, *a psychologist if you want to, you know, talk to somebody.*

I lay on my bed and stare at the ceiling, counting the small scabs of peeling off-white paint and the faint blue blotches of mould over and again. I read and reread the dozens of cards on my desk. The newsagent in town must only stock three styles: the one with the sunset over the lake, the white one with the silver cross, and the black one with the single trumpet lily. *Be assured of our thoughts and prayers. Hoping your memories will be a comfort. Please join us for dinner one night when you're up to it.* And then there's Johnno's, a photo of the hills up behind our place at dusk, glued onto white cardboard. *Shit. I just can't believe it. If you need me, mate, you know where I am.* Buried underneath the mound of cards is my half-written English assessment from before: *The Love Song of J. Alfred Prufrock is a frustrated search about the meaning of existence. Discuss.*

Johnno and I collect firewood in his back paddock, loading it in to the ute in silence. The sun is sinking and a flock of cockatoos flap and screech from a lonely gum, startled by the dull thudding of wood on metal. The sky darkens in degrees and is more purple than blue now. I can just see my breath; suddenly, I'm freezing too. I stare at the sky on the drive home. He loved the sky. *You'll never see stars like that in the city.* He had a favourite sky — petrol-blue, he called it. *I drove your mum to the hospital the night you were born and I just knew everything would be all right because it was the most perfect petrol-blue sky.*

I find Mum sitting on the laundry floor, propped up against the washing machine, holding his red-checked shirt. Her face is soaking wet and she looks like a little girl. It still smells like him.

It's nearly a week before I go back up to the shed. I hear my pulse throbbing right out of my neck as I walk up there with the local copper. I pull my hood up and dig my hands deep into my pockets and keep them there. The door swings open and, for a moment, Dad's there too; it's the woodchip farm smell. I know what Mum means now. I gulp in deep lungfuls of him.

Sorry about this. Just details. You don't have to stay, son.

But I do, I watch him as he squints up at the roof joists and scribbles things in his notebook. He wanders around, picks up a drum of rope and measures the diameter. The colourbond walls start to spin fast and I grip the workbench to stay upright. I lurch outside with the world tilting, my lungs gasping for new air and a thousand hot needles pricking my face.

You right?

I let the tap run through my hands and splash a series of cold, sharp handfuls on my face and over the back of my neck. My hands grip my kneecaps and the gravel at my feet slowly comes back into focus.

I'm finished here now, son. He clenches his thick sausage fingers to block a chesty cough. *Found this.*

I wipe my hands down my jeans and take the diary from him. He keeps walking, clearing his throat all the way to his four-wheel drive down at the house. I watch him go and feel my pulse leave my neck and jackhammer around my skull.

The red tassel lies across August 10, still weeks away.

> *Tim, give them a good run for their money today.*
> *I'm so sorry I can't be there.*
> *Love you mate,*
> *Dad*

I slide down against the peeling bark of the giant twin-forked gum. My fingers run smoothly back and forth across his words, absorbing them like braille. My pulse slips back into a gentle, silent rhythm, and my body is stilled with a new calm. The thin lump behind the page is the blue biro, waiting for me. I pull my hood down and drink in the endless, cloudless mid-morning blue. The soft warmth of the thin winter sun filters through the branches and rests on me. He loved the sky, my dad.

Kate Rotherham is a social worker who lives in northeast Victoria with Roo and their delightful gaggle of small children. She writes when normal people are asleep. Her short stories have been published in journals, magazines and anthologies including *Award Winning Australian Writing 2010, Island, Page Seventeen,* and *fourW*. 'A Favourite Sky' was written in memory of her friend Greg.

The **Rolf Boldrewood Literary Awards** honour Rolf Boldrewood, the pen name of Thomas Browne, who during his time as a police magistrate in Dubbo wrote *Robbery Under Arms,* one of the first major Australian novels. The competition aims to foster the writing of prose and poetry with an Australian content. Prose entries must be no more than 3000 words, while those for poetry have a limit of 80 lines. The winners of both sections receive $500 and a signed, limited-edition bust of Rolf Boldrewood (valued at $100).

Jacqui Merckenschlager

Eyre Writers' Awards

This Empty Space

Afterwards, after the weeping, the remembering,
love and laughter trickled into the void.
This empty space was flooded
by family and friends
and a sunshower sparkled on the wattles.

Afterwards they all went back to distant places,
silence and emptiness slipped through cracks
and hid among his clothes
and lurked between his books and tools,
while rosellas sipped nectar from the bluegums.

Afterwards, he was still there, tinkering,
toying with your feelings, reminding you
of the things he had achieved,
the trees he planted last May,
the letters he wrote when you were only nineteen.

Afterwards the ocean was royal-blue, bottle-green,
hiding shipwreck tragedies, drowned dreamers.
Fishing boats and ferries plied the waves
and tiny penguins nested in the bay.
He walked beside you everywhere, afterwards.

The mining town of Broken Hill, where **Jacqui Merckenschlager** lived as a child, instilled in her a love for the Australian outback, its flora and fauna. This love is evident in much of her writing and helped develop her green thumb. She is a retired teacher and is respected as a self-taught botanist and plant propagator. 'This Empty Space' was written for a friend whose husband died in a farm accident. The poem is Jacqui's second Eyre Writers' Awards success. Her 2009 Tom Black Memorial prize-winning poem 'Mining Town Pianist' considers a woman coping in a 'man's town'.

The **Eyre Writers' Awards**, run by Eyre Writers, are open to short fiction, essay, memoir, rhyming and non-rhyming poetry set to a maritime theme, fact or fiction. First prize is $200 in each section. For more information, contact Dennis Lightfoot on *lincoln5606@hotmail.com.*

LEAH SWANN

Page Seventeen *Short Story Competition*

Street Sweeper

You'll remember this day your dog Winston dies, this day and this night, but right now the afternoon is fresh and untouched by future events. Here you are on the concrete steps, in front of a shabby weatherboard: Mathew Greene at fourteen, with a skateboard under one arm, the other filled with the shaggy warmth of Winston.

Listless, you feel in need of something. But it won't be found in the kitchen — where your mother, Molly, makes jam with Bridget like it's an hilarious science experiment — nor downstairs in the mad slurry of Monopoly money and scone crumbs left by the children. You're too old to play.

Greene senior, the father who gave you Winston on your third birthday, is not here. He married someone else and lives in America with new children. It's no-one's fault; it's just the way things are. Last time he visited, you played footy on the street. You told me it was the best hour of your life.

✳

You hear the women's conversation through the open front door. You're dimly aware that this jam-making business is somehow attached to your mother's need to be accepted by the brigade of

Other Mothers. You can't stand her ostentatious efforts. If she cut off her dreadlocks and removed a few earrings, she might get further. But you can't say such things. You don't want to.

'My goodness, if my mother could see me now,' Molly says. Knives slash and chop on the cutting boards.

'My mother didn't make jam either,' says Bridget. 'But it's a good antidote to the madness of modern life.'

'These mandarins are appalling.'

'Not enough rain.'

'Satisfying to make them into jam, though,' says Molly.

There are cigarette butts in the geranium pot by the steps: Marlboro Lights, Molly's brand. Citrus infuses the air like a pungent teabag. Hearing a cork pop, you know Molly's opened a bottle of wine and your chest kinks with anger. The one bright spot of your day is the evening walk, when you and Molly and your little brother and sister walk the dog. It will be awful if she's drunk — and she could well be drunk by then.

You're hungry but you can't bear to return to the kitchen. You don't want to enter that warm, womanly fug of jam and alcohol and Bridget's cleavage. Now they're testing the jam on a cold saucer; you can hear your mother worrying that it's too runny.

You're itching for something. You don't know what, though later you wonder if you were waiting for the car that screamed around the corner, the car that killed Winston, and the girl in velvet hipsters who tumbled out of the driver's seat, weeping.

You set out to skate from the letterbox to the fire hydrant and back. Winston follows, arthritic and shambling. You've already skated two lengths before the dog's made it to the nature strip to relieve himself. He's wandered out on the road when you hear the car's engine too close and too fast.

'Winston!'

The great bushy head lifts to attention, his eyes obscured by a long fringe of grey and white hair. He doesn't move.

'Winston, come here!'

Ponderous, as if moving through water, the dog raises a paw like a Clydesdale hoof and puts it down again. The red Astra hurtles around the bend. Brakes squealing, the car smashes into Winston and sends him soaring along the road. The Astra screeches to a stop, and the driver climbs out. She's already crying.

Winston must be dead. You run to him and pick up his front and back paws. You're dragging him to the kerb when you see that he's split open — his guts are rolling out. Behind you, the girl gives a short scream.

'Don't worry,' you hear yourself say. 'Don't worry about it. I'll get a spade. I'll clean it up.'

The girl's shoulders are shaking. 'Oh my God, oh my God! I'm so sorry.'

'You can go home, if you want,' you say. *Please go home. Please go. I can't stand it.*

The girl's eyes are dripping black over her lovely face: she's the kind of girl you'd be in awe of in other circumstances. A navel-diamanté winks up at you from her flat belly, making you hot and uncomfortable.

'No, let me help,' she pleads.

'*I* want to do it,' you say. 'Please.'

'Do you want me to go?'

'Yes.'

✳

Running down the driveway, through the noisy kitchen to the back door, you find the spade and walk back through the kitchen. The wine bottle is almost empty. A foaming pot of gold on the stove threatens to boil over, guarded by a giggling Molly with her wine glass and wooden spoon; Bridget's ladling the first batch into washed jars. A row of finished jars sits on the windowsill, back-lit by sunshine, each one full of a dense and radiant orange.

'What the hell's Matt doing with a spade?' you hear Bridget say.

'God knows. Spot of gardening, perhaps?' says Molly. A gale of laughter follows you up the driveway and you think to yourself, *bitch*; but only minutes later she's out there beside you, helping you, proving you wrong.

✻

When you tell me of the evening walks your voice is tender. How the littlies hold hands and walk in front, hauling Winston on the leash, while your mother's beside you, deftly winding the conversation this way and that way, and listening intently to whatever you say about school, dreams, football, skateboards — even girls. You only notice this skilfulness in retrospect. But you bask in her attention; these walks are when you love her best.

She knows how to handle you. When she arrives on the street that unforgettable spring day, Winston spread over the bitumen like the Pro Hart carpet advertisement, she says in a low voice: 'What we need here, Mathew, is a box. Run across to the Stuarts' and see if they have one, as big as you can find.'

Bridget is standing nearby. Molly leans over and says something to her you can't hear. Glad to leave the scene for a moment, you hand Molly the spade and dash over to the neighbours' house.

Molly must have worked like lightning, because by the time you get back most of the dog is in an oversized pillowslip and another, smaller slip. The small one has a faded Thomas the Tank Engine print on it, the one you insisted on having on until you were ten. You set the box onto the nature strip and lift the sacks into the box. Each is knotted, so no furry vestiges of poor Winston protrude. Blood's staining the cotton, fast.

'I think it's best if Georgia and Stefan don't see this,' says Molly, wiping sweat from her forehead.

'I'll take them for tea at my house,' says Bridget.

Once you've carried the box to the backyard, you go inside to clean up. In the bathroom, you wash your hands and face. There are voices outside, followed by Bridget's car driving away. In the mirror you see a whisker poking out of your chin and yank it out with your thumb and forefinger. You walk into the bedroom. Sinking into the bed, your hand stretches by habit to feel Winston's head and swishes through empty air. You lean forward all the way and press your eye sockets into your kneecaps and cry. Tears soak your jeans.

Eventually you go back to the garden where Molly is busily digging under the old mandarin tree. She looks small and skinny with the apron — donned for jam-making — still hanging off her unmotherly form, dust-blonde dreadlocks tucked behind earlobes bristling with silver. There's a tattoo of a sun on her right bicep. The arm that stirred the pot. The arm that dug the grave. It's shaking with effort.

'Let me do that, Mum,' you say.

She hands you the spade gratefully, and wipes at the muck and tears smearing her face.

Later, there will be a memorial service. Georgia and Stefan will toss flowers onto the grave and say poems in Winston's memory. Right now, their absence lets the two of you cry freely. All is quiet, save for the sound of tears and dirt falling over blood-stained pillowslips.

'He was a good dog,' chokes Molly, when it's almost done.

'The best,' you say, and put your arm around her and again you notice the slightness of her, this woman so big in your life.

✳

During the night you can't stop thinking about Winston's body coming apart. You want to stop but your mind keeps going back to it, probing it like a finger on a scab.

You try to think of the mandarins and the hands of the women, their chopping blades, sectioning, stripping, peeling. Dozens of mandarins slashed in half, their dry gold bellies face-up. Pips and pith and shells of orange skin sitting in heaps between the blue packets of sugar. The driver's face comes to mind, and you wonder if she's awake too, disturbed by killing a dog. Despite your efforts, you keep seeing red guts and other stuff, brown and shiny and sausage-like, on the hard road.

Finally you fall into a hot, fitful sleep, only to be woken by the harsh noise of a street sweeper. The vast mechanical brooms whirr through the quiet, breaking it up into so many shards.

✷

When you put on your runners, you slip through the bedroom window and out onto the street. It's late. You pad along, jogging lightly. Cold moonlight spilling over a blossom tree makes it so sharply beautiful, so unearthly — it takes you by surprise. You will always remember its fragrance, its stillness, its lambent white blossoms.

Up the road comes the street sweeper. You avert your eyes from the glaring gold lights, sitting on the truck like upturned jam jars, but nothing can block the noise. It passes you slowly, a moving edifice of brutal efficiency, its raucous vacuum strong enough to suck up a house brick or a dead possum. Even bits of Winston. But Molly did such a good job, there's barely a trace of Winston left; every piece has been wrapped and buried. At least he was saved from that.

As you hurry back along the street to your house, you see a light on in Molly's room. Leaping through your window and sliding into bed, your heart thumps. She's talking to someone on the phone. At this time of night it could only be America. Molly's voice is too muffled to hear what she's saying. Maybe the bad school report. Maybe Winston.

When the conversation ends, you creep into your mother's bedroom. She's in her singlet top and pyjama pants. Her eyes are pink.

'Was that Dad?' you ask, clambering onto the bed next to her.

'Why are you still awake? Were you listening?'

'Couldn't sleep. Winston, I guess. Did you ring him?'

'No — he rang me.'

She looks through the open curtains to the night sky. Her room seems dingy with its peeling paint and op-shop dressing table. Georgia's scrappy bouquet of lavender and jasmine is wilting in the vase.

'You might as well know,' she says. 'He asked if you'd like to go and live with him. And Cady and the little ones. Become part of their family.'

You're surprised at the excitement, even joy, rising inside you. Joy with a seam of dread. It's like someone's opened a door to let in a fresh breeze. To live with him! You take a
deep breath.

'It makes sense, really,' Molly says, rubbing the skin of her forehead with her thumbs. 'You're becoming a man and I don't know how to help you with that. Your father could.'

✱

Years later, you reflect that Molly sent you away at the very moment your body grew stronger than hers; strong enough to crack open drought-dried earth with a spade. Now a grown man, you can see how such strength could have genuinely helped her maintain the house and guard the children. Had you stayed, she might have come to depend on you. Did she know she was protecting you from her own neediness, when she encouraged you — against her own feelings — to say yes to your father's offer?

✱

Several weeks later, you say your goodbyes to Stefan and Georgia at the house. Molly's arranged for Bridget to mind them rather than go to the airport: they've been crying a lot about you going. Closing the front door, you catch sight of Stefan's little sheepskin ugg boots left where he stepped out of them in the hallway. The toes point outwards, the way he habitually stands.

The two of you drive to the airport. After you've checked in your luggage, she waits with you. In her usual way, she keeps the conversation light and funny, teasing you about the American accent you'll inevitably acquire, and the pretty teenager she's spotted that you could 'chat up' on the plane. When the boarding call comes, she gives you a jar of mandarin marmalade.

'Give it to your dad,' she says, and grins. 'Be sure to tell him I've been *making jam*. I'd love to see his face.'

There's a long, awkward hug, and then she holds your shoulders and looks into your eyes, and out of love for her you strive not to squirm.

'You're the best thing that ever happened to me, Mathew.'

Her eyes are bright with unshed tears and she swallows. 'Good courage, son,' she says, and laughs. 'I'm telling you what *I* need! Now remember, if you feel down just go and chat with that girl.'

Courage *is* what you need hours later, when the first real wave of homesickness hits you. Through the window lies a vast mass of sky and ocean. Your tray is flipped open in front of you with a packet of sweet biscuits, tea, and the empty dish that held the lasagne now lodged like cardboard in your stomach. The stricken face of the girl who killed Winston floats towards you, as it does sometimes; it would have been nice to talk to her about it once the shock had passed.

You stack the mess into a pile and fossick in your bag for the marmalade. Your hand closes around the cool glass jar, still sticky from where the old label has been soaked away. Drawing it out, you place it in front of you.

The jar beams on the tray, an orange beacon. Twisting the lid till it pops, you take a spoon and dip it into the marmalade, and listen to Molly and Bridget, their voices coming as though from long ago, a piece of history running through your head:

'Put the jam on this frozen saucer and we'll see if it gels.'

That's Bridget, followed by Molly: 'Oh my God, it's too runny — what will we do?'

'Keep boiling it. Just keep boiling it.'

Holding the spoon, you check the texture of the jam and find it quivers and drips in gelatinous globules onto the empty packets. She did it! A thin twist of peel dangles and glistens. Taking another spoonful, you taste mandarins transformed by sugar and heat. Marmalade coats your tongue, thickly golden. How sweet it is, and how bitter.

Leah Swann lives in Melbourne with her husband and two children. She is a former public relations manager and journalist. She loves listening to stories and poetry, and is writing a novel. Her first book, *Bearings*, a collection of short stories and a novella, was published this year by Affirm Press.

The *Page Seventeen* **Short Story and Poetry Competitions** are held annually, with entries accepted during April, May and June. Winning and shortlisted entries are published in *Page Seventeen*, a magazine founded in 2004 to give new writers an opportunity to see their work published. *Page Seventeen* encourages those with little or no publishing history to submit their work for consideration, as well as those with more writing experience.

www.pageseventeen.com.au

For information on how to participate in *AWAW 2012*, go to
www.melbournebooks.com.au/awaw2012.html